Harton Township 1921

by

Jean Stokes

Contents

Introduction

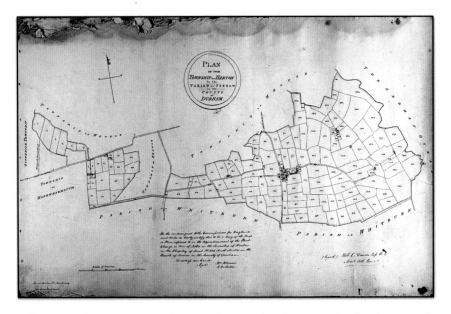

This plan of Harton Township, in the Parish of Jarrow, in the County of Durham, was produced in 1839 and shows the area that will be discussed in this book. This civil boundary existed for centuries. In 1901 the western section was taken into the County Borough of South Shields and in 1921 Harton Township ceased to exist altogether as further land was subsumed into South Shields, leaving just a strip of land along the coast, which was eventually absorbed into South Shields in 1932.

This book wishes to celebrate that until the November 1921 there was such an entity as Harton Township.

The nearby industrial town of South Shields had sought to expand its boundaries since it was made a County Borough in 1850: in 1897 Westoe Township was added; in 1901 the western side of Harton Township and in 1918 the Cleadon Park Estate. The image opposite taken from *South Shields Centenary Book, 1850-1950* visually demonstrates the urban growth of South Shields during those years.

South Shields began its existence as a town huddled along the edge of the river. The beginning of the nineteenth century saw industry boom and the

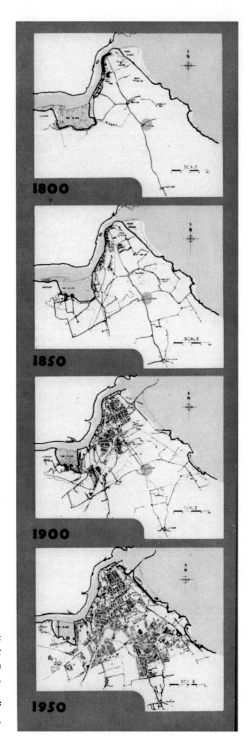

1800

1850

1900

1950

A series of maps from the *South Shields Centenary Book 1850-1950*, showing the urban growth of the town during these 150 years.

The pale green circle marks the site of Harton Village.

3

The upper photograph was taken from the south looking north over the fields of Harton Township towards Westoe Village which can be seen on the left of the horizon. The buildings on the right of the horizon are those of Horsley Hill Farmstead.

population increase exponentially, initially without local government control, leading to crowded houses with lack of sanitation which, in a port where sailors could bring diseases from all over the world, led to a very unhealthy state of affairs.

Although by the end of the nineteenth century new houses had been built on the Lawe, south towards Westoe Village, and west towards Tyne Dock, many of which still exist today, a lot of the town's population lived in the oldest housing in the town. These older buildings were crowded along the riverside in narrow winding streets, often built into the ballast hills, with no water, just a communal stand pipe in the street, and fell far short of the standards required for modern life.

In the twentieth century, once WW1 had ended, the council began a slum clearance policy, made possible by the mayor of the time, Councillor Andrew Anderson who having bought the large Cleadon Park Estate, on the southern border of Harton Township for £18,000, sold it to the corporation of South Shields for the purchase price.

The foundation stone of the first corporation housing development was laid on 3rd November 1920 and the final home completed in 1932. The Cleadon Park Estate offered 1,528 modern dwellings with internal sanitation and running water and gardens full of fresh air far away from the grime and fumes of the industry along the river. Schools and shops were also built to serve this new village community. Council houses would continue to be built throughout the twentieth century and private housing

A photograph taken in 2021 from a similar position now shows rooftops instead of furrows.

estates also proliferated, as the possibility of owning a house, rather than renting one, became more attainable.

Within 100 years all the farms in Harton Township vanished and the fields we see in the top photograph on the opposite page became covered with the houses and roads we see in the photograph on this page. A rural community in 1921 became an entirely urban one, so that in 2021 not one farmhouse or related building exists within the original township boundary, all that can be found are the remains of a few stone walls that once surrounded the farmers fields.

In this book I would like to look back to the beginning of the twentieth century and present a picture of Harton Township as we witness the centenary of its demise. This book is not saying it shouldn't have happened and Harton should have stayed fields and farms, merely it is exploring what was here before.

Harton Township

Chapter 1

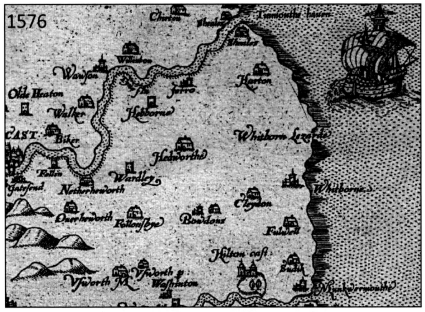

A section from the 1576 Christopher Saxton map of County Durham.

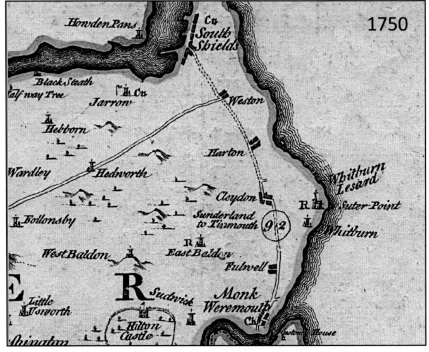

A section from Thomas Kitchin's 1750 map of the County Palatine of Durham.

Introduction

Harton Township ceased to exist in 1921, hence this book written in 2021 marks the centenary of its demise. In this first chapter I wish to present a short insight into the pre-twentieth century life of Harton Township.

I was aware that Harton Village was clearly marked on early maps as can been seen on the opposite examples, but it was the 1768 Richardson map reproduced in Hodgson's 1901 book *The Borough of South Shields* that first alerted me to such an entity as Harton Township. There is the name written clearly along the southern edge of Westoe. Note that South Shields and Westoe are also called townships. So my first question was, what is a township and my second, what were the boundaries of Harton Township?

For centuries in England a vill (Latin: villa) or township was a local division or district of a large ancient ecclesiastical parish, containing a village or small town, usually having its own church. Later, following the Reformation, the sixteenth century saw the development of civil parishes as an area of

Plan of the Townships of South Shields and Westoe in the County of Durham from a survey by Mr Richardson of Darlington 1768.

administration which over time could maintain different boundaries to the initial ecclesiastical parishes.   As indeed is the situation of Harton.   In medieval times a subdivision of St Hilda's ecclesiastical parish in South Shields it became in its entirety the ecclesiastical parish of Harton St Peter in 1864 but by 1890 with the growing population in West Harton, this new ecclesiastical parish of Harton St Peter was subdivided into that of All Saints' in the west and St Peter's in the east.   This dividing up of ecclesiastical parishes boundaries as new churches were built would continue well into the twentieth century.   However the civil township of Harton remained as the original medieval ecclesiastical township until 1901 when a portion was taken into South Shields and then finally in 1921 when the civil township of Harton ceased to be.

The civil administrative area known as Harton Township, whose northern boundary is seen on the 1768 Richardson Survey (see p9) can be seen on the 1863 Ordinance Survey map shown below. It contained a long coastline

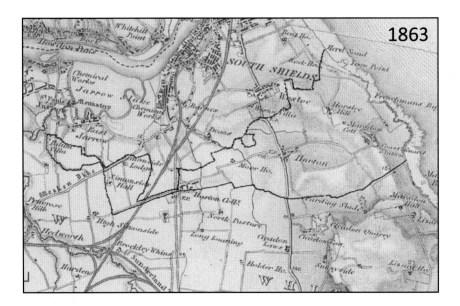

and extended from, although in increasingly slender amounts, to beyond Jarrow Slake. Harton Colliery was in its early existence when this map was surveyed and the township was predominately an area of agriculture with farmers' fields stretching from the west all the way to the rocky coastline, although some small scale quarrying may have taken place from early times.

This 1863 map predates the establishment of the Parish of Harton St Peter, which was established out of St Hilda's Parish in 1864. The first vicar, Arthur A Phillpotts explains in his record written in 1869 concerning the establishment of the parish of Harton St Peter that,

'the Boundaries fixed upon were nearly the same as those of Harton Township, except that Brinkburn and Dene Farm, both of them being in the Borough of South Shields, were included, and those portions of the township which lay beyond the Boldon Lane were left out since they had previously been united to the Parish of St Mary's.'

The areas Phillpotts refers to as *'beyond the Boldon Lane'* are the portions of Simonside which were taken into Harton Township in the seventeenth century. So it is clear that Harton Township existed before the parish of Harton St Peter was created and in this book it is this civil township that is being discussed not an ecclesiastical parish, although it is acknowledged that the beginnings of the township were related to a religious administrative division.

A close up of a section of the left light of The Transfiguration Window in Durham Cathedral created by Tom Denny and installed in 2010; representing the hermit monk who became, at the insistence of the King of Northumbria, the Bishop of Lindisfarne in 685.

Haliwerfolc

In Norman and medieval times the people of Harton Vill (Township) could proudly call themselves Haliwerfloc. That is the people/folk of the saint. The saint being St Cuthbert of Lindisfarne (634-687) whose body now lies in Durham Cathedral.

People of the saint, their land owned by, and their allegiance given to St Cuthbert, or his representatives, the Prior of Durham (later the Dean and Chapter) and the Bishop Palatine of Durham.

All the land between the River Tyne and the River Wear was gifted in the later part of the ninth century to St Cuthbert, that is the community of faithful monks who had taken his body in 875 from Lindisfarne to escape the pagan invaders and who would finally settle at Durham in 995, by King Guthred of Northumbria (died 894/5). The great Saxon historian Bede could not mention this event as it took place about 150 years after his death. However it is mentioned in two early anonymous works, the *Historia de Sancto Cuthberto* and the *Cronica monasterii Dunelmensis*, both refer in broad terms to the land between Tyne and Wear without specifying the vills included in Guthred's original grant. However Harton is categorically mentioned in the 12th century *History of the Church of Durham* written by Symeon, a monk and precentor of Durham who died in 1129.

Initially he describes how the King's gift to the community happened;

'The saint once more appeared to the abbot in a vision, and spoke thus:- "Tell the King that he must give to me, and to those who minister in my church, the whole of the district lying between the Wear and the Tyne, to be held in perpetuity, that it may be the means of providing them with the necessaries of life, and to secure them against want. Moreover- as the land which he had demanded situated between the two rivers was immediately conveyed to him - it was resolved by the assent of the whole people that if anyone gave land to St Cuthbert, or if any land was purchased with his money, that from that time no one should presume to exercise over it any right of service or custom; but that the church alone should possess in perpetuity unbroken quiet and liberty therein, together with all customs.....
(it was in this same vision that the right of sanctuary was created, which prevailed at Durham until 1624)

Later in his account Symeon mentions Harton by name when explaining that the Norman Bishop Walcher (Bishop of Durham 1071-1080) to support three benedictine monks, who inspired by Bede had travelled north to rebuild the monastery at Jarrow, granted to them the vill, or estate, of Jarrow itself and the adjoining vills of Simonside, Monkton, Heworth, Hebburn, Westoe and Harton, *so that they might live in comfort.*

The Convent (Monastery) at Durham quickly gained more land eventually owning most of the land between the Tees and the Tyne plus parts of Northumberland, and Yorkshire. It became a very rich monastery as it gained the tithes, rents and dues from these lands and the work they supported.

A contemporary photograph of Durham Cathedral taken from the south showing many of the remaining monastic buildings of this large and important monastery.

The area between the Tyne and the Wear under the control of these Benedictine monks developed into a group of busy and prosperous communities. Harton was an agricultural vill, the farms being held from the Prior and Convent of Durham either on customary tenure or as bondage tenement. In the former the tenant paid a fine on entering his holding and a rental assessed yearly by the jury of the Halmote Court. He had also to render customary services to the Prior as well as the common services of the vill; to bear arms when called on for the defence of the bishopric and to keep his tenement in repair. Provided he complied with the conditions he held for life and his widow or heirs succeeded to the holding on payment of a fine. Failing direct heirs the nearest blood relative could take up the holding and only in default of such relations coming forward was the holding let out to another tenant. The bondsmen held at the will of the lord, or in this case the agent of the Prior and could not leave the vill without his licence. Part of their rental was worked out in days' work and they were bound in addition to render certain services such as riding on messages, working the demesne land etc., to the Convent. (A considerable change occurred at the end of the fourteenth century when various servile tenures were abolished and they were substituted by penny rents or money rentals.)

An illustration from the 14th-century Luttrell Psalter depicting a medieval harvest. The Luttrell Psalter is an illuminated manuscript that was produced in East Anglia, and dates from around 1320-1340. The text is in Latin, while the marginal illustrations show saints, bible stories and everyday rural life.
Held in the British Museum.

The Lord Prior's court travelled around the Convent's estates three times a year, in the early spring, summer and autumn. For the folk of Harton the nearby manor house at Westoe was the place where these Halmote Courts were held forming a remarkable efficient instrument of local government and jurisprudence. The Halmote discharged functions of a threefold order:

1 It let the lands and tenements of the Convent and regulated and enforced conditions of tenancy.

2 It made by-laws and regulations for the trading and good government of the vills and the prevention of nuisances or trespasses.

3 It inflicted penalties for breeches of these orders and injunctions: for unfair or illegal trading, including the selling of inferior goods or the charging of excessive prices; for assaults and trespasses; the administration of wills; the issues of marriage licences; the appointment of guardians for orphan children; the recovery of debts and the punishment of runaway servants.

The Prior occasionally presided in person, generally it was at least two of the three great lay officials off the Convent; the steward, the land agent or the treasurer together with a jury of four or five of the tenants of each vill, chosen at one court to take office (usually for one year) at the next.

Through these records of the Convent (Conventual Records) we have tantalising snippets about medieval life in Harton vill/township and learn the names of many of the inhabitants of the area 600-700 years ago.

Hodgson in his *The Borough of South Shields,* quotes extensively in his early chapter *The Domain of the Church* from the Halmote Rolls and cites many examples from Harton as well as Shields and Westoe. Volume 82 of the

A border illustration from the 14th-century Luttrell Psalter.

Surtees Society also contains an extensive selection from the records of the Halmote Court of Durham Priory for the period from 1296 to 1384 and the following are a few examples of the type of entries we see in relation to the folk of Harton Township, providing us with names as well as glimpses into their lives:

In 1368 Emma (Halmot Roll 71) the widow of Walter the swineherd, is granted a new tenancy of the property formerly leased by her husband. She pays an initial premium of £3 6s 8d and an annual rent of £1 6s 8d, with some reduction allowed for the first 3 years.

HARTON. Emma quæ fuit uxor Walteri Swynherd venit in cur' et cepit unum bondagium quod prædictus Walterus quondam vir suus prius tenuit: habend' et ten' ad term. vitæ suæ ut de jure viduæ: redd. scaccario Prioris Dunelm' 26s. 8d. et argentum terrarii: incipiendo [etc.] - - Et dat pro gres'm'a v marcas: et condonatur ad 13s. 4d. et non plus, eo quod ædificavit et non tenuit nisi per iij annos.

Halmota prioratus Dunelmensis, containing extracts from the Halmote Court or Manor Rolls of the Prior and Convent of Durham, ed. J. Booth. (Surtees Society, 82: Durham, London and Edinburgh, 1889.)

The court rules on a dispute between Matilda, the widow of John Wymerk, and their son Patrick. Patrick is to make a goodwill payment of 13s 4d to Matilda in two instalments of 6s 8d. Thomas Ward is fined 1s 6d for damage to three hedges.

In 1360 John Colyn is fined 6d for illegally moving the boundary stones in the common field, a frequent offence in medieval times as tenants tried to encroach on land farmed by fellow villagers.

Thomas Colyn (Halmote Roll 76) held a bondage tenement which was taken at his death in 1369, by Dionysia his widow, *of widow's right*, paying 30s for the first year rising to 35s in the sixth and engaging not to marry without the Terrar's leave.

On occasions of the Halmotes, apparently minor officials or servants were billeted on the tenants, for Roger Ward, his son and Thomas Page of Harton were in 1373 (Halmote Roll 69) fined 18d, because they were unwilling to furnish beds at the Halmote.

In 1366 the whole vill of Harton, with the exception of Thomas Page were fined 12d each for failing to attend the court punctually. (Halmote Roll 43)

Adam Carter, with four others was fined in1382 (Halmote Roll 173) because their dogs attacked a flock of sheep in lambing season, worrying three lambs.

Hodgson quotes two references from the Conventual Records of wrecks and wrecking both involving men of Harton. The Harton coastline must have been a treacherous area for sailing vessels making for or leaving the Tyne, abounding with cliffs and hidden rocks. In February 1315 a charge of

A medieval shipwreck depicted in the 14th century.
Held in the British Library.

wrecking was brought against certain men of Harton, Westoe and Whitburn who had broken up the king's ship *The Falcon* which, laden with victuals and other goods from Berwick, had been wrecked by a tempest near Whitburn and carried off certain goods from the wreck.

In 1382 (Durham Halmote Roll 173) Thomas de Neuton and six others, who had taken a cable and other necessaries from a wrecked ship at Harton without the licence of John Godwyn, servant of the Manor, were fined 40d and it was enjoined upon all the tenants of the vill that they are not to meddle with or remove any wreck of the sea without the licence of the Lord or his servants, under penalty of 100s.

The tenants of Harton and Westoe Townships were all bound to buy beer at the Conventual Brewery at Scheles which in the autumn of 1296 (Halmot Roll 5) was let to John Scot and Euota of Jarrow for 20s a year. The tenants were also bound to grind their corn at the mill of the manor, which although always called the mill of Westoe, was situate nearer the vill of South Shields, on the western bank of the inlet which it gave its name and near what is still known as the Mill Dam. We have no record of the date of the erection of the mill but it was repaired in 1347 at a cost of 3s. 2d. In 1364 (Halmote Rolls 27 & 44) and again two years later, all the tenants of Westoe and Harton were ordered to cause to be repaired the pond or dam of the mill. Many other by-laws and injunctions

Border illustration from the 14th-century Luttrell Psalter.

were issued and maintained by the court, such as the tenants of Harton and Westoe Vills were ordered to keep the high road clear of dung (Halmote Roll 158), forbidden to sell growing crops without permission (Halmote Roll 91), not to contaminate the well of Cauldwell (Halmot Roll 108) by using it to wash clothes or to do so in the watercourse near Westoe Chapel (Halmote Roll 160).

An idea of the value of farm stock at that period is furnished by the inventory of goods and cattle of Thomas Page of Harton who died in 1379 (Halmote Roll 151). It included three oxen worth 12s per head; one horse, 16s; one cow, 10s; two others 8s each; one heifer, 4s; one sow, 4s; four pigs, 9s; one pig, 11d; three little pigs, 3s 1d; two carts with wheels sound with iron, with gear, 16s; one plough, with gear, 5s; one fireplace of iron, 8s; one lead, 8s; one winnowing fan with three sacks, 3s; two brazen jars and one washing tub, 3s; also wheat, barley, peas and oats, besides the cost of reaping the same, £6 13s 4d and he also had another horse worth 18s, which the Master of Jarrow had under name of mortuary, (a customary gift formerly claimed by and due to the incumbent of a parish in England from the estate of a deceased parishioner) the entire value of the goods, exclusive of the mortuary, being £13 19s 4d.

The rental account of the priory for 1446 shows that the land at Harton was let to various tenants and brought in annual rents of £24 13s 8d. Other land which was potentially worth £2s 4d per annum lacked a tenant and lay waste. By 1464 the rental income from Harton had risen slightly to £28 12s.

Dean and Chapter

The rental account of the priory for 1539, compiled just before its dissolution, shows annual rents paid by 10 tenants, each paying 54s 7d per annum: William Atkinson, John Brompton, William Brompton, Robert Chambers, Thomas Hutchinson, James Keching, Richard Newton, Richard Pearson, Robert Robinson and John Wilkinson. The total rental return was therefore £27 5s 10d, while the tenants at Westoe paid £26 6s 0d and those at Shields £13 3s 4d, including in this case 7 shillings for the right to brew ale. However there is a separate return for Shields Heugh where one tenant, Thomas Ponchon, paid the surprisingly large rent of £8 and the priory also received £10 annual rent for the mill and £1 10s 0d for the rental of 7 salt pans.

With the dissolution of the monasteries the property of the priory was transferred to the newly-created Dean and Chapter of Durham, although it is unlikely that the Harton tenants noticed the change. A rent roll for 1580 shows that the standard rent for the Harton tenants remained at 54s 7d and that almost all the leases remained in the same families:

1 Andrew Atkinson, presumably the son of William Atkinson.
2 Margaret Harrigate, daughter to widow Brompton by her second marriage, is to have a lease of the family farm but without prejudice to the rights of her mother, presumably the widow of John or William Brompton.
3 Robert Chambers, the same tenant as in 1539 or his son.
4 Thomas Hutchinson, the same tenant as in 1539 or his son.
5 Thomas Keching, presumably the son of James Keching - in his turn he has a son Stephen who shares in the lease.
6 Richard Newton, possibly the same as in 1539 or his son.
7 Thomas Newton, presumably the son of Richard Newton.
8 Thomas Pearson, presumably the son of Richard Pearson.
9 The widow Wilkinson, presumably the widow of John Wilkinson.
The only new name in the 1580 roll is that of Robert Taylor who rents land at the standard annual amount of 54s 7d.

The next major change, though it proved to be a temporary blip, took place in 1649 at the end of the Civil War when the new Protectorate abolished the Dean and Chapter and effectively nationalised its property holdings. The restoration of the monarchy in 1660 resulted in the return of the Dean and

Chapter, and they remained the landlords of Harton for the next two centuries until 1836 when church holdings were brought together under the control of the Ecclesiastical Commissioners.

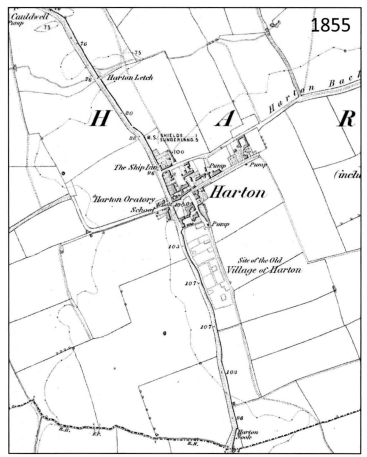

The first Ordinance Survey Map of 1855, shown here as a section between Cauldwell and the Nook, holds an interesting feature; it marks the site of an earlier village of Harton.

On seeing the site of an earlier village marked on this the first ordinance survey map of Harton, speculation brings one to imagine that the village was moved to wipe out one of the numerous plagues that swept the country. There is even a tradition that a sailor who was onboard the wrecked French ship which gave Frenchman's Bay its name, having staggered ashore to find human habitation, came upon Harton and was taken in by the villagers without knowing he carried the plague, which subsequently led to the village having to be burnt down.

Hodgson in his *History of the Borough of South Shields* 1901 addresses this in a footnote on p5:

On the Ordinance Map a field on the north side of the highway through Harton, between Harton Grange and Moor Croft, is marked as the 'site of the ancient village of Harton'. A local tradition states that the population of Harton was almost wholly swept away by an outbreak of plague which led to the demolition of the old village. We have found no evidence in support of the tradition.

So why an ancient village is mentioned on this OS map, why it was abandoned, sadly remains a mystery? Surely if the village had been razed to the ground as part of the civil war or something similar it would have received a mention in the history books? But this OS map appears to be the only mention of it.

Robert Surtees in his *The History and Antiquities of the County Palatine of Durham: Gateshead Section p8,* 1820 describes Harton as:

Harton,
A village near the sea-coast, anciently Heortedun—why not the hill of stags? The whole coast was once a forest, notwithstanding its present naked appearance. Harton was included in Aldwin's donation to the reviving monastery of Jarrow. With the other possessions of that house it became the property of the Convent of Durham; was granted, after the dissolution, to the new cathedral; and is now entirely held by lease under the Dean and Chapter.

Harton was the residence of the family of Smart, of whom came that turbulent Prebendary, Peter Smart, of the fourth stall.

Neither he nor any later gazetteer mentions an ancient village. Surtees does make it clear however that Harton in 1820 remains church land, it is not the Duke of Northumberland nor any other wealthy lord or landowner who owns the land but the Dean and Chapter, as the descendants of the community of St Cuthbert, to whom the land was gifted nine centuries earlier.

Surtees goes on to explain how parts of Simonside came with the remit of Harton Township. Interestingly in his book Harton's description requires eight lines, Westoe a little less than half a page, but Simonside two full pages. In essence although gifted, as all the land between Tyne and Wear was in the ninth century, to St Cuthbert, Germanus, Prior of Durham between 1163-1186, granted Simonside to Hugh de Morwick (the Northumbrian Baron of Chevington). Sibil, his daughter and coheir became the wife of Roger de Lumley, who descendants held Simonside.

Robert first Lord Lumley, fourth in descent from Sibil, forfeited his lands and title in open battle against the canker Bolingbroke *who had supplanted his gracious patron Richard.* Simonside as with Robert's other lands reverted to the Convent at Durham but were almost immediately granted to Sir Ralph Bulmer, and in that family rested until 1522 when Sir William Bulmer exchanged his lands in Monkwearmoth, Simonside and Durham for certain other lands of the Convent in Thorp Hewles, Claxton and Fishburne. On the dissolution Simonside was granted to the Dean and Chapter of the new Cathedral at Durham.

Surtees also explains; *There is a tradition that the village of Simonside was entirely depopulated about two centuries ago by the plague, and the nearest townships divided the deserted lands....parts of Simonside now lie in Harton, Westoe, Monkwearmouth, Southwick and Fulwell.* Hodgson similarly mentions the division of Simonside between neighbouring townships but Surtees writing in 1820 would give the date of this division of the lands as about 1620, Hodgson states it as being 1489.

What we see however is that indeed two bubble shaped pieces of land (see map on p2) to the west of Harton Moor that are named Simonside are part of Harton Township.

Through the seventeenth and eighteenth centuries agriculture continued to be the main employment in Harton. We gradually witness the rise of more prosperous families living in the township. Larger farm holdings replaced

Pockerley Manor House at Beamish Museum gives a lovely insight into what these larger tenant farmhouses at the end of the eighteenth century may have looked like.

smaller ones, which by the nineteenth century required some Harton tenant farmers to employ farm labourers, milk boys and others to assist with work on the farm, often living in cottages linked to the farm. A few large houses were also built during these centuries within the township such as that at Horsley Hill (p94) Harton House (p86) Simonside Hall p122) Marsden Cottage (p164) none have survived to 2021.

The foundation stone for Horsley Hill Farm, one source states, was laid on the 3rd Sept 1743. Described many times as a mansion it is certainly bigger than the usual farmhouse as seen by comparing it with in Pockerley Manor below.

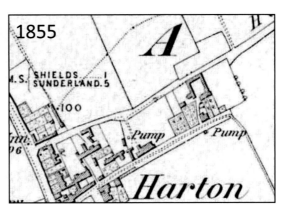

At Harton House, built about 1780, seen on this close up section of the 1855 map, there were extensive laid out gardens and orchards attached to the house, such as those recreated at Pockerley Manor.

It is obvious from the two-line comment at the end of Surtees' description of Harton that some educated, wealthy families must have been living in Harton, the Smart family for one.

A memorial stone and benefaction in St Paul's at Jarrow and a memorial stone in St Hilda's South Shields bear witness to other influential families. (Remembering that these were the only churches in the area at that time.) These are recorded in full in Surtees, chapter on the Parish of Jarrow, in *The History and Antiquities of the County Palatine of Durham: Gateshead Section* p25.

A MEMORIAL STONE PLACED OVER A VAULT
The burial-place of Thomas and Isabella Gibson of Harton, to whose much respected memory this tomb was erected by their son, Henry Gibson, of Newcastle upon Tyne, Surgeon, 1762.

A BENEFACTION
By will, dated 9 Feb. 1768 (proved at Durham in the same year) Richard Walker, of Harton, yeoman, directed his trustees, George Dale and Thomas Brunton, *to place out in their own names, upon security at interest, 60l.; and to pay and distribute the interest thereof yearly and every year for ever, in manner following, viz. five shillings, part thereof each day amongst the poor that attend at Jarrow church the Sacrament at Easter and Christmas; and 2s. 6d. other part of the said interest, each of the said days amongst the poor that attend at Heworth church; and as to the remainder of such interest money, to pay and apply the same towards educating as many poor widows' children within the Constabulary of Monkton, as it will allow.* **The testator also ordered his** *silver tankard and gill* **to be made into a flagon, and delivered to Jarrow church, for the use of the Communion-table.**

The following inscription commemorates the fate of a whole family at St Hilda's. Surtees, Parish of Jarrow, in *The History and Antiquities of the County Palatine of Durham: Gateshead Section* p8:

To the memory of GEORGE YEOMAN of Harton (in this county) Esq., who died January 23, 1785, aged 52 years; also of ESTER his daughter, an infant; and of ANN his daughter, who died on the 11th November 1793, aged 18, cut off by the corroding influence of a consumption, just as she was entering a world in which her beauty, her gentleness, and accomplishments would have attracted universal esteem.

Likewise of George, John, and Henry, his sons, who returning from Quebeck were shipwrecked on the Land's End on the 17th December 1797, GEORGE aged 23, JOHN 20, HENRY 18 years; which unhappy catastrophe, while it filled the heart of their surviving parent with the most poignant sorrow, diffused a gloom over the whole circle of the neighbourhood; for the pleasing expectations which the manhood of George had already confirmed, the less mature years of his brothers promised to fulfil.

Also to the memory of an afflicted Parent's last remaining hope THOMAS, who died March 19, 1799, aged 18 years. This monument, the sad memorial of no common devastation, is consecrated by the widowed Wife, and childless MOTHER. Stranger, if thou hast met with affliction, ponder o'er the rapid destruction of this once flourishing family, and in contemplating the sorrows of a forlorn mother, forget for a while thine own.

On the 19th March 1803, having borne with the meek and resigned spirit of a Christian the repeated deprivations of her husband and children, it pleased God to call from this trial of her fortitude and submission ANN YEOMAN, the wife and mother of the above recorded deceased, aged 60 years: by whose death no vestige of the existence of this family remains save this poor memorial.

It may well be that it was Ann Yeoman's husband who built Harton House which must have been one of the major buildings in the area at that time; judging by its footprint and extensive gardens and orchards (p86).

The Yeoman Memorial Stone in St Hilda's Church, Market Place, South Shields.
Reproduced by kind permission of the churchwardens.

Ecclesiastical Commissioners

In 1836, a year before Queen Victoria come to the throne (1837-1901) the Ecclesiastical Commissioners were formed as a result of investigations following on from the 1832 Reform Act into the inequality of church holdings in England and much of church-owned land came under their jurisdiction.

Living in South Tyneside we still know the land to be owned by the Ecclesiastical Commissioners or Church Commissioners as they became in 1948. (Indeed in 1967 I remember my father buying the freehold property for our family home in Harton House Road from the Church Commissioners.)

During the nineteenth century as travel particularly on the new railways opened up the country many directories and gazetteers listing detailed topographical accounts of places, parishes and counties were written for the traveller.

Three further descriptions of Harton Township are given here each about twenty years apart offering valuable insight into the character of Harton and the changes it was experiencing.

In the *Topographical Dictionary of England* originally published by S Lewis, London, 1848, Harton is given this description:

HARTON, a township, in the chapelry and union of South Shields, parish of Jarrow, E. division of Chester ward, N. division of the county of Durham, 2 miles (S. E.) from South Shields; containing 265 inhabitants.

This place, anciently *Heortedun*, was included in Aldwin's donation to the monastery of Jarrow, and, with the other lands of that establishment, became the property of the convent of Durham; it was granted to the cathedral after the Dissolution, and is now held under the Dean and Chapter.

The township is bounded on the east by the North Sea, and comprises 1390 acres 1 rod 37 perches, of which 884 acres are arable, 445 meadow and pasture, and the remainder roads and waste; the soil is chiefly clay, and coal is found in abundance. On the sea-shore, near Marsden Rock, is a verdant island called the Velvet Bed, which is a favourite resort of

visitors from Tynemouth and neighbouring places; and near it is a remarkable cavern, named the Fairies' Kettle.

A church was erected in 1836, at an expense of £650, raised by subscription; it is a neat structure in the early English style, with a square embattled tower crowned by pinnacles, and contains 280 sittings, of which 138 are free: the living is a curacy, in the patronage of the Incumbent of South Shields. The tithes have been commuted for £5 payable to impropriators, and £249 to the curate of the chapel of Trinity, South Shields.

A photograph in Hodgson of the Oratory at Harton built in 1836 and demolished in 1867 when the current church was consecrated. This low boundary wall still stands between the churchyard and Moor Lane.

This small chapel or Oratory mentioned in the 1848 description of Harton had been erected in 1836 by public subscription. The curate of St Hilda's Rev William Coward having held services at Harton since 1829, a stone building was erected, which was later expanded and a tower added as can been seen in the photograph above. However it was not until December 1857 that the Ecclesiastical Commissioners gave two acres of land to form a burial ground attached to the Oratory. The parish churchyard at St Hilda's in South Shields adjoining the market place, having been closed left the parishioners of Harton with a problem as they had no legal right to be buried in the new municipal graveyard at Westoe not being rate-paying members of South Shields. Hence the necessity for this new churchyard in Harton.

It was not until August 27th 1864 that Harton was created a separate parish and in 1867 the new church was built. The ecclesiastical parish of Harton St Peter, had initially, much the same boundaries as the civil township except it did not include Simonside and it did include Brinkburn and Dene Farm.

In 1870-72, John Marius Wilson's *Imperial Gazetteer of England and Wales* described Harton as:

HARTON, a township in Durham; on the coast, 2 miles South of South Shields railway station. Post town, South Shields. Acres, 1,537; of which 144 are water. Real property, £8,672; of which £4,000 are in mines, and £300 in quarries.

Population of 877.
Houses, 176.

The name is a corruption of Heorte-dune, signifying *the hill of stags*; and, like the names Hart, Hartness, and Hartlepool, commemorates the ancient abundance of harts on the Durham sea board. ...

An extensive colliery at West Harton is 215 fathoms deep.
A cavern on the coast is called the Fairies' Kettle Cave.

A contemporary engraving of Harton Colliery. The first sod was cut on 10th May 1841 and four years later in 1845 the Bensham Seam was won.
(Harton Colliery see page 272, the Fairies Kettle see page 223)

The 1881 census (quoted in *Kelly's Directory 1890*) gives the population of the township as 3,484. There were 601 inmates in the workhouse, leaving 2,883 as the general population which had therefore more than tripled in ten years since *Wilson's Imperial Gazetteer* and the previous census. Most of this increase was due to the huge increase in the industrial working population in West Harton.

Rev Phillpotts the first vicar of Harton St Peter came to the conclusion in 1883 that in view of the increase of the population at the west end of the ecclesiastical parish a new church should be built and a new parish formed in the colliery area. He applied to the Ecclesiastical Commissioners for sites for a church and a vicarage. The site for the church was granted in 1884 and that for the vicarage in 1888. At the time of Rev Phillpotts' death in 1888 the church was almost completed but about £500 was still required to cover the cost. (See document overleaf.) It was consecrated on 11th June 1890 by Bishop Westcott and an order setting up a new parish was made in August 1890.

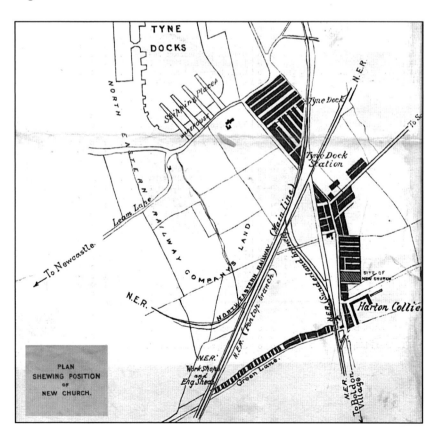

Harton, South Shields.

H ARTON, which was formerly a portion of the Parish of St. Hilda, South Shields, was formed into a separate Parish in the year 1864.

The population was then about 900. A Church was soon built to accommodate 220. During the last four years there has been a large increase of population in that part of the Parish called West Harton, which is close to Tyne Docks, belonging to the North Eastern Railway Company. This population amounts to nearly 3,000, and is increasing; its proximity to the Railway and Tyne Docks being the cause of this increase.

The great majority of the new inhabitants are employed by the North Eastern Railway Company, either on the line or in the railway shops, or are connected with the Docks.

This population is without Church Accommodation, being a mile and a quarter from the Parish Church, which is also too small for them. It has become necessary, therefore, to build a new Church for this part of the Parish. The Ecclesiastical Commissioners, who own the land, have given a site, valued at £600, and have also promised £1,000 towards the Church. The Bishop of Durham's Special Church Building Fund have given £300. The Harton Coal Company have also given £300; other subscriptions have been received, amounting altogether to about £2,360. The Church will cost about £2,650, and an additional sum of about £200 will be required for fencing, drainage, &c., of ground around the new Church.

Only a comparatively small sum can be expected from the inhabitants them-selves, who belong to the working class, and there are no landed proprietors to whom to apply for help. The only employers of labour are The Railway Company and The Harton Coal Company. As already stated, the latter of these Companies has subscribed, but the former, by its rules, is precluded from doing so.

It is necessary, therefore, to appeal to those who are not immediately connected with the Parish, and especially to individual shareholders of The North Eastern Railway Company, in the hope that they will help to supply Church accommodation for this increase of population.

The Church is almost completed, but until necessary funds are forthcoming, cannot be consecrated.

Subscriptions, however small, are earnestly solicited, to enable the Committee to open the Church without a debt, which would be a heavy burden on a congregation composed of the working class. They may be sent to Rev. J. Dixon Hepple, Harton Vicarage, South Shields, or paid to Messrs. Dale & Co., Bankers, South Shields, to the credit of the Harton Church Building Fund.

J. DIXON HEPPLE, Vicar, Harton, South Shields.
C. W. ANDERSON, Belvedere, Harrogate.
LINDSAY WOOD, The Hermitage, Chester-le-Street. } Building Committee.
J. M. MOORE, Harton.
GEORGE MAY, Simonside Hall, South Shields.

Reproduced by kind permission of the vicar and churchwardens of Harton St Peter.

Kelly's Directory of Durham 1890

HARTON is a small village, township and parish, formed 1864 from the parish of St. Hilda, South Shields; it is 2 miles from South Shields, in the Jarrow division of the county, east division of Chester ward, union, county court district and petty sessional division of South Shields, rural deanery of Jarrow and archdeaconry and diocese of Durham. The church of St. Peter is a building of stone, in the Early English style, consisting of chancel, nave, south porch and a tower with spire containing 2 bells: there are 220 sittings. The register dates from the year 1864. The living is a vicarage, net yearly value £330, with residence, in the gift of the Dean and Chapter of Durham, and held since 1888 by the Rev. John Dixon Hepple M.A. of University College, Durham. There are Primitive Methodist and Wesleyan chapels at West Harton. Here is also an extensive colliery, employing a great number of men: connected with the colliery is a reading room for the miners. The Ecclesiastical Commissioners are lords of the manor and principal landowners. The soil is clay; subsoil, sand. The chief crops are wheat, oats and some pasturage. The area of the township is 1,430 acres; rateable value, £17,823; the area of the ecclesiastical parish, 1,200 acres; the population of the township in 1881 was 3,484, which includes 601 officers and inmates in South Shields Workhouse, and of the ecclesiastical parish, 1,567.

A photograph of All Saints Church, Boldon Lane, taken in 1983 by Ken Ludi.

CAULDWELL is a small hamlet in this parish.

Sexton St. Peter's, Walter Tunnah.

POST & M. O. O., S. B. & Annuity & Insurance Office, Harton Colliery.—David Bailey, postmaster. Letters through South Shields arrive at 9.30 a.m. & 6 p.m. Collections at 9.30 & 11.15 a.m. & 4.30 & 7.30 p.m. on week days : sundays at 3.30 p.m. Tyne Dock is the nearest telegraph office

Harton letters arrive at 9.30 a.m. & 4.30 p.m. WALL LETTER BOX cleared at 9.45 a.m. & 4.45 p.m. on week days ; sundays at 3.25 p.m. The nearest telegraph office for this place is Westoe

South Shields Union Workhouse, West Harton, Jas. Craik, master ; Mrs. Ann Craik, matron

Police Office, West Harton, William Deaton, sergeant in charge & 1 constable

SCHOOLS :—

St. Peter's National, Harton, for 70 children ; average attendance, 56 ; Miss Elizabeth Reed, mistress

National, West Harton (mixed & infants), for 140 boys, 140 girls & 140 infants ; average attendance, 111 boys, 97 girls & 91 infants ; Henry Cook, master ; Miss Mary Craigie, mistress ; Miss Elizabeth P. Dixon, infants' mist.

A postcard showing St Peter's Church from the north.
For a brief period Harton Village was connected to South Shields by a horse-drawn omnibus which ran for nine years between 1897 and 1906 and is captured in this image.

Now sections of three ecclesiastical parishes were within the civil township of Harton, St Peter's in the east, All Saints' in the west and St Mary's in the Simonside section. To repeat however, this book deals with the civil township ruled by a council which to make matters more difficult uses the word parish in its title, but this is not to be confused with the ecclesiastical/ parochial parishes councils or boundaries.

The churchyard at St Peter's opened because St Hilda's was full and Harton folk could not by right be buried in the municipal cemetery in Westoe. Westoe Cemetery all too quickly became full and the councillors of South Shields had to apply to the ecclesiastical commissioners for another plot. In 1884 they requested 30 acres of land on the edge of Westoe in Harton Township. They eventually bought this land from the Ecclesiastical Commissioners for £24,000 and it was consecrated in 1890. The architect Henry Grieves was given the job of designing the two mortuary chapels, linked by a gateway (the spire is 103 feet high) as well as a superintendent's house and a board room and an entrance gateway all in spectacular late gothic revival style.

The cemetery became part of the borough of South Shields in 1901.

Harton Cemetery Entrance, South Shields.

Triple-arched, gothic gateway, having a tall, grand central carriage entrance, flanked on either side by a low footway. The central gable has a quatrefoil roundel in its apex, below this are 2 shields inscribed AD 1889. The piers of the arches are buttressed on their east and west faces. All the wrought-iron gates in-situ.
Postcard from the collection of E Lewthwaite.

Two early photographs of Harton Cemetery, a contemporary architectural description explains that, the chapels lie to the east of the entrance at the centre of the cemetery. An H shaped plan, the chapels forming the 2 outer arms, the crosspiece formed by the porch and vestry of each chapel with a grand arched carriage-way at the centre. All is built in coursed rubble, with ashlar for dressings and decorative features and with slate roofs. Designed in a free late gothic manner with Tudor overtones. The most outstanding feature is the very tall and elegant tower and spire which surmounts the central gate-way. Square for the first 2 stages, the archway in the first. Second stage has narrow octagonal turrets at the angles which rise into the third stage. Third stage is octagonal with tall traceried openings. Fourth stage a narrow octagonal stage with pierced parapet. Finally a tall spire. The Superintendents House and Board Room are said to be most picturesque, Tudor in style with upper parts half timbered.

Note in the upper photograph Harton Village can be seen on the horizon as well as Cleadon Water Tower.

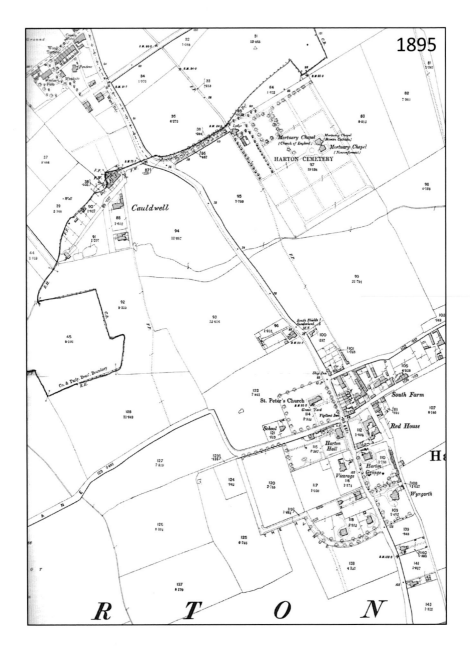

1895

The boundary of Harton Township prior 1901.

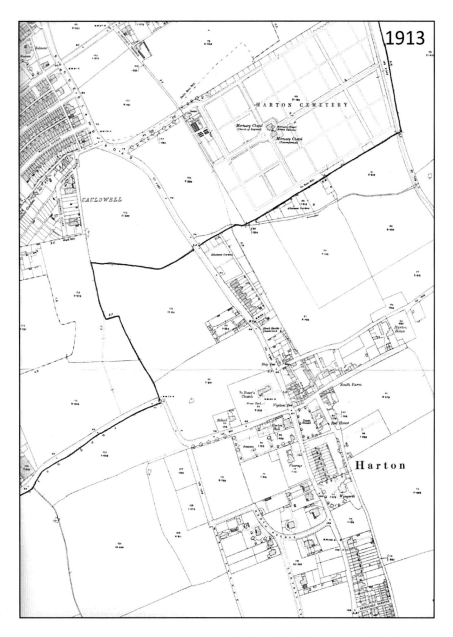

The boundary of Harton Township after 1901.
Notice the cemetery layout has increased and the field layout changed to the south of the
cemetery to denote a planned extension and the area used for Mitchel Gardens prefabs
during WW2. The L shaped land used for the houses of Harton House Road in the 1930s
has also been created. South Shields housing has now reached as far as Cauldwell.

County Borough of South Shields.

PROPOSED EXTENSION.

STATEMENT ON BEHALF OF THE CORPORATION.

PRELIMINARY.

As very few of the residents in Harton Parish can have had the opportunity of perusing and ascertaining for themselves the proposals which are contained in the Memorial of the Corporation to the Local Government Board, it is intended in this statement to set forth for their information some facts and particulars on the subject, and to enumerate some of the advantages which will be conferred upon the inhabitants of Harton Parish by its inclusion within the Borough Boundaries. They will thus be in a better position to decide whether it is to their interest to come within the Borough, or to remain under their present form of local government.

REASONS FOR EXTENSION.

The reasons for taking in the Parish are as follows, viz. :—the smallness of the area of the Borough in regard to its population—the number of inhabitants per acre being larger than any Borough of similar size—that it is rapidly growing; that its growth can only extend in one direction, that is into the Parish of Harton; that buildings have already over-stepped the Borough Boundaries in that

2

direction; that there is a community or similarity of interest between the inhabitants within and those without, evidenced by the fact that the residents in the Parish in great part are employed in business or in the works and commercial undertakings in the Borough; that West Harton in particular is to all appearances, and in every other respect except in its government, part of South Shields; that the Parish is dependent upon the Borough sewers for its drainage; and that for shopping, recreation, amusements and other advantages, the residents mostly resort to the Borough itself. There are other reasons, but these are perhaps the most important of those set forth in the Memorial to the Local Government Board.

ADVANTAGES.

The advantages which the residents of Harton will enjoy by their District becoming a part of the Borough of South Shields are numerous, and may shortly be stated as follows :—

The District will become part and parcel of a Municipal and County Borough which is possessed of the fullest powers of local self-government. As ratepayers in the Borough, they will, by their votes and representatives, have a voice in the conduct of the numerous institutions and undertakings of the Municipality in which they are, or ought, for their welfare, to be deeply interested. As residents over the border they are at present shut out from any share in its concerns, although the prosperity of their district depends upon the commercial prosperity of South Shields.

They will by joining the Borough have, *as of right*, the use of its Parks and Recreation Grounds, Libraries, Reading Rooms, Schools and Technical Classes, and Infectious Diseases Hospitals.

They will be entitled to vote in the election of the School Board, and thus their wishes will be respected in the provision of Schools for their children. Similarly, they will be able to have some control in the election of the Burial Board and in the work which devolves upon that body. They will thus be entitled to vote in the election for, and have representation on the following public bodies, namely :—County Borough Council, School Board, Burial Board, Board of Guardians.

3

They will, through their representatives on the Corporation, be in a position to require that better attention be paid to the paving and flagging and repair of their footpaths and roads, and they will have the benefit and assistance of an efficient staff of Sanitary Officers and Inspectors in the improvement of their dwellings and surroundings.

Instead of a government for local purposes by three separate authorities, viz., the Parish Council, the Rural District Council, and the Durham County Council (the last two of which have other and much larger districts to attend to)—and the Parish and Rural District Councils having besides limited means and powers—they will be a component part of a Municipal Corporation whose powers and duties combine, and in many respects exceed, the powers and duties of the present three governing bodies of the Parish.

In the important matter of Police supervision, they will have the advantage of the Police organisation of the Borough, instead of having to rely upon the provision for that purpose which is made by the Standing Joint Committee of the County Council, a body on which they have so small a share of representation, whereas in the Borough the representatives of the ratepayers have full control of the police.

The Fire Appliances of the Corporation will also be at their disposal, and it will be admitted that the protection which will be thereby afforded to them will be greater than anything they can hope for from a Parish Council.

It remains to be said that the introduction of Tramways and Electric Lighting or either of them in the Parish is impracticable under the present form of Government.

REPRESENTATION.

As the number of voters in Harton Parish does not exceed 800, and the smallest ward, viz. :—St. Hilda Ward has 1,188 voters it has not been found feasible to make Harton Parish a separate Ward, but in the re-distribution of the wards, consequent on the extension, West Harton will form part of the Tyne Dock Ward, and thus the residents of that portion of Harton will be allied to a district for voting purposes

4

in which they are in every way identified, and they may thus be assured of receiving every attention which is due to them.

Harton Village and Cauldwell and district adjoining will be joined to Westoe Ward for voting purposes, and the residents therein will thus be associated with the residents of Westoe in their choice of representatives.

Should the population of Harton increase at any future time to such an extent as to justify a larger representation by them on the Town Council the residents may rest assured that such a state of things will be bound to receive the earnest consideration of the Council.

FINANCES AND RATES.

Finally the finances of the Borough are in every way in a satisfactory condition. The liabilities are more than covered by the Assets and the Debt, which has been incurred in great part in respect of valuable productive undertakings and properties, compares very favourably with that in any other large Municipality.

Regarding the higher rates in the Borough as compared with those in Harton Parish it should be remembered that the provision of Schools, Parks, Libraries, and other institutions for the comfort, benefit, and recreation of the inhabitants, and the thorough Police and Sanitary inspection and supervision in a Borough are necessarily more costly than the administration of a district by a Parish Council and Rural District Council whose powers are insufficient and were never intended to meet the wants of an Urban District like West Harton for instance.

CONCLUSION.

The Corporation confidently believe that the residents of Harton, who thoughtfully consider these facts and weigh the advantages which they will derive from having Municipal Government extended to them, will not allow the question of an increase in their rates to deter them from coming within the Borough.

By Order,

J. MOORE HAYTON, Town Clerk.

January, 1901.

PROPOSED

BOROUGH EXTENSION.

THE CASE FOR HARTON.

A good deal has been said on the one side of this question, and it will probably be of interest to the inhabitants of the Parish of Harton to have the other side of the case put before them. Unfortunately, so far, there has been a distinct tendency to view the whole matter from one aspect only, and without any regard to what the people of Harton may think, or do. Judging from the remarks of some of the Members of the Town Council at their Meeting when the proposed extension was discussed, it would appear that there exists every reason why Extension *should* be granted, and no reason why it *should not*. The wishes of the community to be effected are apparently altogether a secondary consideration, and appear to be completely ignored. But surely the inhabitants of Harton are entitled to be consulted in the matter.

A series of reasons are put forward in the Memorial of the Corporation, which, at first sight, appear to be plausible enough and apparently authentic. One side of a story, however, is generally good only until the other side is told, and we will, therefore, endeavour to see what the other side shows in this case.

The Memorial alleges that the area of the Borough is almost entirely built over ; that the sanitary condition of Harton is unsatisfactory ; and that the inhabitants of Harton have the use and enjoyment of the Borough Parks, Free Libraries, Town Hall (?), Baths, and Wash-houses, etc.

2

The statement that the Borough area is almost entirely built over, is distinctly misleading. There are acres of eligible vacant building land for which not even estate plans have yet been passed, and, even if the area *was* built over, would that be any justification for taking in against its wish, an adjoining Community who, in no sense whatever, injuriously affects or menaces the interests of the Borough? Certainly not.

Then as to the sanitary condition of Harton.—If the allegation on this head holds good in the case of the Parish, it is still more applicable in the case of the Borough, as it can easily be proved that the sanitary condition of Harton will bear comparison any day with that of the corresponding localities within the Borough. Since the establishment of the District and Parish Councils, the administration of the Parish has steadily and immensely improved, and we emphatically say that, if it were in the Borough to-morrow, it would be no better (if as good) *at the same cost.* As regards the "use and enjoyment" of the Borough Undertakings, this is largely a mith. Of what use to the Harton people is the Town Hall, the Marine Parks, or even the Free Libraries? The first-mentioned is out of the question, and the distance of the Parks from Harton renders them useless to the Harton people, and it is very questionable whether they derive any benefit from the Free Libraries. We should think that those Undertakings are "enjoyed" much less by the Harton Community than by the visitors and trippers to the town.

_ The Memorial promises (if extension is granted) all manner of "Boons and Blessings" for Harton (*but it is discreetly silent as to what cost*) in the shape of better lighting, watching, sanitation, and so forth, for instance—the good wives of the Parish will be delighted to learn that they will be free to use the Public Baths and Wash-houses, which are located in Derby Street, some two miles away. But seriously, can the Corporation govern the Parish any better than it is now governed, *at the same cost.* Emphatically "No".

3

The cost of administration in the Parish averages about 3/- in the £, whilst that in the Borough averages over 6/- in the £, and if Harton is taken in, it follows that the rates will be practically doubled, and will anyone seriously contend that the so called advantages (?) will be worth the additional 3/- ? There is only one answer to this, and furthermore, the rates will not stop at 6/- if incorporation is granted, as it must be clear that, if it costs the Corporation 6/- in the £ to govern their present Area with a Rateable Value of £370,000, they cannot for one moment presume to govern an Area twice as large with an accretion of Rateable Value of only about £20,000—especially as they have no profit-earning concerns of their own with which to relieve the Rates. It follows, therefore, that the rates over both areas will increase —goodness knows to what extent—and this increase, although falling in the first instance on the Owners of property and Trades-people, must in the end, inevitably affect the rent-paying community.

Furthermore, one would think that before undertaking the Fatherly care of the Harton people, the Corporation would have endeavoured to complete the many schemes of improvement within the Borough which they have so long talked about, but with regard to which, so little has been accomplished. They are committed to a huge expenditure of Capital in respect of these, notably the Bents Improvement scheme, the New Municipal Buildings, the widening of Fowler Street and Mile End Road, &c., from not one of which the Harton people will derive any direct benefit whatever, and undoubtedly the principal reason for this extension *is to secure the Harton Rateable Value to help to pay the cost of these.*

Another point—the Memorial does not propose to give the Harton people any direct representation on the Council, but to tack on the added area to three of the existing Wards within the Borough without any increase in the number of Councillors, or even Guardians. This practically disfranchises the Harton people, and they may rest assured that the promised Boons, &c., in the shape of

4

better administration will not for some time (if ever) be realised. At any rate, taking East Jarrow as an object lesson on this score, this conclusion would appear to be amply justified. It is a matter of common knowledge that for some years past, the supplications of the East Jarrow (and sometimes Tyne Dock) people have been - "a voice crying in the Wilderness". And what better treatment may the Harton people expect?

Numbers of other reasons could be advanced to show that the would-be anxiety of the "City Fathers" to undertake the welfare of the Harton Community is founded—not so much on the principle of benevolence as on the cold principle of £ s. d., and surely there exists ample scope for the exercise of their powers and capabilities in setting their own house in order before trying their hand at "cleaning up" that of their neighbours.

Every effort is being, and will be, made by the local governing bodies in the Parish to frustrate this attempt of the Corporation to filch away the principle of Local Government from the Harton people, and as, in a matter of this kind, *the voice of the people is always of paramount importance*, it is therefore absolutely necessary that every Parochial Elector should at once make up his mind on the question, and, if he is against the scheme, should not fail to attend the Parish Meeting, and vote accordingly.

By authority of the Parish Council,

GEORGE TODD, *Chairman.*

WM. BAINBRIDGE, *Clerk.*

January, 1901.

1901

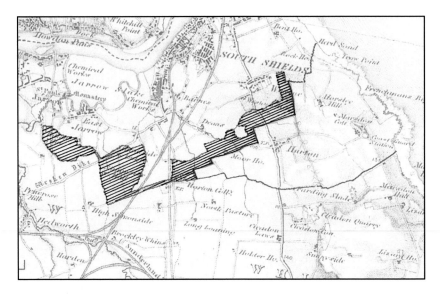

On this 1863 map with the boundary of Harton Township outlined I have shaded in the area subsumed into South Shields in 1901 and hence show the new boundary of Harton Township which would exist until 1921.

Although, as we have seen with the establishment of Harton Cemetery, land within Harton Township had been sold off by the Ecclesiastical Commissioners and it becomes apparent in the next chapter on Harton Farms that fields changed ownership and some farms increased in size and others diminished, the Township retained the same boundary as it had maintained for centuries.

However 1901 marked a change. The western end of Harton Township had become increasingly industrial and houses from Templetown, which was part of South Shields, were starting to blend in with those built in the Township, so that it was only a line on a map that denoted Harton Township from South Shields County Borough. Streets of houses were also creeping towards Cauldwell. No one could deny that South Shields was over crowded and more new housing required.

As early as February 1899 the Borough Surveyor of South Shields had presented a report recommending the inclusion in the Borough of 1,052 acres out of a total of 1,913 acres in Harton Township. His recommendation after meeting considerable opposition was in part approved by the Select Committee of the Houses of Commons and confirmed by the Local Government Provisional Act, no 7. 1st Edward VII, 1901, whereby a portion of the Township of Harton, including Harton Cemetery, Simonside and West Harton, being just over 260 acres in size and with a population of 3,595, was added to the Borough on November 9th

The debate had been recorded fully in the daily newspapers, Rev Hepple writing pages 114 and 115 of the vicar's journal gives his account:

After long and tedious enquiry, during which the inhabitants of Harton successfully resisted the attempt to include the village of Harton within the afore mentioned boundaries an act was passed and in 1901 an order of the Local Government Board came into operation, whereby the boundaries of the Borough of South Shields were extended so as to include so much of the former Township of Harton as lies south of a line extending from Trow Rocks to the south wall of the cemetery, and thence drawn along a small stream to the footpath leading from Cauldwell by the fields. The line leaves the footpath at or near the north stile, and follows this hedge to the elbow of the Moor Lane and thence follows the lane to the west wall of the workhouse enclosure, where it is connected to the original boundary.

Thus a considerable portion of the ecclesiastical parish, as settled in 1890 on the division of the parish by that of the formation of that of All saints Harton Colliery, is now included within the Borough of South Shields. The whole of Cauldwell, the cemetery house and 6 houses at East Harton are now in the Westoe Ward.

The effect of the rearrangement of the boundaries, that the present township or civil parish of Harton now lies entirely (once again) within the ecclesiastical parish of Harton St Peter, with the addition of two fields and the workhouse which are included in the parish of All Saints Harton.

In consequence of these changes the old Harton Parish Council was dissolved, and a meeting convened by the chairman Mr Todd, was held in the schoolroom for the purpose of electing a new Parish Council of 7 members for the reduced township. No poll was demanded and the new council consists of Messers Beazley, Crofton, G Brown, Hemsley, Inman, J B Laidler and Willis.

......the altered circumstances of the township, after consultation with the representatives of the diocese, and with the full concurrence of the vicar of All saints, Mr J Robson, it was decided, that after the 9th November the inhabitants of the Township of Harton who had been taken into the Borough now had their rights of burial in Harton cemetery and consequently must pay fees in Harton St Peter's Churchyard as non-parishioners.

ALL SAINTS' WEEKLY GAZETTE.

No. 409].   Saturday, Oct. 26th, 1901   [Gratis.

THE ANNUAL TEA

For All Saints' Parish will be held next week for the Adults, on Wednesday afternoon, Oct. 30th. This will be followed in the evening by the Harvest Festival Service, at which the special preacher will be the Venerable Archdeacon Watkins, of whose forceful eloquence and masterly scholarship there is no need to remind you.

The Children's Tea, on Saturday, Nov. 2nd, will be followed by two-fold Entertainment in the two School-rooms—in one a description of Iceland (with limelight views) and the boiling geysers and its other wonders, by Rev. J. T. Brown, and in the other a humorous mirth-raising entertainment, of which we must not yet reveal the nature.

After Nov. 9th the whole of the All Saints' Parish will be in the Borough of South Shields, and the Cemetery will be the legal Burial ground for all our people. No burials will be possible in Harton Churchyard (owing to scarcity of space) except for those already having purchased grave or having very near relatives buried there. Should any be wishful to inter their friends in S. Simon's churchyard, information should be obtained from the Vicar of S. Simon's.

On Sunday, Oct. 27th, Sermons will be preached, and the Evening Collection will be in favour of the Ingham Infirmary. All of us know how essentially necessary this is to a district like ours, where accidents are frequent and always possible.

The Churchworkers' Union begins its Session on Tuesday with an address from Bishop Ridley. For a generation the aged bishop has been the veritable apostle to the Indians and Miners of the outlandish parts of Northern British Columbia. 22 years he has been its bishop, and it is with touching pathos that we hear of the fearful loss he has just received in the burning down

An article published on Saturday, 26th October, 1901 about events at All Saints', the second section explaining to parishioners about the change of burial rights.

Reproduced by kind permission of the vicar and churchwardens of Harton St Peter.

On Tuesday, 25th June, 1901 *The Shields Gazette* reported the following:

The Bill confirming the Provisional Order of the Local Government Board for the extension of the boundaries the of the Borough of South Shields, again to-day, came before, the committee of the House Commons over which Sir John Brunner presided. The first evidence taken to-day was that of;

Mr. H. H. Law, M. I. C. R. the Local Government Board Inspector, who presided at the local inquiry. In answer to questions by the chairman, Mr. Law explained what, induced the Board make the Order it was sought confirm. Upon the evidence which was given before him, and also from his inspection of the added areas, he came to the conclusion that it was desirable that that which been included should be a part of the borough. It seemed, to him that the existing boundary at West Harton was an unsatisfactory one, as it not only passed down a road dividing two authorities having different powers, but it also passed through the streets at West Harton irregularly.

The two districts, which the Board had provisionally ordered to be included were Urban in character, whereas the parish of Harton still retained, rural features. The two populations which it was sought to amalgamate seemed to have more in common than they had with the parish, and it appeared to him the needs and requirements of those two places could be the better dealt with by an authority possessing Urban powers rather than by one which did not possess them. He did not think sufficient ground was shown for the inclusion the whole which the Corporation sought to be added—the entire parish of Harton. It therefore became necessary to select a boundary which would follow certain principles. That was to say it should include the two areas Simonside and West Harton. It was also the opinion the Local Government Board that the boundary should follow well defined lines which were easily recognised, and in selecting the boundary he endeavoured to exclude as far possible all that considered was purely agricultural, so after careful consideration he selected the boundary given in the order.

As to the advantages offered by the borough, he was of the opinion that the form of local government which the borough offered to these two areas was better suited to their needs than is the form of government which could be had under a Rural District Council. Moreover he thought the staff of the borough was better qualified to deal with the sanitary requirements of the area than that of the Rural District Council. With regard to what he might call the moral claim of Corporation to the

inclusion of these areas he considered they were, in fact, more closely related to the borough than they were to the parish. Again their existence was in the main due to their vicinity to a large town and that portion of West Harton which immediately adjoined the existing borough boundary was in his opinion an overflow of the borough. He believed that they had a community of interest with the borough they had not with the Rural District.

Harton Parish Councillors.
This photograph is dated 1901, hence it must show the Harton Parish Councillors prior to the reduction of Harton Township as following the 9th November 1901 the council was to be of seven members.

Under the Local Government Act of 1894, Rural District Councils had come into existence. Under the 1894 Act, Harton Township had become a civil parish in South Shields Rural District which also included the civil parishes (townships) of Boldon, Boldon Colliery, Monkton and Whitburn. South Shields Rural District was not a subsection of Durham County Council or South Shields County Borough, but an independent local authority over which Durham County Council had some degree of oversight. Ownership of land was not affected by local government control so the land still belonged to the Ecclesiastical Commissioners. Hence the references to Rural District in the preceding newspaper article. These District Councils particularly had powers with regard to public health, housing and highways.

Hence we see in the following article in *The Shields Gazette* of August 1902 Harton Parish (Township) Council agreeing to send letters to the District Council about sanitation issues and to the Ecclesiastical Commissioners concerning ownership of land.

HARTON PARISH COUNCIL. — The ordinary monthly meeting of the Harton Parish Council was held last evening in St. Peter's Schoolroom, Harton Village.—Mr J. B. Laidler presided.—The Clerk (Mr W. Bainbridge) read a communication from the Clerk to the District Council in reference to the penfold, that it was being put in order at a cost of about £70 and would be occupied at once, and also asking for an agreement as security of tenancy. In reply to complaints about sewer manholes the Clerk also wrote that plugging was considered dangerous to health, but that the District Council would find some other means of remedying the evil if possible. A letter was also read from the Town Clerk of South Shields, offering no objection to the sale of office furniture, and asking for further particulars of fire appliances etc., and a committee was appointed to make the necessary arrangements. On the motion of Mr P. Willis, it was decided to write to the Ecclesiastical Commissioners, drawing their attention to the condition of the wall adjoining the Marsden Road. The question of providing a public hall for the use of the village was introduced by Mr Beazley, who contended that such a building would be self-supporting. A reading room, and playground for the children in connection would be very useful to the people of the village. After some discussion it was decided that the Clerk write to the Commissioners and ask the terms upon which certain land had been granted for the use of the parish, the chairman and Mr Crofton dissenting. The Harton Coronation Committee, which met in connection with the above, Mr Laidler again presiding adopted a financial statement that £35 4s had been received in donations, £23 14s 8d expended on the local festivities, leaving a balance in hand of £6 9s 4d which was, after some discussion, ordered to be banked in the names of the chairman and Mr Inman as a reserve for future requirements.

1921

The 1921 South Shields Corporation Act received Royal Assent on 19th August whereby a portion of the Townships of Harton, Whitburn and Boldon in the rural district of South Shields containing 777 acres and a population of 1,964 was added to the borough on 9th November. The Township of Harton ceased to exist. A 701 acres strip of land along the coast remained in the Rural District of South Shields and for a while became administered as part of the Township of Whitburn. However in 1932 this too was subsumed in the County Borough of South Shields.

All these additions of land were explained in the commemoration book the *Borough of South Shields 1850-1950:*

In 1901 about 360 acres of Simonside and West Harton were added to the borough. A further 778 acres from Harton, Whiteleas and Boldon were added in 1921. By 1932 the population was 113,000 crowded into only 3,400 acres. Another 1,000 acres were added from the Rural District including land from Trow Rocks to Marsden Bay, Horsley Hill and Marsden. In 1950 a further extension with 760 acres at Whiteleas making a total of 5,189 acres as it is today. This meant that in 50 years the size of the town had increased by 50 precent.

The 1921 debate for and against the inclusion of Harton Township into the County Borough of South Shields had been as long and as heated as in 1901 and equally well recorded in the newspapers of the day as well as the minutes of the various committees and commissions involved in the decision. This time it was clearly about the need to have more land to build houses.

Turning once again to the Rev Hepple's diary page 146 we read:

By virtue of the Act obtained by the corporation of South Shields the borough boundary was extended to the south and a new ward called Harton Ward was established. This Ward comprises the Village of Harton and the Cleadon Park Estate, the new houses of which were begun Jan 1921. The ecclesiastical parish of Harton St Peter now lies within the borough area, except for the easterly portion which lies beyond a line from the SE corner of the cemetery to the stile on the footpath to Cleadon Park. This portion of the parish, including the Aged Miners Homes, the outlying farms and Salmon's Hall Cottages also the battery remains within the area of the administration of County Durham.

THE NEW BOROUGH BOUNDARY.

A line drawn from the East wall of the Cemetery to the stile on the footpath to Cleadon Park serves to indicate the Boundary of the new "Harton Ward" of the County Borough of South Shields. The Ecclesiastical Parish of Harton remains as it was before November 1st. The School, however, is now within the jurisdiction of the South Shields Local Education Authority. The New Houses on Cleadon Park Estate are in the Parish of Cleadon.

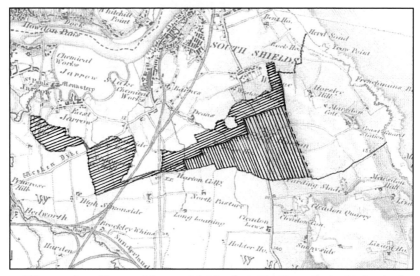

This map shows the remaining coastal strip of what had been the land belonging to Harton Township, which would move in 1921 into the Civil Parish of Whitburn as the Civil Parish of Harton (Township) had been dissolved. Eleven years later in 1932 this coastal strip would be taken into South Shields, which would then have achieved its long term aim of subsuming all of Harton Township.

The Shields Daily News Thursday, 2nd June, 1921 published the following:

BOROUGH EXTENSION BILL. In moving the adoption of the Parliamentary Committees report, J. R. Lawson referred to the South Shields Borough Extension Bill. He said it had passed the Committee of the House of Lords and speaking generally, he thought he could say that to the present they had achieved great success. The Corporation had acquired the whole of the populated district adjacent to the town, and the Park estate, on which the Corporation were projecting their public services, such as the light railway, the housing scheme, the hospital, and a new road or boulevard.

1932

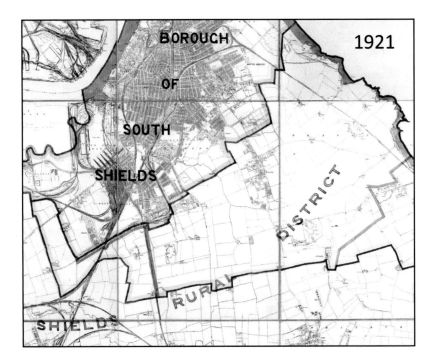

This map of 1921 shows the land which South Shields Corporation hoped to secure. A matter they had been pursuing since 1899. Even in 1921 it was not fully achieved. A large section of Harton Township including Harton Village was taken into South Shields' control, and quickly became covered in both private and corporation housing. These new, on the whole semi-detached houses, offered modern amenities such as indoor bathrooms and flush toilets as well as fresh air away from the industrial river and a garden to thousands of families.

In 1932 the coastline which had once been part of Harton Township moved out of the Rural District Council's control into the control of South Shields and after WW2 a huge housing estate at Marsden was built, followed by the acquisition of more land in 1950 at Whiteleas and Biddick Hall where further council housing took over the age-old farm land. Hence the boundaries of the County Borough of South Shields became much like those sought after for decades and drawn up on this map in 1921.

On Friday, 4th November, 1932 we find this report in *The Shields Daily News*:

SOUTH SHIELDS BOROUGH

Boundary Extension Scheme

APPROVED BY MINISTRY OF HEALTH

Approval has been given by the Ministry of Health to a boundary extension scheme which will add nearly 1,000 acres to the borough of South Shields (says the London correspondent of the "Northern Echo.")

A deputation representing the Corporation attended at the offices of the Ministry as their application was opposed by the Durham County Council.

The area to be added includes Frenchmen's Bay, Hunton Down Hill and Marsden Rock, and is bounded on the south side by the South Shields golf course, which will remain in the rural area.

The addition of this land to the borough will enable the development of housing schemes both by the borough and by private builders.

More than 80 acres had already been secured for this purpose and the schemes which had been held back to await the result of the application will now be proceeded with.

Harton Farms

Chapter 2

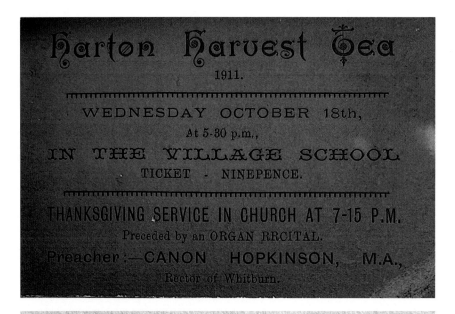

St Peter's Scrapbook vol II 1907-1915.
Reproduced with kind permission of the vicar and churchwardens of Harton St Peter.

Introduction

Life in Harton Township from its early history was based on agriculture, although the industrial revolution did affect it with the growth of Harton Colliery, the railways and the opening of the huge dock nearby at Tyne Dock. However in 1901, when South Shields subsumed the west end of the township, Harton returned to agriculture as its main occupation and remained a basically rural edge to the ever-expanding industry and housing of South Shields.

1930s photograph of the corner of Moor Lane and Sunderland Road.

In 2017 a lady explained to me how as a child just before WW2 she had stood each morning at the end of Armstrong Avenue, which links Moore Lane and St Peter's Avenue, where she was living and watched Mr Wood of Red House Farm in Harton Village amble his dairy cows down Moor Lane to the fields on Harton Moor to graze. Possibly this photograph shows Mr Wood returning back to Red House Farm further up Moor Lane East. Harvest was certainly a great cause for celebration as the scrapbooks of St

The stone section of this garden wall facing Sunderland Road once marked a field boundary.

Peter's Church prove. Each year before WW1 we see a Harvest tea being organised as well as services and other celebrations for the community.

This chapter will discuss the farms that existed in Harton Township at the beginning of the twentieth century, of which not one farmers field, nor one farmhouse, stable or barn remain, merely a few pieces of stone wall that marked the farmer's fields.

Houses and public amenities are necessary and many people remember the joy of coming to a new semi-detached house in Harton. The new roads edged with a grass border and trees. Homes with all the modern amenities including an indoor bathroom and toilet. Gardens front and back with fresh air and bird song. I happily grew up in the 1960s in Harton House Road in a house which had been built in 1937 and took these amenities for granted, but it is sad to think how quickly all the farms disappeared under roads and buildings. Many people have told me stories of how as children in Harton they played on the ruined buildings of the farms. The total demise of the farming life in Harton Township took less than a hundred years to complete.

Ten farms will be discussed in this chapter, all held by tenanted farmers from lease holders, for the Ecclesiastical Commissioners remained the owners of the land. Over time the Ecclesiastical Commissioners did sell sections of land, such as some fields to South Shields Corporation to allow them to establish Harton Cemetery or to wealthy individuals like Mr Moore, but in 1921 we still find seven farms within the truncated Harton Township area, stretching from the coast in the east to the western border with South Shields.

Thursday, 16th March, 1933.

**Not all the Harton Farms (now by this date South Shields Farms) are mentioned in this report but three are:
M A Thornton Harton Farm;
T Hemsley Horsley Hill Farm;
W Snowdon Harton Down Hill Farm; amongst the many others in Cleadon, Whitburn and Boldon at this time.**

"PLOUGHING DAY" AT CLEADON

Farmers Greet New Tenant

Over 40 men and 38 pairs of horses took part in a "ploughing day" at Holder House Farm, Cleadon, South Shields, yesterday.

The property of South Shields Corporation, the farm has a new tenant in Mr W L Dryden, of Sunniside Farm, Cleadon, and in pursuance of custom neighbouring farmers sent ploughmen and ploughs and horses to turn over a field belonging to the new tenant.

The farmers who sent teams were as follow: Mr E. J. Scott, Robin Lea, East Boldon; Mr R. V. Eggleston, Village Farm, Cleadon; Mr J. Simpson, Station Farm, Boldon; Mr F. Paten, Blue House Farm, Whitburn; Mr R. Holmes, Whitburn Moor Farm, Whitburn; Mr S. Gibson, Town End Farm, East Boldon; Mr H. Colley, Westoe Farm, South Shields; Mr S. Gibson, East Farm, Cleadon; Mr F. Orpeth, North Farm, Cleadon; Mr E. Ebden, Glebe Farm, Whitburn; Mrs Ebden, West Farm, Fulwell; Mr S. Hall, Simonside Farm, Simonside; Mr A. Gibson, Farding Lake Farm, Cleadon; Mrs E. Colley, Cleadon Laws Farm, Cleadon.

Mr M A Thornton, South Farm, Harton; Mr W Ramsay, Field House Farm, Boldon; Mr Newby, Mansion House Farm, West Boldon; Messrs Farrow Bros., Mundles Farm, East Boldon; Mr T Hemsley, Horsley Hill Farm, South Shields; Mr W Snowdon, Harton Downhill Farm, South Shields; Mr F Brewis, Cleadon Hills Farm, Cleadon; Mr J Colley, East Farm, Whitburn; Mr M Nichol, West Hall Farm, Cleadon; Mr J Hutchinson, Lizards' Farm, Whitburn; Mr G Ramsay, Wellends Farm, Whitburn; Mr H Roach, Mansion House Farm, East Boldon; Mr E Fairless, Long Loaning Farm, Tyne Dock; Mr W Pratt, Holder House Farm, Cleadon; Mr W L Dryden, Sunside Farm, Cleadon.

The newspaper cutting on the opposite page from *The Shields Daily News* of 1933, shows that even a dozen years after its incorporation into South Shields the number of farms in the area was still large. Horses were still used on these farms, alongside tractors and more modern machinery.

I do not have the space to give a complete history of the Harton farms and families but offer in this chapter some snippets and soundbites to give a glimpse into life on the farms within the township at the turn of the nineteenth century and the beginning of the twentieth. Sadly sometimes there is no image or photograph of that particular farm within the archives,

Two photographs of Cleadon Hills Farm in 2021 offering a suggestion of what the Harton farms would have looked like.

A view over Harton in 2021 reveals rooftops, one hundred years ago it would have been fields that led the eye over to the coast.

A drone flying over St Peter's Churchyard shows the houses stretching to the coast. The green patch mid-distance on the right hand side is Harton Academy playing field; the smaller, paler green area mid-distance on the left is the southern tip of Harton Cemetery.
Thanks to Jamie Hughes.

The largest farm in Harton Township in 1839 was Horsley Hill Farm at 314 acres. The next largest farm in the Township, was South Farm at 136 acres; Harton Down Hill Farm at 127 acres; Harton Farm 122 acres; Red House Farm 111 acres; Harton House Farm 103 acres, Harton Moor Farm 100 acres; Little Horsely Hill Farm 98 acres; Simonside Lodge Farm 70 acres and Low Simonside 67 acres according to the 1839 tithe holding list.

The 1839 tithe map, reproduced on the front cover of this book, and accompanying list which are held in by the Durham Diocesan Registrar and Durham University Library, offer a consistent starting point for this chapter where each of the farms will be looked at individually, though it is appreciated that there may have been changes between 1839 and the period we are focusing on in this book.

Harton Farm

There do not appear to be any photographs of Harton Farm, barns and out buildings other than glimpses of the farm house in the background of images of the village.

Its footprint looks considerable on the map, but it is difficult to know exactly what buildings belonged to it. The churchwarden's plan of 1896 mentioned the house at the bottom of what may be the farm steading as belonging to Mr Scott, steward to Mrs Snowdon. If so it is likely, looking at the map that the farmstead ran from Moor Lane East to Harton Back Lane.

The Farmstead on the 1839 tithe survey is listed as 1 rod and 26 perches large which compares to others such as Harton Down Hill Farm farmstead

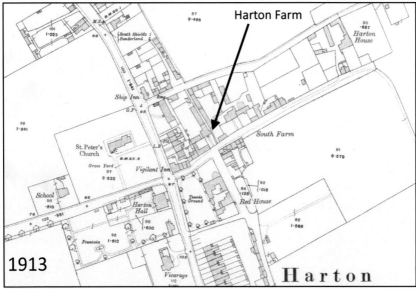

Godfrey Map of Harton Village in 1913 shows the foot print of all four Harton farmsteads, just as we see in other villages where the farmhouses are built in close proximity to start a community and offer protection. However although the other three are mentioned by name Harton Farm is not. The garden path to the farmhouse is clearly marked and it almost faces Red House Farm and is right next to South Farm, which too has a garden path from Moor Lane East leading to the farmhouse.

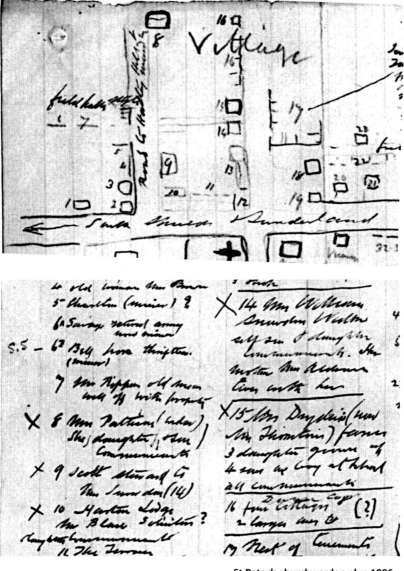

St Peter's churchwarden plan 1896.

9 Scott, steward to Mrs Snowdon (14).

14 Mrs William Snowdon, widow,
self, son and daughters communicants. Her mother Mrs Alderson lives with her.

at 1 rod 32 perches. The farmhouse itself stood on Moor Lane East facing south up St Mary's Avenue.

Harton Farm is listed as a farm of 122 acres, 1 rod and 31 perches in the 1839 tithe holding list and by the 1881 census it is being run by a young farmer and his wife; William and Jane Snowdon, both 24 years of age. William is the eldest son of William and Annie Snowdon of Harton Down Hill Farm and I have marked on the section of 1839 tithe map how propitious a

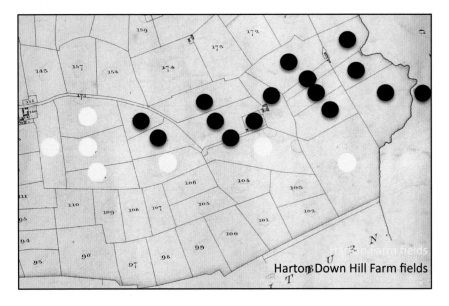

Harton Down Hill Farm fields

William Snowdon the younger had married Jane Alderson on 20th November 1879 at St Peter's Church Harton. He died in 1883 at the age of 26 leaving his wife to run the farm and three small children to care for.

In the 1891 census Jane Snowdon, widow 34 born in South Shields, is recorded as the farmer of Harton Farm. Living with her at that time are: her three children who were all born in Harton William 10, Mary 8 and Anne 7; her widowed mother Mary Alderson, born in Scotland, now 73 years old; Margaret Purvis 24, a general servant from Whitburn and Geoffrey Tate 15, a milk-boy from Harton.

Hugh Scott 55, named on the census as agricultural labourer from Heddon-on-the-Wall, Northumberland, with his wife Ann 60, from Ponteland and their grandson Hugh Warcup 4 years old born in Harton, are listed in the

This photograph was taken looking down St Mary's Avenue towards Moor Lane East and shows Harton farmhouse overgrown with ivy and most probably awaiting demolition. The walls of Red House farmstead are on the left of the photograph and Caffrey's corner shop on the right. Just to the right of the farmhouse's garden fence is part of the salt path which ran from Shields to Hartlepool sneaking between Harton Farm and South Farm, today we see a section of this behind where this building stood, leading from the council garages and between the houses onto Marsden Road.

A photograph from the 1930s when the road adjoining Sunderland Road at the Ship Inn corner, originally known as Harton Back Lane, was about to be widened. The house seen in the middle of the road would seem to have been the house Mr Scott and his family lived in, belonging to Harton Farm, but has the appearance of being larger than the two roomed property they are said to occupy in the 1891 census.

This view west along Moor Lane East, taken in the late 1940s shows Harton farmhouse set back from the road with the new Vigilant and the top of St Peter's steeple visible behind it.. *Reproduced by kind permission of Janice Wright.*

next property on the census sheet. The property they lived in only had two rooms.

In 1901 Jane Snowdon, aged 44, is still running the farm. Her children: William 20, Mary 18 and Anne 17 are all working on the farm. Jane's mother Mary Alderson 82, was living at the farm with William Alderson 42, Jane's brother, listed as managing the farm and Leopold Stephenson 18, working as a milk-boy.

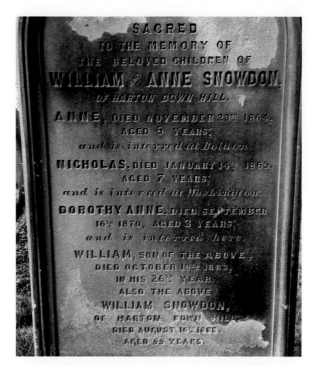

One of the Snowdon family headstones in St Peter's Churchyard. This records the death of four children of William and Annie Snowdon: Anne aged 5 in 1864, Nicholas aged 7 in 1865, Dorothy Anne aged 3 in 1870 and William aged 26 in 1885; plus William Snowdon senior in 1888 aged 55.

Headstone of Mary Alderson who died in 1901 aged 84 and her daughter Jane Snowdon who died in 1913 aged 62, in St Peter's Churchyard.

South Farm

I cannot offer an explanation why this farm is called South Farm, it is not the southern most farm building in the Township and its fields lie to the west and are not the southern-most.

Equally I cannot offer an image of the farmhouse, all I can offer are the railings in front of its garden. The footprint of its farmstead on the 1913 map is also difficult to establish. It may have owned various farm labourers' cottages further east along Moor Lane East, as the statement of probate granted in 1936 following the death of Robert Simon Dryden states that he

DRYDEN Robert Simon of 3 Drydens Cottages South Farm Harton Village **South Shields** died 12 August 1936 Probate **Durham** 7 September to Mary Hardy (wife of James Hardy) and Lilian Thompson (wife of James Spence Thompson). Effects £955 16s. 5d.

but whether these are the ones we see here on the 1913 map I cannot say with any confidence.

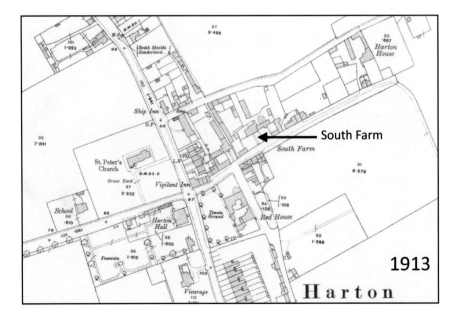

In these two 1920s photographs of Moor Lane East, the top one looking east, the bottom one looking west, the railings that marked the fort garden of South Farm and the trees in the garden are visible. These photographs also give an image to the collection of buildings on the north side of the road we see as a footprint on the map opposite.

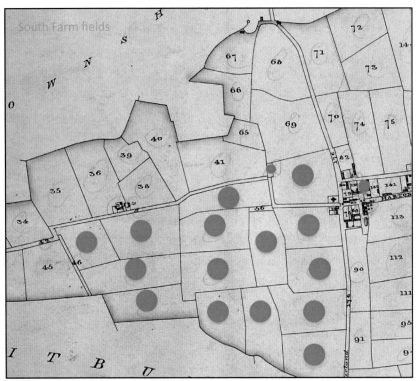

South Farm fields

St Peter's Churchyard granted by the Ecclesiastical commissioners in 1857 would take the most north east field of those belonging to South Farm in 1839, and the development of Harton Hall, the Vicarage, Harton Lea and other houses would eat into the fields along the west edge of Sunderland Road.

In 1839 South Farm was the second largest in Harton Township being a farm of 136 acres, 2 rods and 35 perches. It was farmed for generations by the Dryden Family. Robert Dryden senior died in 1888, leaving his wife Mary Ann Dryden with seven surviving children, the eldest Jane Ann Dryden, 16 years old at the time, the youngest William Lawson Dryden only 4 years old.

On the night of the 1901 census Mary Ann is not in residence at the farm nor is her eldest son, Robert Simon, then 24 years old who was married and living in a cottage nearby. Those listed are: Jane Ann 29, Elizabeth 28, Edith 25, John 21, Albert 19, William then 16 and Neil McCormerick a 15 year old employee. Mary Ann would marry again to another local farmer and become Mrs Thornton of Sunniside Farm.

Hence in 1901, both Harton Farm and South Farm were being run by widows with the support of their children. The same we shall find is true for Harton House Farm just a little further up Moor Lane East.

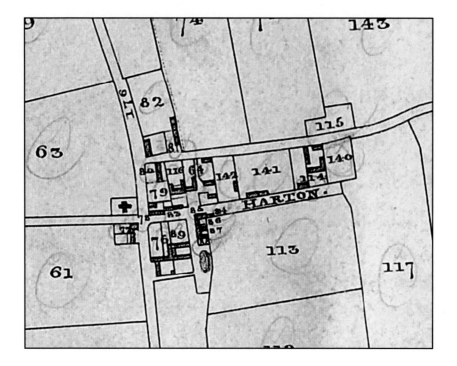

In 1839, South Farm farmstead was shown as number 64 on the tithe map, where 116 was Harton Farm and 114 Harton House Farm. Numbers 141, 142 and 140 were rented by Thomas Davison, who would also farm fields 142 to 148, but this did not include a farmstead within the Township, so maybe this was merely a section of a greater farm with the farmhouse in Westoe or other local area. There seems to be a similar situation with fields 65, 66 and 67. This could all have changed as the century progressed and South Farm taken over these plots in the village or even been given other fields by the Ecclesiastical Commissioners to compensate for the loss of the churchyard field and others.

In 1839 there was indeed another farmstead in the village marked as number 76 on the tithe map. It backed onto Red House Farm which was number 89, and stood where the village shops are now, farming fields 69 to 75. Two fields from this farm would become Harton Cemetery reducing what was relatively a small farm of 87 acres 2 rods and 7 perches to something even smaller. It is not mentioned on the 1881, 1891, or 1901 census, when only the farms discussed in this chapter are named. So it would seem plausible that the other local farms were allowed to absorb these fields by the Ecclesiastical Commissioners to compensate for fields

NOT A COLLIERY DISASTER, ONLY A POTA

A portion of the crowd outside the barn.

The news spread like wildfire that Mr. Dryden, of Harton South Farm, had decided to open his potato pit and sell out retail to the public. People began to arrive at 4.30 a.m. in the morning and by starting time, 10 a.m., the crowd

The Sunday Pictorial

This refers to

In 1917 this was not a South Shields Farmer, rather a Harton one.
St Peter's Scrapbook vol III 1915- 1922.

ATO SALE BY A SOUTH SHIELDS FARMER.

A little buyer sings to the crowd.

Two successful buyers return from market.

numbered thousands. The village constabulary, numbering one, in P.C. Simpson, had the task of its life. The buyers started at single file, but gradually closed up to six and seven deep.—(*Sunday Pictorial* exclusive.)

April 1st AD 1917.

The Potatoe Famine Que to the War.

Wednesday, 28th March, 1917.

STEALING POTATOES FROM A FARM AT HARTON.

Magistrates' Warning.

A charge of stealing three stones of potatoes valued at 4s 6d, the property of Mrs Thornton, at Harton South Farm, on the 17th inst., was preferred at the South Shields County Petty Sessions, yesterday, Col. Allison presiding, against Wm. Johnson (66), labourer, Back Edward Street, South Shields; John Kelly, senr. (61), miner, Bents Cottages, South Shields, and John Kelly, junr. (27), 22 Berwick Street, South Shields.

Albert H. Dryden, manager for Mrs Margaret Thornton, of the South Farm, Harton, said he examined the potato pit on the farm on Saturday afternoon, the 17th inst., and saw that everything was in order. On the following morning, from what was told him by the police, he examined it again and found that a quantity of potatoes had been stolen. He identified the potatoes produced as Mrs Thornton's property.

Sergt. Oliver, of Whitburn, stated that on Saturday night, the 17th inst. he was on duty in company with P.C.'s Simpson and Reed near Mrs Thornton's potato pit, when he heard a noise. On proceeding to the pit to investigate he saw the three defendants coming away from it, and proceeding in the direction of Westoe, each of them carrying a small bag of potatoes. He took them into custody and took them to Westoe Lane Police Station. In reply to the charge Johnson said "All right." The other two made no reply.

P.C. Simpson gave corroborative evidence.

The defendants pleaded guilty and said they were sorry.

Supt. Yeandle said the three defendants belonged to South Shields. It came to the knowledge of the police, through a rumour, that it was intended to raid the potato pit on Mrs Thornton's farm, and a watch was kept. The capture of the defendants was the result of the watch. There had been no attempt made to raid it since.

The Chairman (Col. Atkinson) said the defendants would be fined 40s each, and he wished to give the warning that if there was any more of this sort of thing the offenders, when brought before them, would be sent to prison.

The Newspaper article on the previous page and the one opposite may well be linked. On March 28th 1917 we read that Albert H Dryden manager for Mrs Margaret Thornton of the South Farm, Harton brought an action in the civil courts against some thieves who had stolen potatoes from their farm store. Then with glorious supporting photographs we see that 1st April 1917, three days later, Mr Dryden decides to open his potato store and sell direct to the public. The clue seems to be in the date and the statement by the churchwarden handwritten on the newspaper cutting, *This refers to the potato famine due to the war.*

What we see in the large photograph is the long pantiled roof of the potato store, which surely can be related to the footprint of the farmstead on page 70, and allows us to imagine exactly where these people were standing.

A newspaper article of 1936 notes the death of Robert and Mary Ann's eldest son, like his father at an early age. Robert senior was 45 when he died in 1888, Mary Ann would die in 1940 at the age of 89.

SHIELDS FARMER'S DEATH

One of the Oldest in The Borough

By the death of Mr Robert Simon Dryden, of South Farm, Harton, in the Ingham Infirmary yesterday, South Shields has lost one of its oldest farmers.

This is so, notwithstanding the fact that Mr Dryden was only 59. Mr Dryden's father, Mr Robert Dryden, died 48 years ago. Mr Dryden was born at Harton, and was only a few months old when his father took over the tenancy 59 years ago.

Mrs Dryden married again and became Mrs M. A. Thornton, of Sunniside Farm, Harton.

Mr Dryden leaves a widow, two sons and two daughters.

Thanks to Mrs Janice Wright, granddaughter of Mr Robert Simon Dryden.

Red House Farm

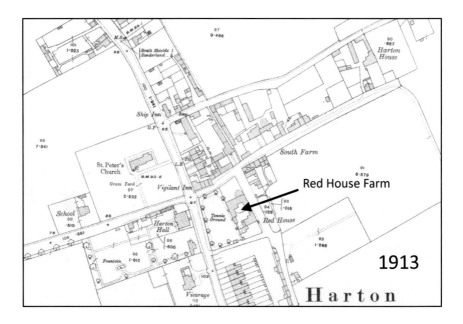

Red House Farm

1913

H a r t o n

There are no pictures of the farmhouse for Red House Farm, but a few of the farmstead, which was large at 2 rods and 2 perches. The farmstead stood on the southern corner of Moor Lane East, where it joins St Mary's Avenue. A horse gin can be seen in the picture below and the picture opposite offers us a glimpse into the farm yard itself. The lane running to the south of the farmstead from Sunderland Road to St Mary's Avenue is still used as a popular thoroughfare. The farmstead marked on the 1839 tithe map which was next to Red House Farmstead was replaced for a short while with a

Red House farmstead was demolished in the early 1950s and bungalows now cover the site.

The Wood family farmed Red House Farm for 64 years. Robert and Mary had moved from a farm in Cleadon to Red House Farm some time in the middle of the 1890s, as the 1891-92 Wards Trade Directory gives John Snowdon as the farmer (a large, local farming family) however in the 1897-98 directory we find Robert Wood listed as the farmer of Red House Farm.

In 1901 Robert was 53, Mary 44, Annie their first daughter 22, Robert who would take over the running of the farm, was 20, Ethel 17, Fred 11 and Grace 8. John Robinson who was 14 was employed as a milk boy. In the 1911 census Annie is no longer living on the farm but the other girls are listed as dairy maids and the two boys are working on the farm. At this time

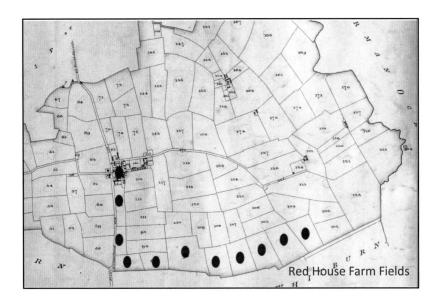

Red House Farm Fields

In 1839 Red House Farm was 111 acres, 1 rod and 20 perches in size and stretched along Sunderland Road and what is now Prince Edward Road. The fields along Sunderland Road would become the site of large residential houses in the late nineteenth century such as Wyngarth, Moor Croft, The Poplars and South Croft. To compensate for this loss as Moor Farm ceased to exist it would seem that Mr Wood farmed fields which had one belonged to Moor Farm. Mention has been made of him taking his dairy cows each morning down Moor Lane to graze on Harton Moor. The newspaper article on page 84 states that Red House Farm was 300 acres, so must certainly have taken on more fields to have tripled in size

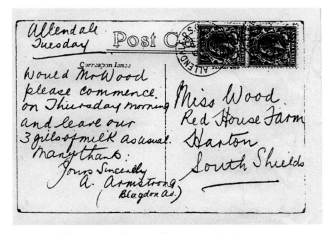

A postcard from the collection of Ernest Lewthwaite.

A photograph of the harvest from the early 1900s and a family photograph of Mr and Mrs Woods, Mary and Robert and three of their children, Ethel, Grace and Fred. Mary would die in 1913 at the age of 56 and Robert in 1932 at the age of 84. They are buried in St Peter's Churchyard.

A transcript of an article which appeared in the Shields Gazette on the 9th November 1951.

Another Farmer is Leaving Shields

With the encroaching of land for housing and other purposes yet another of South Shields' few remaining farmers will soon be leaving the district to resume farming in another part of the county.

Red House Farm, Harton, which once extended for 300 acres has now been whittled down to a farmhouse and some buildings wedged in by houses in St Mary's Avenue on one side and a row of shops and a garage on another.

All Moving
So on November 23 the tenant Mr Robert Wood, his wife, daughter and grandson will be moving with their furniture, remaining cattle and farm implements. They are going to a 78 acre farm bought by Mr Wood at Margery Flatts a short distance from Lanchester. When Mr Wood leaves Red House Farm, he will be severing a 64 year link with the holding, having gone there as a boy of seven when his father left Cleadon to take over the tenancy.

At one time the farm, owned by the Ecclesiastical Commissioners, stretched from Harton to Lizard Lane and included the land between Prince Edward Road and Marsden Road and down to Cauldwell. Today, fields of turnips, potatoes, corn and other crops have given way to schools and housing estates. The beginning of the end came when the new High School for boys was built 15 years ago. Since then more and more of the land has been acquired for building purposes. During the last few years Mr Wood has had part of Harton Moor Farm for grazing his cattle.

The farmhouse itself, thought to be at least 200 years old, was last year included in a list of buildings considered of special architectural interest by the then Ministry of Town and Country Planning. It is now feared it will be demolished for possible future development.

Red House farmyard can be seen on the very left of the black and white photograph, with Caffery's the corner shop and Harton Farm all awaiting demolition

A section of Red House Farm crenellate farmyard wall still exists in 2021.

Harton House Farm

If George Yeoman who died in 1785 did build Harton House for Ann, *he built her a new house with gardens and orchard,* then it must have been built in the middle to late 1700s, which ties in with the newspaper report of 1950 on the pervious page, claiming Red House Farm to then be 200 years old.

Maybe Harton House was not originally a farm, but in the 1839 tithe record we find it referred to as a farm of 103 acres, 2 rods and 17 perches, with a farmstead of 3 rods and 10 perches, which is the largest in the township. The 1839 tithe holdings list gives Ralph Watson as the landowner and the occupier.

Ralph Watson married Mary, a young widow with three children when Ralph was 69 years old and Mary was 43. Tragedy struck and Ralph died a few months after their marriage. Mary inherited Harton House Farm and on the 1851 census she is listed as a land proprietor. She owned the farm for 30 years. In 1881 she left Harton House Farm, two years before her death at the age of 78. She is buried in St Peter's Churchyard.

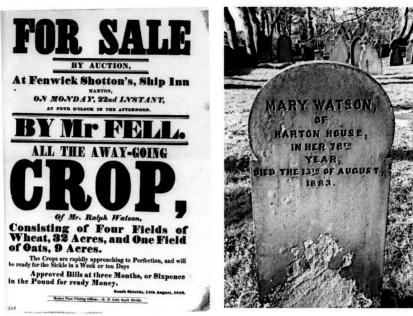

Sale of crops from Mr Watson and Mary Watson's grave in St Peter's Churchyard.

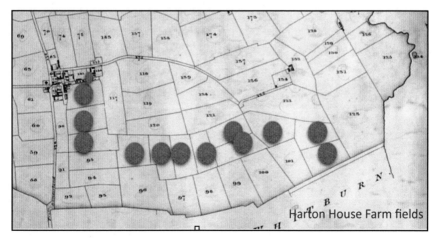

Harton House Farm fields

As can be seen from the above tithe map, Harton House Farm owned the fields in front of the house and then eastward towards Redwell Bank.

In 1886 Harton House Farm was put up for sale and the Pattisons were the next owners. James Pattison only farmed the land for four years before his untimely death and his wife had to take over the running of the farm. So as with nearby Harton and South Farms, a young widow was left to run the farm.

The grave of James Pattison of Harton House, who died in 1890 aged 47; St Peter's Churchyard.
A newspaper article on Saturday, 8th February, 1890 records his untimely death.

THE SHOCKING DEATH OF A HARTON FARMER.
INQUEST AND VERDICT.

Yesterday an inquest was held at Harton Village, before Mr J. Graham, coroner, concerning the death of James Pattison, farmer, who was found dead in his dairy at Harton House Farm, on Wednesday morning. When the body was discovered, it will be remen. ered, there was lying beside it a single-barrelled, muzzle-loading gun, and the head and face of deceased were fearfully disfigured, pointing clearly to the conclusion that death he been caused by the discharge of a gun. The jury gave a verdict that death was due to a gunshot wound, accidently caused.

Mary Pattison must have been widowed at 33 or 34 with three boys, 12, 8 and 6 and a daughter, 11 years old. The 1891 census confirms this and also shows that she had three live-in servants to assist her: Robert Walker 19, was an agricultural labourer; Margaret Bainbridge 23 and Margaret Ray 21, were general domestic servants. The census lists houses before and after Harton House where families of agricultural labourers lived, so maybe these were linked to the farm or at least the occupants worked at Harton House Farm. The census records that Harton House had more than five rooms, but those next to it on the census list are family dwellings of only two or three rooms.

On Monday, 8th September, 1890, the same year as the death of her husband, Mary had to deal with the following incident,:

FIRE AT A HARTON STACK-YARD.

About four o'clock yesterday afternoon, David Carr, managing hind for Mrs Pattison, of Harton House Farm, Harton, brought information to Westoe Branch Police Station that a haystack on the farm was on fire. With assistance, Sergt. Burton got the hose and manual engine to the spot without much delay. He found a large stack, valued at £50 in flames, and within a few feet of it was another larger stack, and adjoining this the outbuildings. The engine and hose were got ready, but there was no supply of water near at hand, and it had to be brought in buckets from a pond between two and three hundred yards away. Under these circumstances there was no hope of getting the fire out, and attention was directed to the saving of the large stack immediately adjoining. In the meantime, a messenger had been despatched to the Central Police Station, South Shields, for a standpipe, and when this was brought it was fixed to a hydrant, and a plentiful supply of water was obtained, and the fire speedily subdued, though only a small portion of the stack was saved. The other stack was fortunately prevented from taking fire. Inspector Hume was on the spot soon after the news reached South Shields and materially helped in the operations. The stack was insured for its full value in the North British and Mercantile Insurance Company.

The newspaper article names David Carr as the managing hind for Mrs Pattison of Harton House Farm. On the 1891 census he is living next to Harton House in a two roomed property with his wife Mary Ann, both being 26 years old, and their one year old twin sons David and James. David senior's occupation is given as cart-man

In the 1901 census Mary and her three sons are still living in Harton House, and she is listed as the head of the family, a farmer and an employer. There are no live-in servants at this time. Next to them is still David Carr his occupation now being given as a self-employed general cart-man. His family has now grown to four children; they are living in three rooms. Others living next to them are listed as hinds on the farm. Indeed the churchwarden's plan of 1896 (p65) says there are 4 cottages and two larger ones standing in front of Harton House. So this is most probably where Mary's workforce lived. However this does not fully tie in with some of the

Our Harton Park and Recreation Grounds, South Shields

In this photograph from the *Smiths Dock Monthly* magazine of April 1924, we see the WW1 memorial the firm placed in their workers' recreational park in Harton (now the playing fields of Harton Academy). In the distance at the bottom of the field we catch a glimpse of Harton House. Closer inspection reveals two houses. A plastered and painted one but behind it a much larger house, possibly five windows wide, so the same size as the

Looking back to the map on page 84 we see there is indeed a large house and garth set back from the road facing south to part of the garden, and also another house which looks like a lodge house, which would seem to be this white house. This ties in with the photograph below which was taken in 1931 when they were widening Harton Back Lane and making it into Marsden Road. Here we see Harton House farm, with two large barns, a house facing south with three chimneys, and in front of that is another substantial property, which one assumes this is the rear of the house whose front is painted white. Was this one of the larger *cottages* mentioned in the churchwarden's plan? Sadly it is impossible to say with any certainty. If it had been divided up the census would have recorded it as a tenement and

Both these photographs were taken in 1931. The upper one shows, on the right hand side, the extensive barns behind Harton House, extending right to Harton Back Lane/Marsden Road. Note also the newly planted trees.

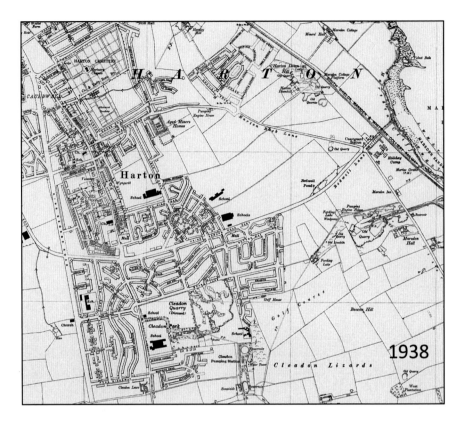

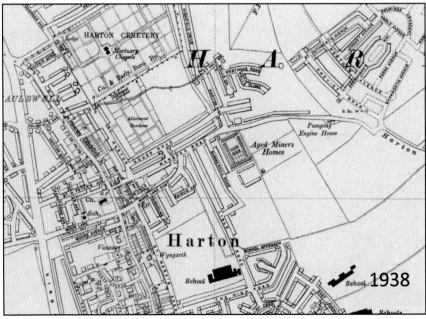

The map opposite, which has a further blown up section underneath is from 1938 and shows the roads and houses then under construction. Harton House Farm and all the buildings connected with it have been razed to the ground and replaced by semi-detached houses and bungalows. It sat on the south side of Marsden Road but gives its name to a long road on the north side of Marsden Road. See also the fields that once belonged to the farm filling up with housing estates.

Horsley Hill Farm
& Little Horsley Hill

This sweeping view across fields, taken looking north from Quarry Lane in 1928, shows us Horsley Hill farmstead in the distance just off the right of middle with Little Horsley Hill farmstead just appearing on the very far right of the horizon. The collection of building to the left on the horizon are the houses of Westoe Village. Today a similar view is only of rooftops, as seen in the photograph below.

Unlike some of the other farms in Harton Township thankfully there are a number of photographs in the archives of South Tyneside Libraries and *The Shields Gazette* of the impressive farm known as Horsely Hill Farm; though sadly none of its smaller counterpart.

The main house was more a mansion house than a farmhouse, as the following photograph from the 1930s shows. Attached to it were a number of outbuildings, barns, stables and a collection of cottages for agricultural workers. In front of the house was a large duck pond.

In 1839 Horsley Hill Farm was the largest farm in Harton Township at 314 acres. It appears by 1891 to have absorbed the 98 acres of Little Horsley Hill farm and the two were then run as one farm.

In the photograph above we see the five bay mansion house that was Horsley Hill Farmhouse. The considerable outbuildings and other cottages within the farmstead can be seen in the footprint below; also its proximity to Little Horsley Hill Farm.

A larger section of this 1921 map is given on the following page where it is compared with the 1954 map to clearly show the growth in housing, and the demise of the farm. over that 33 year period.

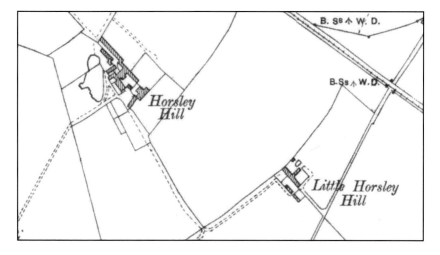

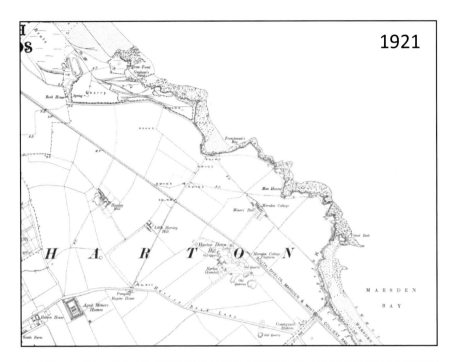

1921

1954

The farmhouse can still be seen on the 1954 map surrounded by housing. This shows exactly where the farm was, not at Horsley Hill roundabout as many of us might expect. The photographs below give a further indication of its position. Taken in 1935, when homes were beginning to encroach on fields, from the aptly named Northfield Road, which remains a cul-de-sac.

The enlargement of the background of this image shows, like the footprint on the map, the extent of the associated buildings and the proximity of Little Horsley Hill.

The colour photograph is taken from a similar position to the 1935 photograph but eighty six years later.

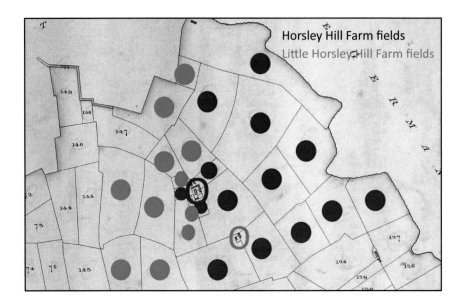

Horsley Hill Farm was extensive as well as impressive and the farmers who farmed there were well known within Harton Township and beyond. Their farm stretched from Frenchman's Bay to Trow Point.

The mansion house at Horsley Hill was built for Robert Stote of Hedworth and his wife Anne nee Watson. Its foundation stone was laid on 3rd September, 1743. By 1830 the tenant farmer was Henderson, a later farmer would be called Hemsley, and many who still recall the farm talk of it as Hemsley's farm, commemorated in a local street name, Hemsley Road.

Robert Surtees in his *History and Antiquities of the County of Durham*, written in 1816 wrote in the Gateshead section, under the Parish of Jarrow, about the history of the Stotes family:

The family of Stote long held considerable leasehold possessions in Hedworth. Stotteshouse is mentioned in 1538, and a very numerous race may be traced from the commencement of Parochial registers. Robert Stote (many generations of Stote men are called Robert) appears amongst the Disclaimers at the visitation of 1615.

He adds in his footnotes:

The Stote's of Horsley Hill, ancestors of Roper-Stote-Donnison Roper, Esq. are of this family.

In 1773 Robert Stote was able to add greatly to his fortune through the death of a relative by marriage, James Donnison, who owned the estates of Farrington and High Ford, near Silksworth. Robert Stote died in 1796 and was buried in St Hilda's Churchyard. He had disinherited his son Watson, and the land and fortune passed to his three daughters. Margery, the middle daughter never married and lived at Horsley Hill all her life, becoming famous for her healing elixirs, for which people would travel for miles at the turn of the nineteenth century. Madame Stote, as she became known, died in 1842 at the grand old age of 97, leaving a fortune of £20,000 Ownership passed to the Fox family of Westoe Village.

Hodgson in his *The Borough of South Shields from its earliest period to the close of the nineteenth century* first published in 1901, discusses the Fox family of Westoe:

The Fox family were for generations engaged in commerce and shipping on Tyneside. The first one connected by residence with South Shields was George Townsend Fox, who on July 7th, 1807, married Ann Stote Crofton, the only child of a South Shields shipowner and heiress to the Stote property at Harton.

After his explanation of the famous career of Ann's third son, William who became PM of New Zealand in 1873, he completes his discussion of the Fox family by saying that,

The family still hold property in Westoe as well as the two farms at Horsley Hill which belonged to the Stotes.

The 1839 tithe holdings state that Margery Crofton Stote and Mary (nee Stote) and Thomas Wilkinson Esquire are the landowners of Little Horsley Hill and Horsley Hill. Ownership was on a lease hold from the Dean and Chapter, later the Ecclesiastical Commissioners, and the landowners frequently rented out the farms to tenant farmers. The occupiers of both farms in 1839 are given as John Mallam, William Sanderson and John Henderson.

Horsley Hill farm was farmed by generations of the Henderson family. Mr

On the 14th September, 1867, one advert stated:

Potatoes, fresh taken up every Morning and delivered to James Ellison, Market-place, South Shields, grown on J. Henderson's, Esq., Farm, Horsley Hill near Marsden. Quality of which cannot be excelled.

On Wednesday, 29th July, 1868, it was reported:

TYNESIDE AGRICULTURAL SOCIETY'S SHOW AT HEXHAM.

The annual show in connection with the Tyneside Agricultural Society was held yesterday at Hexham, and it proved the most successful that has yet taken place. The visitors numbered 1,500, being about double to that any preceding year. The total number of entries was about 230, this being greatly in excess of the numbers also shown on any former occasion. One of the most excellent features in the exhibition was the presence of cattle. The show of sheep was capital. The horses exhibited cannot be so highly praised. The shepherds dogs exhibited were very good animals.

Mr. John Henderson, Horsley Hill, near South Shields, officiated as one of the judges in connection with the show. The annual dinner was held in the Town Hall, and was largely attended. The

Mr Henderson died in 1885 and the obituary printed in *The Shields Gazette* on Monday, 19th January, gives a further idea of the extent of the farm he ran. Sadly he and his wife did not have any children and so the farm and all the contents were sold. The stock lists which name pedigree horse after pedigree horse is indeed very impressive as can be seen on the following pages.

It is with regret that we record the death of Mr John Henderson, which occurred at his residence, Horsley Hill, last night.

The deceased gentleman, who was in his sixtieth year, has for a considerable time taken an active part in the public life of South Shields. For many years he was member the Guardians, and seven

years ago succeeded the late Mr Anderson as chairman, and has since filled the position with great ability.

In a bye-election in 1877 he was returned to the Council as a representative for Westoe Ward, and served in the Council until 1880. Mr Henderson was a member of the directorate of South Shields Gas Company for 15 years.

He was probably one of the must prominent agriculturists in the North of England, and regularly acted as judge of stock and horses in all the principal agricultural shows of the country. He had a large farm at Horsley Hill, and another in the North of Ireland, upon the latter of which he was an extensive breeder of stock. A few years ago be took the first prize at the Royal Agricultural Show, held at Birmingham, for horses and was at that time said to possess the finest breed in England. He was secretary the East Chester Ward Agricultural Association for a considerable time, and also prominent member the Newcastle Farmers' Club. For many years in South Shields, Mr Henderson carried on the business of agent and valuer, and on the death of Mr Broughton, between two and three years ago. was appointed the representative of the Ecclesiastical Commissioners in this district.

It is nearly two years since Mr Henderson's health first began to fail, and since then he has been gradually sinking. A week past night he was seized with a fit of convulsions, after which he was not able to leave his bedroom. He was well known in all the agricultural circles of the north, and the news of his death will be received with deep regret. Mr Henderson leaves a widow, but no family.

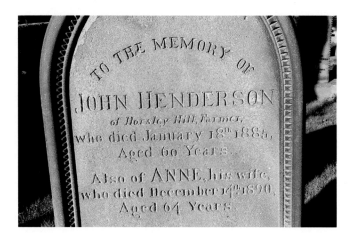

MR ARTHUR T. CROW has been favoured with instructions from John Henderson, Esq., who is leaving the Farm, to SELL BY AUCTION, on MONDAY, 4th February, 1884, the VALUABLE DRAUGHT HORSES, &c.

CATALOGUE:

Lot 1.—Grey Mare, Rising 5 years, 16·2 hands, by Pencote, dam a Clydesdale Mare.

Lot 2.—Grey Mare, Rising 6 years, 16·3 hands, by Emperor.

Lot 3.—Brown Mare, Rising 8 years, 16·2 hands.

Lot 4.—Bay Horse, Rising 5 years, 16·3 hands, by Pencote, dam a Clydesdale Mare.

Lot 5.—Grey Colt, Rising 5 years, 16·3 hands, by Pencote, dam a Clydesdale Mare.

Fat Bullocks, Heifers, and Geld Cows. 10 Prime Fat S.H. Bullocks. 7 Neat Cutting Fat Heifers. 3 Splendid Fat Geld Cows. Implements of Husbandry; Carts, Hay Rake, Grub Harrows, Corn Bins, Cart, Shaft and Trace Gears for 4 Horses, and a

WELL-WON OLD LAND HAY STACK,

About 35 Tons.

The Sale to commence at 12 for 1 o'Clock to a minute.

These three newspaper articles relate to the sale of the stock, crops and furniture at Horsley Hill Farm: the top article is from Friday, 1st February, 1884, during Mr Henderson's illness; the lower article from Tuesday, 1st September 1885; the one on the opposite page from Tuesday, 17th March, 1885; the latter two were subsequent to his death.

HORSLEY HILL.
WESTOE, SOUTH SHIELDS.

MR A. T. CROW has again the honour of of announcing instructions from the Executors of the late John Henderson, Esq., to SELL BY AUCTION, at Horsley Hill, Westoe, on FRIDAY, September 4th, 1885, the away-going CROPS, consisting of

11 ACRES OF WHEAT, and
7 ACRES OF OATS.

The Straw to remain on the Premises.

The Sale to commence at 4 for 5 o'clock precisely.

HORSLEY HILL FARM, WESTOE, SOUTH SHIELDS.

MR ARTHUR T. CROW,

In conjunction with

MR ADAM TINDALL,

Has received instructions from the Executors of the late Mr John Henderson,

TO SELL BY AUCTION,

On Monday, 23rd March, 1885,

THE Valuable FARMING STOCK, &c., upon the Premises. Catalogue:—

POWERFUL DRAUGHT HORSES.

Lot.

1. Grey Mare, Darling, 10 years, 16 hands, by George 2nd.
2. Bay Mare, Damsel, 10 years, 16 hands, by Premier, in foal to Royalty.
3. Bay Mare, Jessie, 8 years, 16 hands, by The Swell.
4. Grey Mare, Polly, 7 years, 16·1 hands, by Emperor.
5. Brown Horse, Duke, 5 years old, 16·3 hands, by The Duke.
6. Brown Horse, Lofty, 5 years, 16·3 hands, by The Duke.
7. Brown Horse Cob, Bob, 9 years, 14·2 hands.
8. Grey Horse Cob, Charlie, 9 years, 14·2 hands.
9. Bay Draught Colt, rising 3 years, by Viceroy, dam lot 2, unhandled and possessing ample bone.
10. Grey Draught Colt, rising 2 years, by Breastplate, dam lot 1, unhandled and possessing ample bone.
11. Brown Half Bred Cob Horse, Prince, 6 years old, 15 hands, accustomed to all harness.

SPLENDID S.H. COWS, FAT CATTLE, AND GRAZING STOCK.

18 Grand Dairy S.H. Cows, calven and to calve.

8 Prime Fat Geld Cows.

2 Fat S.H. Bullocks.

2 Neat Fat Heifers.

Prime S.H. Fat Bull (3 years old.)

2 Yearling S.H. Queys.

24 Prime Fat Wedders.

FARM PRODUCE.

A Prime Stack Well-won Old Land Hay (about 30 Tons).

4 Wheat Stacks and Straw.

50 Tons Swede Turnips.

4 Tons Regent Potatoes.

Also, the Large Collection of Implements of Husbandry.

Also, the Surplus HOUSEHOLD FURNITURE, consisting of Brussels and other Carpets, Feather Beds, Mahogany Wardrobes, Tables, Kitchen and other Tables, Dresser, with Shelves; Chairs, Couches, &c.

The Sale to commence at 10 for 11 o'clock to a minute.

Manor House, Sunderland, March 7th, 1885.

The photographs on this page show the expansive pond which sat in front of the farmhouse.

On the opposite page is a rural scene of the roads leading to Horsely Hill Farmhouse. Haystacks and a horse and cart are visible on the left-hand side of the image in the middle ground.

By 1901 the next prominent tenant of Horsley Hill Farm, Mr Hemsley, had arrived; he and his family would farm the area until 1944

In the 1901 census living at Large Horsley Hill Farm were:,
John Hemsley 52, farmer; Jane, 42, wife; their children Thomas 16, Jane 13, Annie 9, Maggie 7; their niece Margaret 18; Isabella Geddes 24, a general servant; Johnson Kirton 29, ploughman on the farm; Charles Hill 28, milkman, and Edward Davison 18, milk-boy.
In the four cottages attached to the farm were the following:
Cottage 1: Margaret Nixon 71 a widow; her daughters Catherine 30, and Elizabeth 27, both dairy-maids on the farm.
Cottage 2: Thomas Best 36, a hind on the farm; Emily 45 his wife.
Cottage 3: unoccupied.
Cottage 4: Charles Johnson 33, stock-man on the farm; Alice 28 his wife; Charles Nixon an adopted son of 10 months; Mary Heslop 36, a visitor on the night of the census.

At Little Horsley Hill Farm lived: Ann Smith 76, a widow listed as a farmer; her two sons, Aaron 43, and Enoch son 35; her grandson John 11; Elizabeth Burnhope 18, a general domestic servant.

On Thursday, 1st June, 1944, the local newspapers reported an accident which befell Mr Thomas Hemsley, John Hemsley's eldest son, who was now running the farm.

Sadly he did not recover as the entry below, from *The Newcastle Journal*, **Wednesday, 11th October, 1944**, lists the sale of items from the farm following his demise.

It is interesting to note the degree of mechanisation that is now part of farm life.

Shields Farmer

TOSSED AND GORED BY BULL

Mr Thomas Hemsley. of Horsley Hill Farm. South Shields, was tossed and gored by one of his own bulls yesterday in the field where the bull was kept.

After receiving medical attention he was taken to Ingham Infirmary suffering from general injuries—his condition today was stated to be "very poor."

Mr Hemsley. who is over 60. took over Horsley Hill Farm on the death of his father many years ago.

It is believed that Mr Hemsley entered the field to quieten the bull. which was knocking its horns against a barn door, when he was attacked.

An assistant cowman. Ernest Malcolm Sidebottom. of 15 Winterbottom Street was told of the accident and ran to the field where he saw Mr Hemsley pinned to a wall by the bull.

He seized a hay-fork and drove the bull away until other men arrived and were able to drive it back to its stall.

HORSLEY HILL FARM. SOUTH SHIELDS Re the Estate T. Hemsley. deceased THE northern agricultural CO-OPERATIVE SOCIETY. LTD. favoured with instructions from Lloyds Bank Limited. Executor and Trustee Dept., 102, Grey Street. Newcastle-on-Tyne,

SELL BY AUCTION on MONDAY. NOVEMBER 6. 1944.
4 HORSES. Quiet and good workers all yokes.
1 RED AND WHITE SHORTHORN COW.
2 STRONG STORE PIGS

IMPLEMENTS.—I 1940 Model Case Tractor, complete with power take off, rubber tyres front and rear, set of Opperman wheel strakes for same, iron wheels front and rear; Miller, tool bar for Fordson Tractor, complete; Miller, low crop wheels R and F, complete, never been used: Blackstone Potato Digger; Vacca Milking Machine (4 unit), complete with electric motor; Sterilising Chest; 1 Bissett 6ft. cut power drive Binder, only cut 12 acres; Four-wheeled Tractor Trailer, rubber tyred: 1-2-Wheeled Tractor Trailer on rubbers: 1-3- Furrow Tractor Plough; 2-2-Furrow Tractor Ploughs; 1 Set Disc Harrows; 1 Self-lift Tractor Cultivator; 1 Tractor Hay Sweep.

All the above Tractors and Tractor Implements are excellent condition, and worthy closest attention buyers.

1 Ruston Proctor 48" drum Thresher and Bottler; 1 Brooks Electric Motor, 440 volts, 12 h.p.. Pulleys, Belting and Shafting for the above; 1 Bentail R.6.X. Mill; 1 Newman Electric Motor on iron stand 400/440 volts. 1.5 h.p.; Metropolitan Electric Motor, 440 volts, 5.5 h.p. and Turnip Chopper all on one stand; 1 Electric Motor, 440 volts, 1.5 h.p.; 1 Teasdale Hay Chopper; 1 Power Barrel Root Cutter; 1 Set. Emery Wheels (power driven), brand new; Wolf Electric Hand Drill; 1 Wolf E.S.I. Clasp. Horse with tractor drawbar and shafts; 3 Hay Bogies (metal wheels); Hay Bogie (rubber tyres); 1 Coup Cart and shelvings, rubber tyres; Coup Carts and shelvings. on iron tyres; 1 Nicholson Hay Rake: 1 Barford Hay Tedder; 1 Kearsley Grass Cutter' 1 Bamlett Grass Cutter; 1 Paddy Hay Sweep; 1 Gate Hay Sweep; 1 Blackstone Swath Turner; 2 Hay Poles; j Massey-Harris Self Binder, complete with 2 sets canvases. horse pole and tractor drawbar; 1 Com Drill; 1 Manure Drill; 1 Turnip Drill; 2 Horse Cultivators; Cambridge Drill Roller-1-2-Furrow Horse Plough; Digger Ploughs; 2 Drill Ploughs; 2 Scufflers: 1 Potato Digger; 1 Flat Roller; 1 Scrubber; 1 Set Spike Harrows; 1 get Grass Harrows; 1 Set Saddle Harrows- 1 Cambridge Roller; 1 Concrete Flat 'Roller; 2 Potato 2 Machines and 1 Winnowing Machine- 3 Barrows —2 with rubber tyres; i Hand Turnip Chopper; 3 Sack Barrows; Bins- 2 Sets Block and Tackle: Zinc Tanks; T 2 Stack Nets: 4 Stock Sheets; 2 Wooden Tool Chests; 3 Grindstones; 1 Cake Crusher; 2 Hay Spades; 4 doz. Potato Swells, nearly new; Vice; 1 Large Hand Drill; 1 Anvil; 4 Paraffin Tanks with hand pumps fitted; 1 Portable Hen 2 Portable Silos; 1 Large Implement Shed; Large Quantity Binder Twine; Sundry Ladders; Earthenware Troughs; 200 Fencing Posts, new and varied selection; other Timber:

Large Quantity Hand Tools for carpenter's and mechanic's shop; Many Spare Parts for Implements: Varied quantities Nails. Screws. Bolts, etc.; Varied assortment Hay Porks and Rakes: Turnip Hoes, Grapes, Drags, Hacks, Spade, Scythes, Melts, Shovels, etc.

Harton Down Hill Farm

Harton Down Hill Farmhouse photographed in *The Shields Gazette* **7th March, 1934.**

Cleadon Hills Farmhouse in 2021, built, one assumes, of the same local rock and in the same solid square style as Harton Down Hill Farm house.

This is the only photograph I have found of Harton Down Hill Farm. It was the home of the Snowdon family, a farming family with extensive connections to various other farms in the wider area. Their eldest son would move into his own farm, Harton Farm, but died young and his widow would then run the farm (p66).

Harton Down Hill Farm in the 1839 tithe inventory was a farm of 127 acres, and like Horsley Hill Farm stretched right to the cliff edge, including interestingly a small island now locally known as Camel's Island, but then a significant tourist attraction known as the Velvet Beds (p213). The early maps show that the hills of Harton Down Hill were once quarries and in the early nineteenth century became home to a coastguard station.

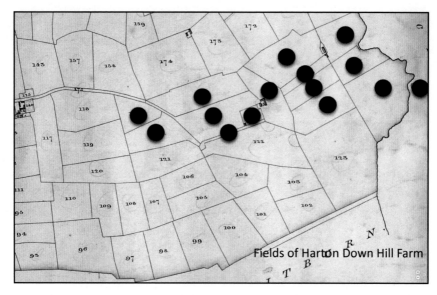

Fields of Harton Down Hill Farm

Harton Back Lane led from Harton Village to the lane which provided access to Harton Down Hill Farm. Marsden Cottage (p164) was a large, privately owned residence with its subsequent drive leading off from Harton Down Hill to its position on the eastern side of the hill, nearer to the coast.
Down Hill Farm house lay sheltered from the sea blasts behind the hill.

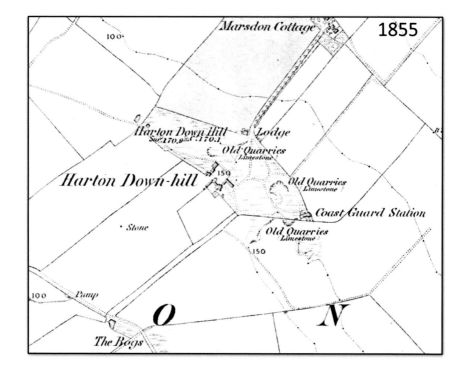

1855

The following report appeared in the local newspaper on Saturday, 17th November, 1866:

Yesterday, a severe gale from the north and northeast, with heavy and continuous showers of rain. was experienced on this coast. The sea broke heavily on the bar, and along the coast, and in the presence of such tempestuous weather, considerable anxiety was evinced for the safety of shipping.

About six o'clock last night the inhabitants of and around Marsden were thrown into a state of excitement by noticing a vessel, which was making for the Tyne, in dangerous proximity to the rocks a little above the Marsden Grotto. Anxiously the course of the vessel was watched at Marsden by Mr. Wm. Allen; and providentially, at the same time, Mr. Snowdon, of Down Hill Farm, near Marsden, was in the act of riding to South Shields, when his attention was directed to the vessel's lights. Knowing that the vessel must be in danger by seeing her lights so near land, Mr, Snowdon, with great foresight and precision immediately summoned his hinds, and proceeded to the coastguard house to cart the rockets and lines down to the rocks, to be in readiness. However, ere the short time elapsed between Mr. Snowdon seeing the danger and the lines being carted, the coastguardsmen--John Williamson and Wm. Odgers—also on the alert, saw the vessel strike the rocks at the portion of the coast known as the "Blow Hole." They, too, gave the alarm, and ran for the rocket apparatus; but, though only a very few minutes elapsed between the time when the alarm was first given and the apparatus being down to the edge of the rocks, it was found that the crew had landed, safe and sound.

The barque, which proved to be the *Sovereign*, belonging to Mr. I. Dale, of North Shields, had most fortunately been driven ashore on a flat, jutting portion of rock, with the bowsprit overhanging the rock known as the "Blow Hole". The moon at the time shone out between a cleft in the clouds, and the crew were enabled to see a ready escape front their perilous position, by dropping from the bowsprit down to the rock, where they were received by Mr. William Allen, of the Marsden Grotto. The men. as they landed, were taken, some to the residence of the coastguard, and others to the house of Mr. F. Shaw, where they were most kindly and hospitably treated.

Harton Down Hill Farm like all those in Harton Township, supplied the ever increasing population of South Shields with food, sold directly to grocers and butchers in the town or wholesale as these adverts show.

Wednesday, 22nd December, 1880:

CHRISTMAS BEEF.

GEORGE McGREGOR, Butcher, King Street, South Shields, again returns his sincere thanks to his patrons and the general public for favours that have hitherto been accorded him, and begs to intimate that he has procured for the Festive Season four prime English HEIFERS, fed by John Henderson, Esq., Horsley Mill Farm; also, one score of half-bred SHEEP, from the same feeder; likewise half-a-score of Dairy-fed PORKERS, from William Snowden, Esq., Harton Down Hill Farm. The whole of the above Stock will be sold at reasonable prices.

The farms in Harton Township tended to be mixed farms with crops and animals as these two adverts show.

The Durham County Advertiser 28th July, 1905:

HARTON DOWN HILL FARM, SOUTH SHIELDS.

SALE OF AWAY-GOING CROPS.

MR WM. CHRYSTAL' honoured with instruc' tions from the Exors. of Robert Snowdon Esq., will Sell by Public Auction, on Friday, the 4th August, 1905, 29 Acres of Away-Going Crops.

13 Acres Wheat.
16 Acres Short Oats.

Sale at 6 o'clock p.m.

To meet at Farm Buildings.

TERMS—Cash less 2½ per cent., or 3 months' bill on approved joint security.

Auction and Estate Offices,
Houghton-le-Spring.

Like Mr Henderson, at near by Horsley Hill Farm, Mr Snowdon was a prominent member of the township. His funeral in 1888 was attended by some of the most influential, local men of the time such as: Mr J M Moore, the Town Clerk of South Shields and Alderman Readhead.

FUNERAL OF MR SNOWDON OF HARTON.

This afternoon, the remains of the late Mr William Snowdon, farmer, of Harton Down Hill, were interred at the Harton churchyard. The whole of the houses in the vicinity of the churchyard had their blinds down, and a large concourse of people assembled at the grave to witness the solemn service. The officiating clergymen were the Revs. Arthur Watts and W. C. Carr. The coffin was of polished oak, with brass mountings. The funeral cortege left the residence of the deceased about two o'clock, and the hearse was followed by eight carriages. The chief mourners were the two sons of the deceased, John and Robert Snowdon, Robert Snowdon, of Bishop Auckland, Robert Snowdon, of Leamington, and John Snowdon, Washington. There was also a number of private carriages in attendance, including that of Mr J. M. Moore, Town Clerk of South Shields, and Ald. Readhead. The following friends of the deceased walked in order to the cemetery : Councillor Bowman, R. Chapman, R. Lawson, John Collie, Dr. Robson, and Ald. Wardle, South Shields ; Mr R. Crow, Sunderland ; Geo. Ripton, Harton; George Forster, North Biddick Farm, Washington ; John Clark, Horsley Hill ; L. M. Snowdon, Marsden ; Mr Patterson, Harton ; Robert and Henry Burdon, Cleadon. There were also several of the employees of the deceased present at the grave.

The footprint of Harton Down Hill Farm on the 1855 map and the census returns show that there were a number of workers' cottages at the farm. The site also offered accommodation for the coastguard before their purpose built station (p248) and it would seem likely that they maintained a look-out post at the site, which offered a such vantage point.

The panoramic view north east and south east along the coast from Harton Down Hill.

By the time of the 1891 census Whitburn Colliery was in production and the Marsden Rattler running as transport to and from the colliery, hence we find coal miners living amongst farm labourers in the cottages of Harton Down Hill Farm.

The 1891 census lists three families living in separate dwellings at the farm:

Cottage 1: Burtis Gray 30, coal miner; his wife, Hannah 30; their children Hannah 8, Elizabeth 4, and Burdis 3 years old..

Cottage 2: William Tate 43, coal miner; Frances his wife, 39; Elizabeth their niece 9 years old.

Cottage 3: Edward Robson 66, an agricultural labourer; Jane 53, his wife; Hannah 13, their daughter.

William had died in 1888 and the farm was then run by his son Robert Snowdon 26. Also living in the farmhouse on the night of the 1891 census were: Annie, his mother, a widow 63; Sarah, his sister 28; Dorothy White 20, a general domestic servant; Annie Gibson 19, also a domestic servant; William Henderson 18, and Geoffrey Olive 21, both agricultural labourers on the farm.

The 1901 census still has Robert as the head of the farm unmarried and now 36 years old. With him live: his sister Sarah 37 and her husband Alfred Johnson, 37 a general merchant; their three children Annie 7, William 4, and Jenny 3 years old; Thomas Blair 21, a ploughman on the farm; Edward Brown 15, worker on the farm; Jane Gilroy 21, a general domestic servant, and Isabella Bell 37, also a general domestic servant.

A second Snowdon family headstone shows that Robert died in 1904 aged 39.

In the four cottages attached to the farm we find:

Cottage 1: Henry Edgar 44, a coal miner, an underground hewer; his wife Rose 38; and their children John 17, a coal miner, an underground putter, Henry 13, Mealy 11, Robert 9, George 7, and Rose 4; with Ann Oakley 66, Henry's widowed mother-in-law.

Cottage 2: Joseph Barnes 52, horseman on the farm; Mary 48, his wife; their children Mary 22, Annie 19 and Albert 14, an underground horse driver in the coal mine.

Cottage 3: George Montgomery 42, coal miner, an underground hewer; his wife Mary 35; and their children Mary 14, Edward 12, Sarah 7, Ada 4 and Anne 1 year old.

Cottage 4: William Hunter 40, a coal miner underground shifter; Maria 40,

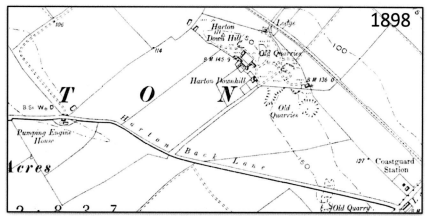

This map of 1898 shows an extension to Harton Back Lane which now joined Redwell Bank, where the new coastguards houses (p248) were situated, plus the South Shields, Marsden, Whitburn Colliery railway line and a Pumping Engine House is mentioned, which supplied water to Whitburn Colliery from a deep shaft to an underground stream.

Looking north east toward Harton Down Hill in 2021

Harton Moor Farm

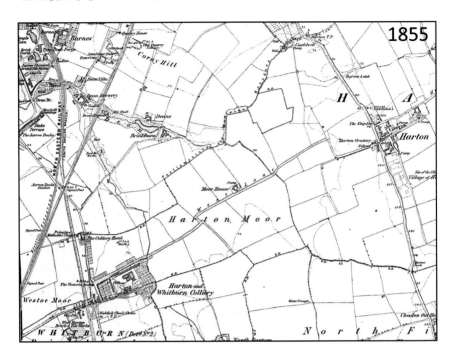

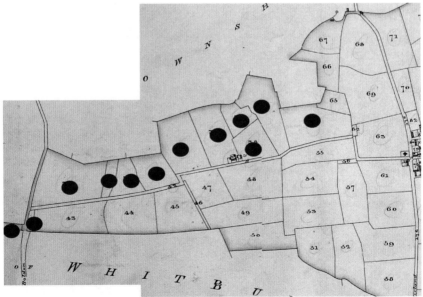

The 1855 map opposite shows the site of Harton Colliery. Harton Moor Farm was on the opposite side of Harton Lane to the colliery but the western-most field of this farm was already witnessing the growth of workers' houses along Boldon Lane (p188).

In 1901 all of Harton Moor Farm was taken into South Shields, but it already appears to have ceased functioning as a farm. By this time housing had spread along its four most western fields and a football pitch had been erected in the next one. The 1901 census still names the farmhouse, but two families are now living there, one a mining family and the other a younger family with the head of the house recorded as a hind on a farm, but which farm and whether the remaining fields of Moor Farm had been taken over by Mr Woods of Red House Farm is not certain.

We once again do not have any pictures of the farmhouse, but just a little distance to the north, over a couple of fields, we find Brinkburn Farmhouse, and there are some historic images of this farmhouse in the South Tyneside Libraries collection. It is shown here to give some indication of what Moor Farm house may have looked like. In 1839 Moor Farm was a farm of 100 acres with a farmstead of 1 rod and 29 perches. All of the fields, at that

A photograph of Brinkburn Farmhouse taken in 1942. The house still exits today standing at the bottom of Ashley Road, South Shields.

What does exist in South Tyneside Libraries archive of photographs that relate to Moor Farm are these two glorious images of some of the fields belonging to the farm.

They are from about 1900 and are of the same stile shot from both directions; the top one is looking north towards the newly built Stanhope Road and the lower one looking south along the path over Harton Moor.

The roofline in the centre of the horizon of the bottom image is more likely to be Harton Laundry than Harton Moor Farm. There are two possible paths shown on the map opposite that this lady and these girls might have taken; it could be that they even started from the path in front of Brinkburn Farmhouse

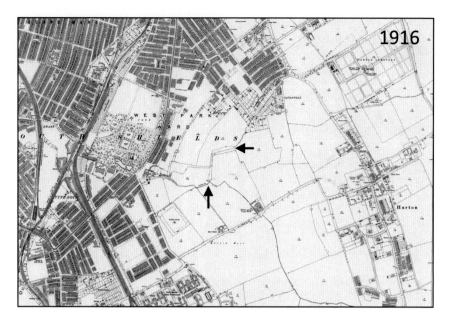

Moor Farm, seems to have changed hands quite regularly and adverts for new tenants in the local newspapers give a little more information about the farm. Such as this one from December, 1832:

TO BE LET BY PROPOSAL,

For such a Term of Years as may be agreed upon, and may be entered upon immediately, or at May-Day next,

HARTON MOOR HOUSE FARM, in the Township of Harton, and Parish of Jarrow, containing 100 Acres or thereabouts, of excellent Arable and Pasture Land, desirably situated for Manure, Lime, and Markets, being one Mile from South Shields, and five from the Market Town of Sunderland. The Poor Rate is exceedingly low in this Township, and the Farm pays a small Modus in Lieu of Hay Tithe. There is an excellent Thrashing Machine on the Premises. For further Particulars, apply to Mr. John Straker, Jarrow Lodge, who will send a Person to show the Farm, and by whom Proposals in Writing, will be received until Saturday the 22nd of December.

Jarrow Lodge, Nov. 28, 1832.

In December, 1857, there is another notice seeking a new tenant for Harton Moor Farm, but this time the farm is quoted as composing about 90 acres, and now in the occupation of Mr John Potts. A new tenant having been secured Mr Potts then advertises the sale of his farming stock and *implements of husbandry*, which gives a further insight into the make up of Harton Moor Farm in 1858:

HARTON MOOR FARM, NEAR BROCKLEY WHINS STATION.

MR. MOSES PYE is favoured with instructions from Mr. John Pott, to SELL BY AUCTION, on *Monday, May* 10*th*, 1858, the FARMING STOCK, IMPLEMENTS of HUSBANDRY, &c., upon the above Farm, comprising.—

Brown Horse, aged.
Brown Horse, six years old.
Brown Harness Horse, rising four years old.
Grey Colt, rising three years old, by Thornhill.
Two Fat Heifers.
One Fat Pig.

Long Cart and Coup, 2 Iron Ploughs, 2 Pair Harrows, Harness for Two Pair Horses, Water Barrel, Hack, Forks, Gripes, Shovels, &c., &c.

Sale to commence on the arrival of the Two o'clock trains from Newcastle, Sunderland, and Shields.

Sale Offices—28, Groat Market, Newcastle, and 13, Russell Street, North Shields,
May 6th, 1858.

In the 1891 census: Henry Colley 40, from Bolam Northumberland, is the farmer at Moor House Farm; his wife Isabella Colley 38, was born at Newburn, Durham; Mary Isabella 6, his daughter born in Whitburn; his sons Thomas 4, and Ralph 2, were both born at Harton; living in the farmhouse are also Ann Potts 18, and Bella Potts 19, both domestic servants from Harton; Alfred Bulmer 19, an agricultural labourer, from Wark, Northumberland; Edward Charlton 14, an agricultural labourer, from St Andrews, Middlesex.

By 1901 Mr Colley had moved his family to a nearby farm at Westoe; still remembered locally as Colley's farm. The farmhouse at Harton Moor Farm would be lived in by two families:

John Horn 59, a coal miner, a shifter underground, born in Yorkshire; Louisa 54, his wife born in London; Matthew 25, and Thomas 17, their sons, both working as coal miners underground; Frances 15 their daughter; all three children had been born in County Durham.

Also living in the farmhouse is the Muckle family: John W Muckle 29, a hind on a farm, from Cramlington Northumberland; his wife Isabella 24, born in Whitburn; their two young children Elizabeth 2, born in Northumberland and William 5 months old, born in Harton.

In 1901 the land which had been Harton Moor Farm, plus the buildings of the farm were removed from Harton Township in the expansion of South Shields.

A photograph from the 1950s of Colley's Farm in Westoe. Demolished to make way for South Shields Marine and Technical College.

Simonside Farms

The Rev William Adams and Mary Pigott Cay.
Occupied by Robinson Cook.

Samuel Blenkinsop and Isabella Straker, Trustees of Samuel
Blenkinsop, Nicholas Blenkinsop and William Ord.
Occupied by Thomas Stothard.

Henry Major Esquire. Occupied by himself.

John White. Occupied by himself.

The Rev John Brewster the Elder and Rev John Brewster the younger.
Occupied by Matthew Maughan.

Robert Ingham Esquire.   Occupied by John Clark.

Only a small section of Simonside ever came into Harton Township's
jurisdiction. The 1839 tithe map shows two farms within the Simonside
area of Harton Township and the 1851 census shows the same names
connected with these fields.

In 1851 Low Simonside Farm was farmed by Robinson Cook 58, his wife
Jane 55, and their four children all born in Simonside. An aged relative of 80
and a farm servant Edward 14, also lived in the farmhouse.   The farm
consisted of 70 acres and 21 perches, within that the farmstead covered an
area of 2 rods and 6 perches.

At Simonside Lodge Farm now lived Luke Blenkinsop 33, who is recorded on
the census as a farmer, with a housekeeper and three other servants.   In
Simonside Lodge itself lived two of Blenkinsop's sisters and his niece, plus a
housekeeper. So it would seem that the Trustees no longer rented the farm
to Thomas Stothard, but that a member of the Blenkinsop family had
decided to run it himself. This farm was slightly smaller than Low Simonside
Farm, both being smaller than other farms in Harton Township, at 67 acres,

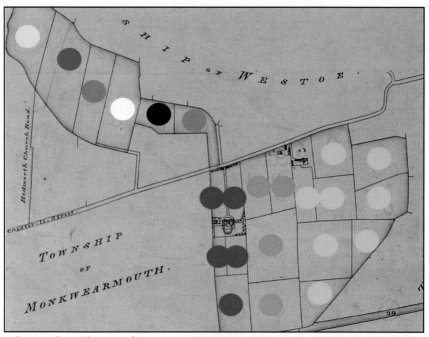

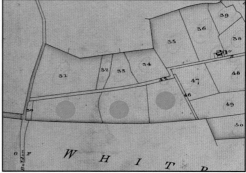

The complete tithe map of Harton Township shown below, serves to place these other two maps in context.

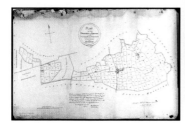

3 rods and 31 perches, with the farmstead and garth accounting for 2 rods and 20 perches.

The fields joining Bilton Villa had different owners and may have formed part of other farms not in Harton Township. The names of the owners and tenants of these fields, taken from the 1839 tithe list, are shown in the table opposite, which in turn relates to the maps above.

The various census returns between 1851 and 1901 show changes of ownership and the reduction in size of these farms. Fields were taken away for other purposes than farming. In 1841 the fields farmed by Robinson

Cook of Low Simonside Farm which were accessed along Green Lane, became the site of Harton Colliery.

The south eastern fields of the Blenkinsop Simonside Lodge Farm became a series of terraced houses for mining families and others working on the nearby railway. Madras Street, Tennent Street, Wenlock Road etc still stand as a reminder of the industry that once abounded in the area. Shops and small manufacturing businesses grew along Green Lane. Behind them the land owned by Westoe Township witnessed the development of masses of railway lines feeding Tyne Dock Staithes and the erection of a huge engine house. The fields farmed by Simonside Lodge Farm were further reduced with the building of St Simon's Church, St Simon's vicarage and a school in

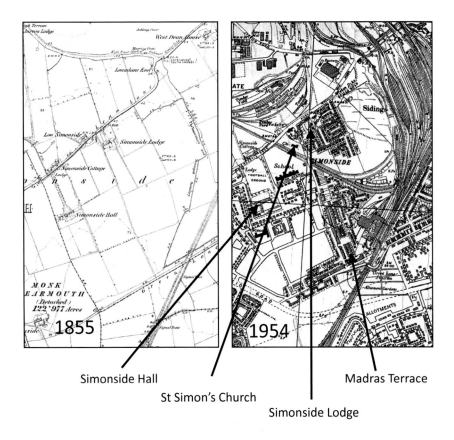

Simonside Hall   Madras Terrace

St Simon's Church

Simonside Lodge

The 1855 map shows the field boundaries as well as the boundary of Harton Township and can be compared with the map of the same area 100 years later.

the 1880s on what had been the north east corner of the farm. So by the 1891 census we can appreciate why there is only one farm mentioned within the Simonside area of Harton Township.

Bilton Villa, Simonside Hall and Simonside Lodge are all mentioned in the census as homes of wealthy businessmen (p200) and though they did have a certain amount of land attached to their property, it was not enough to constitute a farm; more likely providing paddocks for their horses.

So it seems that over time the two separately managed farms reduce to one. They may not have been amalgamated as the land could have been rented to other interested parties by the Ecclesiastical Commissioners; owners could change as quickly as tenants. In 1891 the only farm recorded in this area of Harton Township is given the all-embracing title of Simonside Farm on the census. The farmer was Joseph Richardson 64, his wife Margaret 70, both their son John 32, and their daughter Margaret, 23, worked on the farm and James Taylor 23, was a live-in employee, a general farm labourer.

The 1901 census records Simonside Farm as being run by the same family. Joseph Richardson is now 74 years old and recorded as a farmer and a gardener, so maybe this farm was already dwindling in size, his wife Margaret 80, and their son John 42, who is also recorded as a farmer and gardener.

In 1901 this area of Simonside was subsumed into South Shields.

Residential Harton

Chapter 3

Two aerial photographs by Fred Mudditt - Fietscher Fotos Ltd taken in 1975 and 1971 showing the urban growth in what had been the agricultural heart of Harton Township in 1921.

Introduction

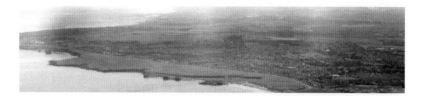

At the end of the nineteenth century and beginning of the twentieth century Harton Village began to expand and became more than farms and workers' cottages, for it began to be seen as a desirable place to live for those wishing to escape the industrial pollution of South Shields. Some upwardly mobile families: solicitors, newspaper editors, ship owners, initially moved into newly-built single detached houses then the more middle class families came to live in the new terraced houses that began to be built. Any green belt between Westoe Village and South Shields was disappearing and the next village on the main road was Harton.

West Harton had witnessed the growth of Harton Colliery and the railways which passed between it and Simonside to Tyne Dock. Working class homes grew at a rapid pace here and these would be taken into South Shields in 1901 to join with their near neighbours Templetown and Corstorphine Town.

By 1920, following WW1, the County Borough of South Shields began their first council housing estate at Cleadon Park, to the south of the township. Slums in the industrial town were to be cleared in the acknowledgement that everyone deserved fresh air and modern amenities. It appeared clear to the council members of Harton Township in 1921 that the reason to take over Harton was to provide land for housing for the ever increasing population of South Shields.

Just as today in 2021, when we see estates encroaching on the edge of villages and towns, we are caught in the dilemma between losing precious green fields and the acknowledgement that everyone has the right to live in a pleasant environment. The incorporation of Harton Township in 1921 shows how quickly farm land can disappear yet I for one have had a pleasant life living in one of these *new* houses in Harton.

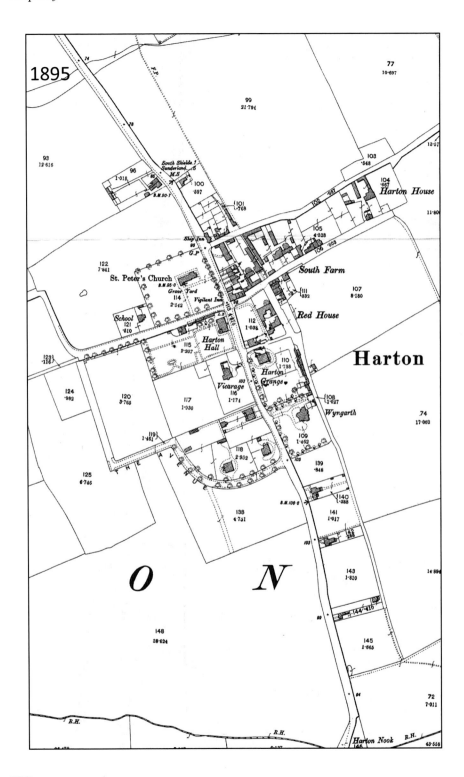

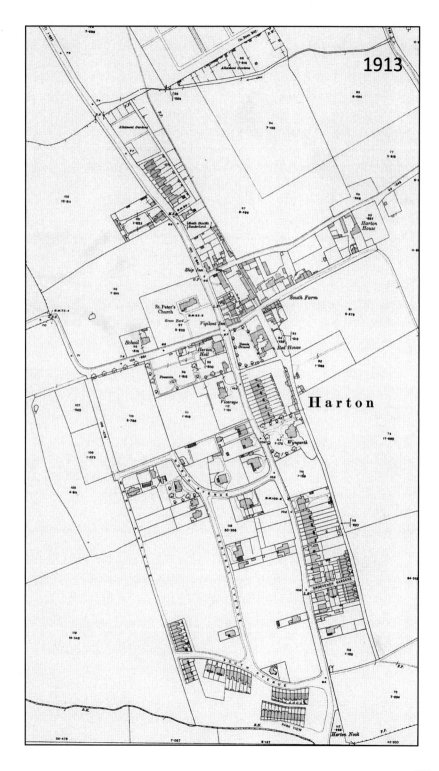

The Village

In 2017 I wrote a book about Harton Village in 1900 and I do not intend to repeat that information here.   Rather I want to pick up the thread a little from where I left off and look primarily at the early twentieth century and the growth of houses in and around the village between 1901 and 1921.

The Victorian period (1837-1901) had witnessed a natural growth of houses in and around the village as the middle classes and upper middle classes of South Shields, moved *into the country* just as so many of us aspire to do, but still requiring to be near to their places of work.   Large detached or semi-detached houses were built on the edge of the village around farm buildings and workers' cottages.   Then later, but before the WW1 as seen in the section of the Godfrey map opposite, terraces or large semi-detached houses were built, most of this development taking place along the main road from South Shields to Sunderland which ran through the village.

A comparison of the two maps on the preceding pages, from 1895 and 1913, shows this organic growth. The Oratory would be demolished in 1867 to make way for the new St Peter's Church soon accompanied by a grand vicarage. A new school would be built by Mr Moore in 1875 as a swap to replace the earlier school building of 1846 which he had acquired. Mr J M Moore, Town Clerk of South Shields, would also demolish earlier Georgian houses to build his new Harton Hall in 1881. The Grange, one time home of South Shields Borough Engineer Mr M Hall, built after 1855, would be demolished in the new century and replaced by Grange Avenue, the old Vigilant Inn would be demolished in 1925 and replaced by the building we see today.   Harton Lodge was demolished in 1931 to allow Harton Back Lane to be replaced by the much wider Marsden Road and many other old buildings belonging to the village vanished to be replaced by new housing, such as the cottages and houses in St Mary's Avenue, replaced by a terrace and bungalows.   In the 1950s the village pond would be filled in and farmhouses razed to the ground. The old blacksmiths which stood behind The Ship Inn meeting its fate in 1964 to make way for the pub car park.

Only three sets of buildings shown on the 1855 map (p21) currently exist in the village: The Ship Inn; the cottages to the east, behind The Ship Inn; The Terrace to the south between The Ship Inn and The Vigilant.

An early photograph of the Ship Inn shows it without the addition of the semi circular bay windows, Harton Lodge is not visible but further up the road is The Terrace and then centre in distance the white building is the original Vigilant pub.

This early photograph is of the corner of Moor Lane and Sunderland Road and shows the house and shop which stood on the corner demolished in 1881 to make way for Mr Moore's Harton Hall, which after his death was converted into three properties with shops beneath.

A view of Moor Lane East showing the old Vigilant pub on the corner. This was demolished in 1925 and replaced by the current building.

The area behind The Vigilant once looked like this; is now a car park and bungalows.

Today to take this photograph we would be standing outside The Vigilant pub looking up Moor Lane East. None of the buildings in this image exist in 2021.

Harton Village pond looking north, none of these buildings nor the pond exist in 2021.

The building on the left of this photograph stood where the forecourt of Harton Garage now stands, the other large house was Harton Grange, built after 1855 and when this photograph was taken up for sale. It would eventually be demolished and replaced by Harton Police Station, which is now in turn waiting demolition.

The Ship Inn is just visible on the extreme left of this photograph, the large house behind the trees is Harton Lodge which was demolished in 1931 to allow Marsden Road to be built.

On this page are images of some of the houses built in Harton Township prior to 1921. Although changed by the addition of porches, new windows and other modern aspects, these and many other houses from the same period are still providing family homes.

Houses began to stretch long Sunderland Road as can be seen in the above photograph with houses heading north from The Ship Inn and in the image below a terrace built in 1907 in the grounds of Harton Grange, with a row of what were already then mature trees. These trees are marked on the 1895 map.

Two photographs taken in 1912, showing the houses leading out of the village on Sunderland Road towards the Nook.

By comparing the 1895 map (p130) with the 1913 map (p131) it can be seen that none of these terraces existed before 1895. Individual houses did stand on Sunderland Road, in their own grounds and most remain to this day. Later in the twentieth century semi-detached houses would be added to completely line the street with housing.

After 1921, that is particularly between the two world wars and immediately after WW2 a huge spurt of council and private housing took place quickly covering all the Harton farmers' fields mostly with semi-detached housing, roads and other amenities necessary for modern living.

A photograph of South Avenue. The gable of which can be seen in the image below.

These three images narrow images above are details from photographs taken in 1928 taken from Quarry Lane during the second stage of council housing to be built on the fields between Quarry Lane and Prince Edward Road.

The top two are from the same photograph enlarged, so they provide a continuous view of the village at that time, from Wyngarth and St Peter's Steeple, to south Avenue and the Nook. Cross referencing can be made with the 1921 map on the next page. All the gaps seen in the housing and the fields were to be covered with further houses, shops, a cinema, a library, a methodist church and a catholic church.

The lower photograph shows the new Cleadon Park Estate and Cleadon Park Farm, known locally as Veitch's Farm, which stood at the bottom of Quarry Lane. (All that remains of this farm are the stone walls that now form the front garden wall of houses along this part of Sunderland Road.)

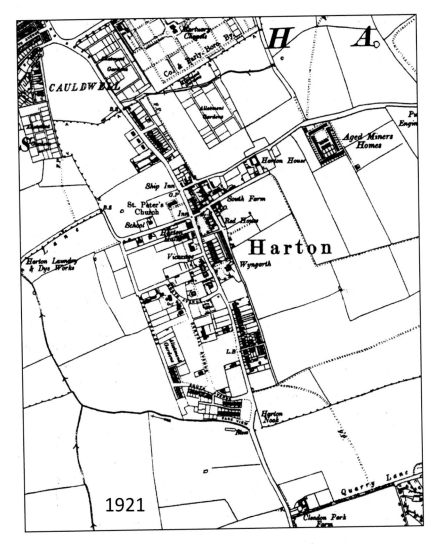

The enlarged background details opposite from photographs taken in 1928, from Quarry Lane looking over in a westerly direction across the fields of Veitch's farm, give a record of the size of residential Harton Village at this time, which links in superbly with the map above.

There is not enough room in this chapter to state when each house or street was built, but at the end of this section I have attached a copy of the enumerator's list for 1911 which states the name and address of each person living at that time in Harton Township. The above map of 1921, which although ten years after the list, serves to provide a breathtaking snapshot of Harton Township.

An Advert for Cleadon Park Estate. Indoor bathrooms, full electric light and gardens back and front were the standard for each house.

Opposite is a map of 1938, showing the development of Little Horsley Hill Estate. Note that Little Horsley Hill Farmhouse had been demolished but Horsley Hill Farmhouse and Harton Down Hill Farm still exist.

Cleadon Park Housing Estate

B RIGHT REEZY RACING

Those seeking Houses within quick and easy access of the centre of the town will find ideal conditions combining comfort and convenience at Cleadon Park.

4 Roomed Houses, 11/11 per week including rates
5 Roomed Houses, 14/11 per week including rates
6 Roomed Houses, 16/4 per week including rates

Electric Light throughout.   Bathrooms.
Gardens back and front.

Write : HOUSING MANAGER, TOWN HALL
SOUTH SHIELDS
Telephone—210

for particulars of vacant houses and full information

The Harton Township boundary pre-1921 ran up Prince Edward Road, so Quarry Lane, Veitch's Farm and the new Cleadon Park Estate (the South Shields's first Corporation estate) was not built in Harton but on the southern border. The land had been bought by the then Mayor of South Shields Councillor Andrew Anderson, for £18,000 and he allowed the Corporation to buy the estate at no more than its purchase price. The Mansion House went on to become Cleadon Sanatorium opened in 1921 for the treatment of sufferers in the early stages of TB. Of the surrounding land, 131 acres were dedicated for housing and the remainder for other public purposes such as education and recreation.

The foundation stone of the first house was laid on 3rd November 1920. Over the next 12 years 1,528 houses were built. The houses were of varying sizes, the largest being six-roomed houses which comprised living room, parlour and scullery the ground floor with four bedrooms above with bathroom and lavatory. Most had a large back garden and a garden at the front.

Cleadon Park offered clean air and a healthy environment for families from the overpopulated, polluted areas of South Shields which were in their turn being cleared. With the Cleadon Park scheme such a success the council followed it up with many others. They built 396 two bedroom bungalows on five estates

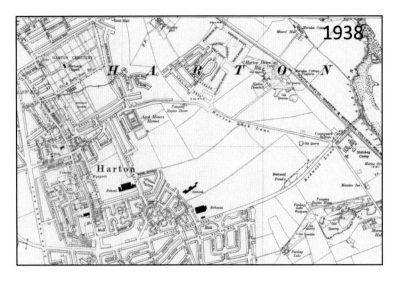

between 1933 and 1934. Just before the commencement of WW2 they completed 608 houses on the site of Little Horsley Hill Farm land. Council building also began around the southern end of what is now Centenary Avenue where it joins Prince Edward Road and schools were erected. After the war work started on the 2,072 houses of the Marsden Estate, which took over most of the remaining fields of Red House Farm, Harton Farm, Harton House Farm and Harton Down Hill Farm.

In the 30 years after Cleadon Park's completion the corporation built more than 6,000 houses, well over a third on land which had once been in Harton Township.

Opposite is part of a page from *The South Shields Centenary Book 1850-1950* **showing the new houses of Marsden Estate and their modern conveniences.**

New houses and bungalows on South Shields Corporation's Marsden Estate, showing typical interior views of the modern corporation house

Mr Moore of Harton Hall died in 1911 and by that time he had acquired a number of fields from the Ecclesiastical Commissioners, much to the concern of the vicar, who felt the vicarage being surrounded. His land was subsequently sold off for private building plots and the individual houses that form Moore Avenue were built. His land also encompassed Armstrong Avenue and Forster Avenue named after his grandson who died in WW1.

The two photographs on this page show the development of houses around St Peter's Church. The top shows houses extending down Moore Avenue (West Avenue and King George Road do not yet exist) and the lower one shows work going on in the fields to the north of the church.

Opposite is an advert from a private builder, William Leech, who is offering:

Here is the home you have been waiting for. Delightfully situated in a modern garden city one mile along the Marsden Road these labour-saving homes are well within the reach of every pocket.

Private builders also bought land from the Ecclesiastical Commissioners and a large number of houses were constructed such as those in Harton House Road, Marsden Road and many others during 1930s and after WW2 in what had been Harton Township so that by 1954, thirty three years after its demise, the map of what was Harton Township now looks like this:

The photograph above shows: the awning of the Ship Inn Off Sales Department; next to it the Smithy on Marsden Road; the old cottages next to that; then further along Marsden Road some of the newly built semi-detached houses that were erected in the 1930s.

Population of the Parish in 1871.

No. of Houses. 170 -

Males 648. Females 628. Total 1276,

Harton village only.

ho. of Houses 33.

Males 108. Females 118. Total 226.

These figures do not include Brinckburn.

Reproduced by kind permission of the vicar and churchwardens of St Peter's Harton.

A record written the Rev Phillpotts' diary related to the 1871 census shows that there were only 33 houses in Harton Village at that time. Although like for like comparisons are not possible, as there are always so many variables to consider, in whatever sense 33 houses compared with 197 dwellings in 1911 does give some understanding of the growth around the village before it was taken into South Shields.

The 1911 census follows a different format to preceding census returns and each family is recorded on a separate sheet. Along-side this information is the enumerator's summary book. On the next pages are tables which are a copy of this 1911 summary book giving a list of the name of each occupant in Harton Township (this being ten years after West Harton, Simonside and Cauldwell were taken into South Shields) the location/name of the property and the number of occupants on the night of the census. This information should be read in conjunction with the 1913 map on page 130. It also lists unoccupied houses as well as the buildings that are not used as residences, so we can see where the new building is taking place and which terraces had been completed and were fully occupied.

Please note the enumerator's handwriting was not always easy to read and I apologise for any errors I have made in transcribing the names. On a few occasions I have added questions marks to signify that I am not in any way confident that I have the correct name.

	Property	Type	Occupier and number resident.	
1	Trow Rocks (Red House)	Maisonette	Mr McDonald	7
2	Trow Rocks (Red House)	Maisonette	Mr Spooner	6
3	Trow Rocks (Red House)	Maisonette	Mr Hall	8
4	The Nest, Trow Rocks	Maisonette	Mr Hicks	3
Frenchman's Point Powder Magazine				
5	Frenchman's Point	Maisonette	Serg Green	4
	Frenchman's Point	Maisonette	unoccupied	
Salmon's Hall, eight dwellings				
6	Salmon's Hall	Maisonette	Mr Varley	5
7	Salmon's Hall	Maisonette	Mr Waggott	3
8	Salmon's Hall	Maisonette	Mr Shotton	13
9	Salmon's Hall	Maisonette	Mr Carwood	12
10	Salmon's Hall	Maisonette	Mr Burn	10
11	Salmon's Hall	Maisonette	Mr Sparks	10
12	Salmon's Hall	Maisonette	Mr Miller	4
13	Salmon's Hall	Maisonette	Mr Auty	8
14	Marsden Cottage	Maisonette	Mr Elliott	3
15	Coastguard Station	Maisonette	Mr Miller	3
16	Coastguard Station	Maisonette	Mr Graham	6
17	Harton Down Hill	Private House	Mr Snowdon	9
18	Harton Down Hill	Maisonette	Mr Kirton	5
19	Harton Down Hill	Maisonette	Mr Reay	4
20	Harton Down Hill	Maisonette	Mr Lowdon	8
21	Station Cottage	Maisonette	Mr Nicholson	10
22	Little Horsley Hill	Private House	Mr Phillip	6
23	Horsley Hill Farm	Private House	Mr Hemsley	8
24	Horsley Hill Farm	Maisonette	Mr Thwaites	8
25	Horsley Hill Farm	Maisonette	Mr Wilkinson	7
26	Horsley Hill Farm	Maisonette	Mr Walker	4

	Property	Type	Occupier and number resident.	
27	Horsley Hill Farm	Maisonette	Mr Wade	7
Horsley Hill electrical Pumping Station				
28	Ailsa	Private House	Mr Brown	6
29	Flatbush	Private House	Mr Lawlan	3
30	Stonecroft	Private House	Mr Guy	4
31	Seatondale	Private House	Mrs Anderson	3
	Woodcote	Private House	Unoccupied	
32	Glenfield	Private House	Mr H Crofton	3
	Richmond Villa	Private House	Unpccupied	
33	Highbury House	Private House	Mrs W Brown	6
34	West View	Private House	Mrs F C Laidler	7
35	Ship Inn	Public House	Mrs Waugh	7
36	Laidler's Cottages	Maisonette	Mrs Wayman	7
37	Laidler's Cottages	Maisonette	Mrs Smith	1
38	Laidler's Cottages	Maisonette	Mr Bell	3
39	Laidler's Cottages	Maisonette	Mr J Murphy	4
40	Laidler's Cottages	Private House	Mr J Carr	5
41	Harton House Farm	Private House	Mrs Pattison	6
42	Pattison's Cottages	Maisonette	Mr Earle	8
43	Pattison's Cottages	Maisonette	Mr Rainey	3
44	Harton Village	Maisonette	Mr Townsend	3
45	Harton Lodge	Private House	Mr R Blair	5
46	The Terrace	Maisonette	Mr Staddon	5
47	The Terrace	Maisonette	Mr Allan	3
48	The Terrace	Private House	Mrs Kate H Deans	2
49	The Terrace	Private House	Miss Hall	3
50	The Terrace	Private House	Mr Beazley	4
Harton Village Warehouse				
51	Vigilant Inn	Public House	Mr Woodall	5

	Property	Type	Occupier and number resident.	
	Harton Village	Maisonette	Unoccupied	
52	Harton Village	Maisonette	Mr E Hutchinson	3
53	Harton Village	Maisonette	Mr Aggie?	6
54	Wood's Buildings	Maisonette	Mr Wilson	3
55	Wood's Buildings	House and shop	Mrs Owen	3
56	Harton Village	Private House	Mr Eley	6
57	Harton Village	Private House	Mrs Dryden	4
58	Dryden's Cottages	Maisonette	Mrs Clark	1
59	Dryden's Cottages	Maisonette	Mr Coulthard	8
60	Dryden's Cottages	Maisonette	Mr Scott	4
61	Dryden's Cottages	Maisonette	Mr J Pattison	2

Harton Village   Blacksmith's Shop

Reay's Buildings   Tenemented properties 5 dwellings

	Property	Type	Occupier and number resident.	
62	Reay's Buildings		Mr Savage	6
63	Reay's Buildings		Mr Anderson	3
64	Reay's Buildings		Mr Wray	5
65	Reay's Buildings		Mr White	5
66	Reay's Buildings		Mrs Stephenson	3

Harton Village   Warehouse

	Property	Type	Occupier and number resident.	
67	Moore's Building	Maisonette	Mr R Dryden	
68	Moore's Building	House and Shop	Mr Caffery	

Urwin's Cottages   Tenemented properties 8 dwellings

	Property	Type	Occupier and number resident.	
69	Urwin's Cottages		Mr J Barnes	5
70	Urwin's Cottages		Mr Brockbank	7
71	Urwin's Cottages		Mr Bacon	4
72	Urwin's Cottages		Mr Jones	4
73	Urwin's Cottages		Mr Appleton	4
74	Urwin's Cottages		Mrs Harland	2
75	Urwin's Cottages		Mr Urwin	2

	Property	Type	Occupier and number resident.	
	Urwin's Cottages		unoccupied	
76	Red House Farm	Private House	Mr Wood	7
77	Shewan's Cottages	Maisonette	Mr G Hutchinson	3
78	Shewan's Cottages	Maisonette	Mr J Hutchinson	3
79	Shewan's Cottages	Maisonette	Mr Arold	8
80	Shewan's Cottages	Maisonette	Mr Lunn	2
81	Shewan's Cottages	Maisonette	Mr Noble	3
82	Red House Cottage	Private House	Mr Marshall	7
	4 Grange Ave	Private House	Unoccupied	
83	5 Grange Ave	Private House	Mr A Purvis	
84	6 Grange Ave	Private House	Mr H Reid	
	7 Grange Ave	Private House	unoccupied	
85	8 Grange Ave	Private House	Mr R Purvis	
86	9 Grange Ave	Private House	Mr Rudd	4
	10 Grange Ave	Private House	Unoccupied	
87	11 Grange Ave	Private House	Mr Coxon	3
88	12 Grange Ave	Private House	Mr A Crofton	2
89	13 Grange Ave	Private House	Mr Appleby	5
90	14 Grange Ave	Private House	Mr Pottinger	6
91	15 Grange Ave	Private House	Mr Mostyn	3
92	Wyngarth	Private House	Mr Fenwick	5
93	Moorcroft	Private House	Mr J B Laidler	3
94	The Asplay?	Private House	Mr Grieves	6
95	1 Linden Gardens	Private House	Mr Stansfield	5
96	2 Linden Gardens	Private House	Mr Darling	5
97	3 Linden Gardens	Private House	Mr Harvey	1
98	4 Linden Gardens	Private House	Mr Davidson	4
99	5 Linden Gardens	Private House	Mr Blues	4
100	6 Linden Gardens	Private House	Mr Lawrence	3

	Property	Type	Occupier and number resident.	
101	7 Linden Gardens	Private House	Mr Barbour	7
102	8 Linden Gardens	Private House	Mr Guthrie	6
103	Aubrey House	Private House	Mr Brown	7
104	Highfield	Private House	Mr Moore	3
105	Fife House ???	Private House	Mrs Clark	2
106	Westcombe	Private House	Mr W McDonald	5
107	Dalni	Private House	Mr Black	4
108	Dunira	Private House	Mr Lockey	3
109	Westholme	Private House	Mr MacQuarrie	7
110	Glenthorn	Private House	Mr Eltringham	2
111	Grosvenor House	Private House	Mr Johnson	3
112	Selwood Cottages	Private House	Mr Wilson	4
113	Southcroft	Private House	Mr Hodgson	3
114	Grosvenor Gardens	Private House	Mr J K Todd	7
115	Grosvenor Gardens	Private House	Mr W Todd	7
116	Grosvenor Gardens	Private House	Mr Rae	3
117	Grosvenor Gardens	Private House	Mrs Tudor	5
118	1 Belgrave Gardens	Private House	Mr J H Smith	6
	2 Belgrave Gardens	Private House	Unoccupied	
119	3 Belgrave Gardens	Private House	Mr Stonehouse	2
120	4 Belgrave Gardens	Private House	Mr Tupin?	4
121	5 Belgrave Gardens	Private House	Mr Harker	4
122	6 Belgrave Gardens	Private House	Miss Allen	1
	7 Belgrave Gardens	Private House	Unoccupied	
123	8 Belgrave Gardens	Private House	Mr Smith	9
124	9 Belgrave Gardens	Private House	Mr Hart	2
125	10 Belgrave Gardens	Private House	Mr Hudspeth	5
126	11 Belgrave Gardens	Private House	Mr Mason	6
127	12 Belgrave Gardens	Private House	Mr Warner	3

	Property	Type	Occupier and number resident.	
	13 Belgrave Gardens	Private House	unoccupied	
128	St Leonards	Private House	Mr Stephenson	6
129	Argue House?	Private House	Mr W Wilson	8
130	Lindisfarne	Private House	Mr Muit	5
131	Northside	Private House	Miss Pridham	1
132	Swedehope	Private House	Mr R Lockey	4
133	1 Park View	Private House	Mr Lawrie	5
	2 Park View	Private House	unoccupied	
	3 Park View	Private House	unoccupied	
134	4 Park View	Private House	Mr Newby	2
135	5 Park View	Private House	Mr Woodcock	4
136	6 Park View	Private House	Mr Giles	3
137	7 Park View	Private House	Mr Smith	3
138	8 Park View	Private House	Mr Eales	3
139	9 Park View	Private House	Mr Reah	6
	10 Park View	Private House	Unoccupied	
140	11 Park View	Private House	Mr Carr	5
141	12 Park View	Private House	Mr Taylor	3
142	13 Park View	Private House	Mr Wishart	7
143	South Avenue	Private House	Mr Bains	3
144	South Avenue	Private House	Mr Hammond	2
145	South Avenue	Private House	Mr Glover	2
146	South Avenue	Private House	Mr Wake	4
147	South Avenue	Private House	Mr Cooper	6
148	South Avenue	Private House	Mr Emmerson	7
149	South Avenue	Private House	Mrs Robson	8
159	South Avenue	Private House	Mr Johnson	4
151	South Avenue	Private House	Mrs Wynne	5
152	South Avenue	Private House	Mrs Bunn	1

	Property	Type	Occupier and number resident.	
153	South Avenue	Private House	Mr Powell	4
154	South Avenue	Private House	Mr Hardy	4
155	South Avenue	Private House	Mr Harrison	2
156	South Avenue	Private House	Mr Murphy	6
157	South Avenue	Private House	Mr Bovill	8
158	South Avenue	Private House	Mr Burdis	6
159	South Avenue	Private House	Mr Nellist?	5
	South Avenue	Private House	Unoccupied	
	South Avenue	Private House	Unoccupied	
160	South Avenue	Private House	Mrs Hair	5
	South Avenue	Private House	Unoccupied	
	West Avenue	Private House	Unoccupied	
161	West Avenue	Private House	Mr Clark	3
	West Avenue	Private House	Unoccupied	
	West Avenue	Private House	Unoccupied	
	West Avenue	Private House	Unoccupied	
	West Avenue	Private House	Unoccupied	
162	West Avenue	Private House	Mr Aubin	4
163	West Avenue	Private House	Mr Doughty	2
164	West Avenue	Private House	Mr Turnbull	4
165	West Avenue	Private House	Mrs Bailey	4
166	West Avenue	Private House	Mr Pyle	5
167	West Avenue	Private House	Mrs Burton	8
168	West Avenue	Private House	Mrs Lightley	1
169	West Avenue	Private House	Mr McDonald	2
170	West Avenue	Private House	Mr Freeman	4
171	Aberdeen Villa	Private House	Mr Bogle	7
172	Craigmore	Private House	Mr Maltman	7
173	Inglethorpe	Private House	Mr Chapman	6

	Property	Type	Occupier and number resident.	
174	Aldersyde	Private House	Mr Westcott	7
175	Woodside	Private House	Mr Hughes	5
Woodside Cottage One house tennemented property, two dwellings				
176			Mr Tetley	5
177			Mr Locking	4
178	St ?	Private House	Mr Hill	3
179	Heathfield?	Private House	Mr Milstead	4
180	Hawthorn Cottage	Private House	Mr Forsyth	2
181	Belle Vue	Private House	Mr Scott	9
182	Fairholme	Private House	Mr Morris	5
183	Inglewood	Private House	Mr Marsh	6
184	Harton Lea	Private House	Mr Annand	9
185	Rose Villa	Private House	Mr Thornton	4
186	Laburnam Villa	Private House	Mr Cadle	6
187	Hawthorn Villa	Private House	Mr Crofton	5
188	The Vicarage	Private House	Mr Ashworth	7
189	Harton Hall	Private House	Mr Corringham	3
	Lodge		Unoccupied	
190	Gardner's Lodge		Mr Blackburn	5
Harton School				
Harton Church				
	Harton Road	Cottage	Unoccupied	
191	Phillipsville	Private House	Mr P Willis	5
192	? Cottage	Maisonette	Mr M Willis	6
193	Willis' Cottages	Maisonette	Mr Nixon	2
194	Willis' Cottages	Maisonette	Mr Bowman	4
Harton Road Shop				
195		Two flats in one house	Mrs Thompson	5
196			Mr Bowe	5
197	Upton House Harton Road	Maisonette	Mr Henderson	9

Cauldwell

With the 1901 South Shields Borough Extension Order Cauldwell was removed from Harton Township and added to South Shields hence the names of those living in Cauldwell do not appear on the enumerator's list of 1911. The two maps below show this dramatic change of boundary line.

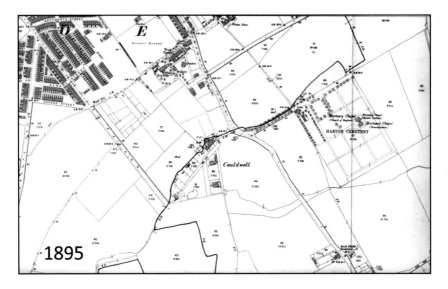

1895

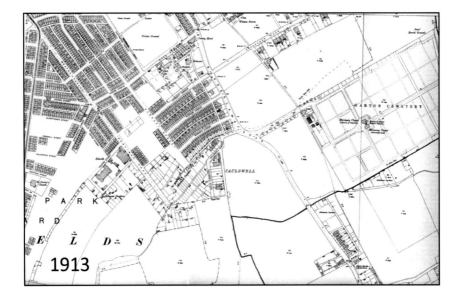

1913

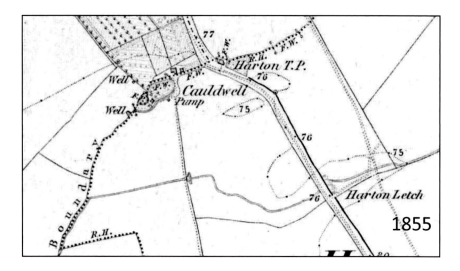

1855

The 1855 map above shows that none of the buildings at Cauldwell exist prior to that date. There may indeed have been one small building to collect the tolls at the Harton turnpike marked on the map as T.P. but if so it did not exist by 1895. The turnpike trust that had run the road from 1796 having been dissolved by this date. The terrace, the large house and the two large semi-detached villas built at Cauldwell after 1855 still exist, although now surrounded by other more recent housing.

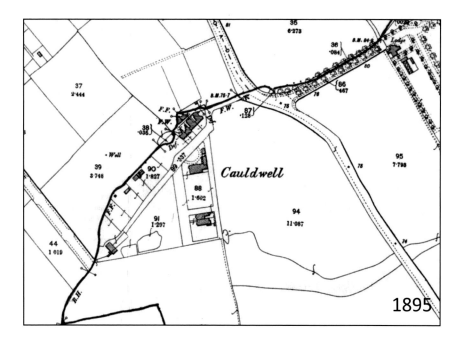

1895

A photograph of Cauldwell Terrace from about 1899.
Surrounded by fields one can see in the distance on the right of the terrace a clear view of Mortimer Primary School and the caretakers house.Mortimer Infant and Mixed Junior School was opened on 1st September 1896 with accommodation for 612 pupils. The three storied senior school was opened on 12th August 1901 and does not appear to be constructed when this photograph was taken.

On the early maps showing Cauldwell Terrace there appear to be four houses but all the census returns suggest five. The lower photograph does show that the central house with four gables is indeed two houses. However the situation is far from clear as the 1881 census states there are 18 houses at Cauldwell, 10 occupied and 8 uninhabited with no information as to who lives where, merely a list, but there are four families with servants, suggesting they lived in the larger houses. I have added information about their places of birth to highlight that even in this small settlement of houses families obviously moved constantly around the UK seeking employment.

In the order they appear on the census:

1 Elizabeth Watson widow 54, laundress born in Rothbury Northumberland; her daughter and son both born at Harton both are in employment, Elizabeth Ann, 22 single, as a domestic servant and James 18, as a cooper.

2 Peter Sinclair Haggie 30, a rope manufacturer born in Gateshead; his wife Jane 23, from Wigin Lancashire; Jane Thew Ramshaw 23, from Workington, Northumberland, cook and Isabella Saul 19, from Chester le Street Durham, a housemaid.

3 William Henry Rooke 31, commercial clerk in chemical works, he and all his family born in South Shields; Hannah, 31, his wife, James William 7, Harry Stanley 6, Charles Winn 5, Robert Percy 1, and John Williamson under one month old; Mary Ann Cosgrave from Scotland 20, general domestic servant and Mary Ann Purvis 46, a visitor, a professional nurse.

4 Edwin Wareham 32, lab proprietor he and his wife and first 3 children born in Dorset and his youngest two born in Cauldwell; Rosa his wife 31, Fred 10, Charles 8, Rosa 6, Fanny 4 and Sydney 2.

5 Jas Graham Tatters 39, analytical chemist, born in Durham; Isabel his wife 34, from Northumberland; their son Hugh Lee 13, born in Penzance Cornwall; Edith Mary 9, born in Plymouth and Ethel Annie 3, born in South Shields; Jane Ann Oliver 14, a domestic servant from Jarrow.

6 Robert Detchon 55, commercial clerk graving dock, from Northumberland; his wife Margaret 50 from Scotland; their six children Elizabeth 26, James 22, Robert 16, George 13, Arthur 11, and Henry 9, all born in Northumberland; Elizabeth Barron 44, their domestic servant from Heworth Durham.

7 Joseph Richardson 35, a tailor, at present a cart-man; Mary 29, and their two children Arthur 11 and Florence 1, all of South Shields.

8 George Emms, 40, gardener; his wife Caroline 37 and their three elder children Albert 18, Herbert 13, and Rosamund 11, all born in Norfolk; their five younger children, Rebecca 8, Mary 6, George 4, John 3, and Thomas 8 months, all born in South Shields.

9 Samuel Taylor 40 a common labourer born in Derby; his wife Catherine 34 from Scotland; their daughter Margaret 12, also born in Scotland; Samuel 6 born in Nottingham; Michael 4, born in Newcastle upon Tyne and Catherine 11 months old, born in Yorkshire.

10 Mary Ann Reay widow 45 laundress from Durham; Mary Ann her unmarried daughter 26, James her son an agricultural worker aged 24, and George 14, a scholar, all three born in Harton.

It is similarly difficult to make sense of who lived where within Cauldwell from the 1891 census, but it does offer an insight in that although it presents 21 houses, it informs us that seven of them have only two rooms. These are clearly not the terrace, the semi detached villas or the large house, but may include a coachman's house or the lodge linked to this house. Happily the churchwarden's plan once again provides much of the answer, although some of it is difficult to decipher, it provides enough hints to cross reference it with the 1901 census.

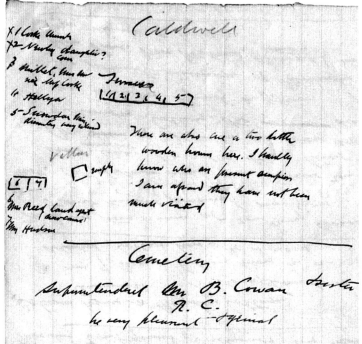

Re-produced by kind permission of the vicar and church-wardens of Harton St Peter.

The churchwarden's plan clearly shows a terrace of five houses where lived: *1 Cooke Church? 2 Newby daughter?? 3 Mr and Mrs Millet née? ? Cooke 4 Hellyar. 5 Snowdon Miss dissenter very retired.* In the two semi-detached villas: *6 Mr Reed land agent (new comers)* and *7 Mrs Hudson.* The large house is shown to be empty and there is no mention of the lodge or a coachman's house, but this sentence helps us understand the number of two roomed houses, *There are also one or two little wooden houses here. I hardly know who are present occupiers. I am afraid they have not been much visited.* At the gate house of the cemetery lives the *Cemetery* Superintendent Mr B Cowan and sister? R.C. He very pleasant and genial.

In the terrace there are two occupants in 1901 that appear to match the churchwarden's plan, further proof how quickly these families moved from what must have been rented properties:

1 The Terrace Robert Bell 59, from South Shields, wife and 5 children.

2 The Terrace unoccupied.

3 The Terrace William Read 39, from Gainford, his wife and six children.

4 Hannah Newby 62, a widow, from Easington and her 5 children, four in employment one as an architect the others as school teachers.

5 Esther Cook widow 63, from Durham, two daughters and two grandchildren whose surname is Millet.

The 1901 census also lists two families that match directly the churchwarden's plan, Reed and Hudson, so we can confidently say they were living in the large semi-detached houses: John T Reed, estate agent and auctioneer 39, an employer born in South Shields; Jane his wife 31, from Newcastle upon Tyne: Wilfred 7 born in South Shields; also Catherine Rainey 18, a general domestic servant born at Eighton Banks, Durham and her sister Elizabeth 16. At the adjoining house lives Eleanor Hudson 65, a widow born in Durham and Mary Johnson a domestic servant 27, from Scotland.

There are very few photographs of Cauldwell in the South Tyneside Libraries archive, this black and white image showing the rear end of the villas was taken on the 12th March 1943 by Amy Flagg recording one of the bombings in the area that left a huge crater in the adjoining allotments. It shows the new 1930s semi detached housing across the street which is now called Cauldwell Villas. The colour photograph is a contemporary one of the front of the two victorian properties.

The Large house is empty but in the attached cottage/lodge which it is stated has two rooms, lives: Thomas Parker 34, horse keeper at the coal mine (underground) from Norfolk; his wife Annie 32, also of Norfolk; their two sons both born in South Shields, Ernest 6, and Albert 3.

A house behind the Terrace is empty, then 5 cottages are mentioned which may all constitute the wooden ones mentioned by the churchwarden: one with four rooms occupied by Joseph Eley 50, Farmer from Suffolk, his wife and two children; in the other two roomed properties we find John Burdis 54, a coal miner, a shifter underground, from Jarrow, his wife and three children; David Bowman 59, from North Shields, a coal miner a shifter underground, with his wife and two sons the eldest at 19 already employed in the coal mine as an underground shifter; Thomas Ostons 43, from Berwickshire, a cart-man, his wife and five children; in the final cottage Edward Chapman from Norfolk 28, a coal miner hewer underground and his wife and five children.

At Harton Cemetery Lodge the 1901 census records: Bernard Cowan 52, from Northumberland; his wife and two step-children; Rachel 17, a domestic servant.

During the later Victorian period Cauldwell House is frequently advertised as up for rent, and it does not seem to have provided a family home for any long term occupier. The rental notices from the newspapers give some idea of the size of the property which has in the course of the twentieth century been divided to offer smaller sized accommodation. On Friday, 10th December, 1886, *The Shields Gazette* reported on the the marriage of Miss Florence Margaret Stevenson, third daughter of J. C. Stevenson, M.P. of Westoe. The marriage took place in Shotley Bridge. The reporter waxes lyrical about the weather conditions up in the Derwent Valley and in Harton Township.

Snow lay on the hill sides, and away on the vales as far as the eye could reach, and the magnificent panorama, as viewed from Cauldwell, the temporary residence of Mr J. Stevenson, M.P., was greatly admired by those to whom was new.

Thursday, 12th October, 1899, the property is once again empty and up for rent.

```
              TO LET,
THE   FOLLOWING   SELF - CONTAINED
   HOUSES :—
Cauldwell House, Fifteen Rooms, Bathroom, w.c ,
Coach-house, and Lodge.
   3 Dacre Terrace, Eight Rooms, Bathroom, and w.c.
   5 Dacre Terrace, Eight Rooms, Bathroom, and w.c.
   3 Ogle Terrace, Nine Rooms, Bathroom, &c.
Selbourne House, Selbourne Street, Eight Rooms,
Bathroom, and w.c.
   55 Trajan Avenue, Eight Rooms and Bathroom.
   5 South View Terrace, Eight Rooms, Bath, and w.c.
   6 Kensington Terrace, Seven Rooms, Bath, and w.c.
              Apply to
      VASEY & REED,
25 KING STREET, SOUTH SHIELDS.
```

The area around Cauldwell was also full of allotments as we see in the 1913 map and these too are frequently advertised for rent in the local newspapers.

Saturday, 30th September, 1899.

```
MARKET GARDEN TO LET, at
   Cauldwell.—Apply to D. Brows, House
Agent, 34 King Street, South Shields.
```

In 1901 Cauldwell ceased to be a part of Harton Township and became part of South Shields.

Westoe Park Estate

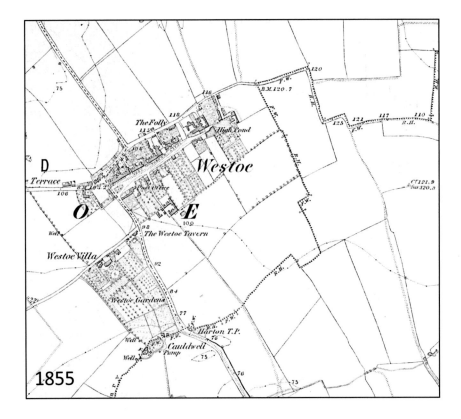

This detail of the 1855 which shows part of the northern boundary of Harton Township can be compared to the 1897 map opposite which shows a further close up section of the same boundary at the east end of Westoe Village, both maps using a dotted line to denote the boundary. This plot of land was sold in 1878, three years after the death of the previous landowner, Robert Ingham, by the Ecclesiastical Commissioners to a consortium of six, local, affluent, business men.

Miss Amy Flagg, in her notes on Westoe Village, refers to this development as the Westoe Park Estate. The intention of these business men was to build large villas for their respective families, each standing in extensive grounds with an average accommodation of twenty rooms. Five of these six houses would be in Harton Township until the boundary changed in 1901.

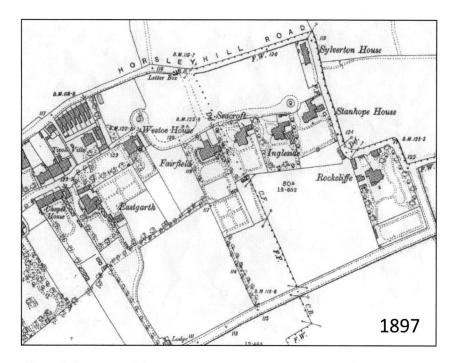

Five of these grand late Victorian mansions are captured in the aerial photograph below; Sylverton House, Stanhope House, Ingleside and Seacroft can be clearly seen, Fairfield only partially glimpsed on the left was not in Harton Township and Rockcliffe that was, is out of the photographer's frame, being more to the south east. Between the end of WW2 and 2015 they were all demolished, many being left empty and vandalised before this fate befell them. The post-war world had moved on and houses that needed servants to run them were no longer required. They have in turn been replaced by collections of modern housing.

The St Peter's churchwarden plan of 1896, offers this insight; *New Westoe to the East of Westoe Village are five detached houses: Rockcliffe, Alderman Mabane, solicitor; Stanhope House, Alderman Wardell, wood merchant; Seacroft, Sir Chapman, accountant; Ingleside, Alderman Rennoldson. These with the exception of the Chapmans have all their interests in Shields and scarcely recognise the fact that they are in Harton Parish. There is also a new house, Sylverton House, Mrs Wadham, a widow. Her husband was a publican. They are dissenters.*

Reproduced by kind permission of the vicar and churchwardens of Harton St Peter.

Few photographs exist of the Westoe Park Estate houses, above is one of Stanhope House dated 1886. Further information about these houses and the families that lived in them can be found in Dorothy Fleet's book, Westoe, printed in 2019 and available from the South Shields Local History Group.

The census return of 1901 confirms the churchwarden's names and provides information of others living in the house on that day: At Seacroft were Dora and Henry Chapman (aged 44 and 51 respectively) and seven of their eleven children plus their sister-in-law and three domestic servants. Mr Chapman is recorded as a chartered accountant; at Ingleside Gertrude and James Rennoldson (40 and 47) their daughter (they would have three children, one did not survive to adulthood) and three domestic servants, Mr Rennoldson is recorded as a solicitor and notary; at Stanhope House Mary and John Wardle (60 and 66) with four of his children and two servants, Mr Wardle is recorded as a timber merchant and saw miller; at Rockcliffe are Isabella and John Readhead, (49 and 51) with four of their surviving five children and 3 live-in servants, John Redhead had newly moved into Rockcliffe, it was Thomas Grieves Mabane a solicitor and town councillor, twice voted as mayor of South Shields, who had built the house, Mr Readhead is recorded as an engineer and ship builder; Rockcliffe also had a lodge house and there lived John Pairlie 46 and his wife Mary 45 with their six children, John is recorded as a gardener and their eldest son William 25 as a coachman; at Sylverton House the 1901 census records Alice Wadham 54, a widow, her unmarried daughter of the same name 22 and her married daughter Blanche 25, with her husband William Grant 28, who was a jeweller and an employer, together with two general domestic servants.

Marsden Cottage

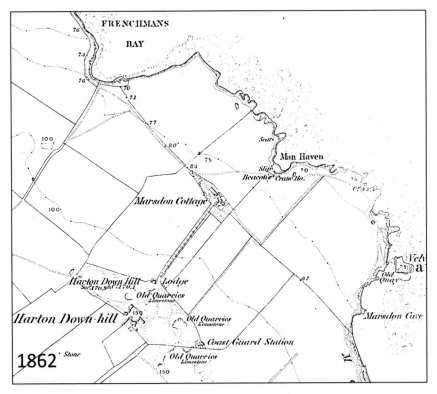

Marsden Cottage is a rather misleading name for what can be seen from the above map and the photograph opposite as a rather imposing residence with various out houses and buildings associate with it and the most impressive view along the coastline. Access was via a drive from the lodge house situated at the foot of Harton Down Hill. Marsden Cottage was built in the Georgian period and was initially linked with some very powerful and influential ship owning and ship building families in South Shields.

The Cottage was built by William Barras (1752 -1818). William was a member of a wealthy land owning family from Whickham. The Barras fortune had developed through *wayleaves*, tolls levied by landowners for allowing coal to be transported across their land. William also had large shipping interests. His brother John Barras established a brewing business in Gateshead around 1775. The Barras brewery was one of the original five companies that formed Newcastle Breweries Ltd in 1890.

A photograph of Frenchman's Bay showing Marsden Cottage sitting on the cliff tops with its commanding view. This cliff top area remains an area of staggering beauty having been gifted to the National Trust on 1st April 1987 by the then owners, South Tyneside Council.

A photograph of the rear view of Marsden Cottage.

By 1809 William and his family were in residence at Marsden as on the 30th of December a coming of age party was given for William junior at Marsden Cottage.

By 1830 the family had moved on and Marsden Cottage was put up for *Sale by Auction*. The house was described as:

A Mansion House called Marsden Cottage, with coachhouse, stables and outbuildings all in perfect repair, and 27 acres of grassland; delightfully situated on the sea coast between South Shields and Whitburn. A commodious lodge at the entrance to the premises affords an excellent convenience for brewing and washing. There is a warm bath, water closet, force pumps, spring of excellent water and large tanks for rainwater. The furniture may be taken at a valuation.

A further newspaper advert on published on 31st May, 1830 gives more detail even mentioning London manure and a peacock:

MR. FELL has the honour to announce for SALE by AUCTION, on TUESDAY, the 8th of June next, at noon, on the premises, that most delightful Marine Residence, situate about a mile and a half from the mouth of the Tyne, in the county of Durham, called MARSDEN COTTAGE, surrounded by 27 acres of most productive land, 2½ acres of which are in tillage, and the remainder fine old grass, which is free of hay tithe, with a Lodge at the entrance of the grounds. The house contains a handsome entrance hall, dining-room 21 feet by 18, library, breakfast and bath rooms, butler's pantry, two kitchens, dairy, pantries, &c. on the ground floor, with cellars underneath; drawing-room, five lodging rooms, and dressing-room on the first floor, with servants' apartments in the attic; detached are, double coach-house, two stables, cowhouse, pig-sty, dog kennel, &c. A spacious tank retains the rain water, and a never-failing spring out of the limestone rock supplies the house with soft drinking water, which is conveyed by a force pump to a room at the top of the house for the convenience of the upper story, the water-closet, and the bath. The sea view and adjacent scenery from the house is the finest that can be imagined, commanding a South view of the beautiful Ruin, Castle, Light-house, and Village of Tynemouth, together with the Spanish Battery and Clifford's Fort. In the immediate neighbourhood stands the majestic and celebrated Rock of Marsden, which is visited and admired by thousands who annually repair to it and the adjoining caves, which here abound so richly in the natural beauties of the

…shore. From Manhaven (a part of the estate and only a few …rods from the house), boats can put out to sea at almost any time, so …that a yacht or the shipping may be boarded with little difficulty. The property for several years past has been in the occupancy of the proprietor, Wm. Barras, Esq., who has spared no expense to render …replete with every comfort and convenience, suitable for the re-…dence of any family of distinction. It is held by lease from the …Dean and Chapter of Durham, for 21 years from 1827, renewable every seven years. Immediate possession may be had, and a prin-…cipal part of the purchase money may (if required) remain secured …upon the property. Immediately after the sale of the estate, that of the farming stock and implements of husbandry will commence—…they comprise strong coop and pony carts, with harness and gears, …an plough, large double roller, stone and wood troughs, ladders, …and hurdles, a large quantity of London and stable manure, some …excellent hay of last year's growth, a new hay rick, cover, and …same, a pair of powerful and active draught horses, two superior milk …cows, goat, two pigs, a town built gig and harness, elegant peacock …in full feather, poultry, &c. And, on Wednesday and following …days, the whole of the valuable and fashionable furniture, grand hori-…zontal piano-forte by Broadwoods, eight-day clocks and time-pieces, …antique, Oriental, and English china, dinner and dessert services, …glasses of every description, patent mangle, chamber, kitchen, dairy, …and laundry requisites and utensils of the most approved kinds.— …Catalogues of which may be had (price 6d. each) after the 25th …instant, at the Durham Chronicle Office; Hue and Cry Office, …Newcastle; Mr. Reed, Printer, Sunderland; Messrs. Barnes, …South Shields; and of Mr. G. W. Barnes, Printer. South Shields. …N.B. The furniture. &c. may be inspected between the hours of …twelve and three o'clock on Thursday, Friday, and Saturday pre-…ceding the sale.

…South Shields, 18th May, 1830.

The property came into the ownership of other wealthy influential South Shields families most preferring to use it as a summer residence. In 1863 it was up for auction again and this time was acquired by Thomas Salmon (1794-1871) a notable solicitor in South Shields. He was one of the leading promoters of the Town Improvement Act and following the incorporation of the Borough in 1850 he was unanimously elected the first Town Clerk, a post he held until his death in 1871. He rendered singular service in the establishment of the separate Customs Port of South Shields, the creation of the Local Marine Board, and the establishment of the Pilotage Commission. He filled many public offices being Clerk to the South Shields Poor Law Union and Burial Board, Superintendent Registrar for the Union and Vestry Clerk, a

MARSDEN COTTAGE.
MR GLOVER
Has the honour to announce that he has been favoured,
by the Executors of the late Mrs Roxby,
with instructions to
SELL BY AUCTION,
At Marsden Cottage, the Summer Residence of the
Deceased Lady, on MONDAY, June 15, 1863, and
following days,
THE whole of the Valuable HOUSEHOLD
GOODS, consisting of Dining, Drawing, Library,
and Breakfast Room FURNITURE, comprising Dining,
Drawing, Breakfast, and Library Tables, Mahogany
Chairs, Sofa, Conches, a very superior Rosewood Cot-
tage Pianoforte, by Collard and Collard, Rosewood
Couch, Mantel Mirror, large Mirror with Console
Table (Marble top), Rosewood Chairs, Easy Chairs,
Rosewood Oval Table, Rosewood Inlaid Table two
elegant Time-pieces, Occasional Table, Two Rosewood
Whatnots, Canterbury, Two richly-gilt Chinese Cabi-
nets, a very excellent Teak-winged Bookcase inlaid,
Mahogany-winged Bookcase (glassfront), an elaborately
carved Oak Cabinet, Oak Library Table, Oak Chairs,
Walnut Centre Table, Oak Couch, Easy Chair, Mirror,
a quantity of Cut and other Glass,
A VERY RICH DINNER AND DESSERT
CHINA SET,
Elegant Mahogany Bedstead and Chintz Hangings,
Mahogany Four-pole and Iron Bedsteads, a very su-
perior Mahogany Wardrobe, Lady's Wardrobe (plate
glass front), Mahogany Dressing Tables with Marble
Tops, Feather Beds and Hair Mattresses, Bed-room
Chairs, Toilet Ware, Mahogany Chests of Drawers,
Brussels and Kidderminster Carpets, Hearth Rugs,
Stair Carpets, magnificent specimen of Antique China,
one of the finest private collections of Shells in the
North of England.
Close Carriage with Rumble (nearly new), Open
Carriage in perfect condition, Coup Cart, two double
sets and one single set of Harness (almost new).
VALUABLE SCREEN.
FROM 40 TO 50 OIL PAINTINGS AND A
FEW ENGRAVINGS,
Among which is a Grand Gallery Painting, by Rubens,
Nymphs and Satyr; the Abdication of Napoleon, by
the celebrated French Painter, Horace Vernet. In the
English School—two by Train (one of which is a View
of Loch Awe, very fine); several Marine Views, by P.
Anderson, and Huggins; The Piper, after Wilkie;
others by Reynolds, Gainsborough, &c., &c.; four first
class Pictures of the Dutch School, by Ostade, Teniers,
Jean Stein, and Pollenberg; four fine Paintings, by
Pother. Several fine Engravings—the Death of Nelson,
after Drummond, finely coloured; Death of Nelson,
coloured, &c., &c.
From 360 to 400 VOLUMES OF BOOKS; a choice
Collection of HOTHOUSE PLANTS, with the whole
of the Garden Implements; a few doz. of Wine; about
10 tons of Hay; Hen House with Wire Fence; the
WHOLE OF THE KITCHEN REQUISITES.
To those who are furnishing and require good and
substantial Furniture, to the lover of the elegant and
antique, to the admirer of Works of Art and Virtu, and
to the Conchologist, this sale presents a rare oppor-
tunity.
Sale to Commence at 11 o'Clock each day.
The Furniture can be Viewed on THURSDAY and
FRIDAY, June 11 and 12, from 11 to 3 o'Clock in the
Afternoon.
South Shields, May 30, 1863.

This advert printed on the 4th June, 1863 for the sale of the contents of Marsden Cottage presents a staggering list including: a grand gallery painting by Rubens; others by Reynolds and Gainsborough and more. Even with questions of attribution as we understand them today, the list of contents belonging to Anne Roxby, a member of the Forsyth shipbuilding family who had married Captain James Wardle Roxby in 1814, is remarkable, especially as they treated Marsden Cottage as a summer residence and had their town house in Ogle Terrace.

Vice-President of the Mechanics Institute and a director of the Savings Bank. In 1865 Mr Salmon was presented with a valuable testimonial in acknowledgment of his services in connection with public matters, while his portrait and bust were placed in the (Old) Town Hall.

Photograph of Thomas Salmon, Town Clerk of South Shields from 1850-1871. He lived at Marsden Cottage from 1863-1871. On his death in 1871 the house passed to his son John and he and his family lived there for almost twenty years. Hence Marsden Cottage became locally known as Salmon's Hall.

On the death of Thomas Salmon, Marsden Cottage passed to his son John Salmon (1824-1912) He was an interested amateur sailor and made good use of the proximity of Man Haven (p216). On the death of his wife John left Marsden Cottage and relocated to Cleadon Park and by the time of the 1891 census Marsden Cottage had been leased to the Whitburn Coal Company. From this time onwards it was often referred to as Salmon's Hall.

Once the coal company took over the lease it converted the outbuildings into cottages and divided the main house into separate dwellings for men working at the nearby Whitburn Colliery. At the 1901 census it was providing homes for thirteen mining families.

The 1901 census states that two families were living in the Marsden Railway cottage, which may have been the lodge of the grand house at the end of the drive, by then very near the South Shields, Marsden and Whitburn Colliery Railway line. One family, living in a single room, was John Hewitt 20, coal miner, a hewer underground, his wife Mary 20, and their eleven month old daughter Mary, the second family were the Edgar family and they had three rooms. Henry Edgar 44, a coal miner, a hewer underground, his wife Rose 38, and their six children the eldest being John 17, a coal miner, a putter underground, also Henry's mother-in-law Anne Oakley 66.

One of the cottages (not the lodge) attached to Marsden Cottage which after 1891 would become the home of a mining family. The Hall is just visible behind the cottage.

The cottages and converted outbuildings attached to the main house offered five separate homes for coal-miners' families:

1 John Auty 35, a coal miner a hewer underground, his wife Elizabeth 34, and their eight children ranging from 4 months old to 13 years old live in a three roomed accommodation. Their eldest son Samuel 13, working in the mine as a horse driver underground.

2 James Scrimgour 35, a coal miner, a hewer underground, his wife Dorothy 33, and their four children aged 9 years to 7 months lived in a two roomed property.

3 Thomas Dunlavey 41, a coal miner, a hewer underground, his wife Mary 39, and their five children lived in a three roomed accommodation. Their eldest son Michael 16, was a coal miner a horse driver underground.

4 James Elliott 57, coal miner, underground stoneworker, his wife Isabella 56, their son William 21, a stone mason, their daughter Margaret 24 and their granddaughter Isabella Smith 2, lived in a three roomed property

5 Edward Jones 45, a coal miner, a hewer underground, his wife Margaret 39, and their eight children ranging from 19 years old to 11 months old. Their eldest son John 15, was a coal miner, a horse driver underground. They lived in a four roomed property.

The Hall itself appears to have been divided into accommodation for four families:

1 Robert Waggott, 49, a winding engiineman at the colliery, his wife Mary 47, and Jane their unmarried daughter 18, having three rooms.

2 Edward Phillips, 57, a coal miner, a shifter underground, his wife Mary 57, and their five sons, the eldest four; Peter 26, James 21, David 19, Robert 15, all working underground in the coal mine. They lived in four rooms.

3 Peter Phillips, 57, coal miner, a hewer underground, Alice 48, his wife and their eight children in four rooms. The three eldest children were working; Mary 20, as a dressmaker from home, Julia 16 and Maggie 14, as farm workers. This family lived in four rooms.

4 Thomas Varley, 55, coal miner, a hewer underground, his wife Catherine 51, their five children and one grandchild lived in accommodation that offered five or more rooms. The eldest son Thomas 25, is a widower and one presumes the father of Cecil who is 9 months old, he and his next younger brother, John 23, are working like their father as hewers underground.

Marsden Cottage was a fairly remote place for these families to live, only accessible via the coastal footpath or by farm tracks over Harton Down Hill. To help get their workforce to and from work the Harton Coal Company built a station called Marsden Cottage Halt on the colliery railway line. The mineral line ran coal from Whitburn Colliery and limestone from the quarry kilns to the staithes on the Tyne.

Marsden Cottage know locally as Salmon's Halt, trains stopped if they were hailed.

When the line opened in 1879 the owners put on 6 passenger trains a day in line with the miners shift pattern to get the workforce who lived in South Shields to Whitburn. In 1888 the Board of Trade sanctioned the running of passenger lines along the line and a timetable was issued. Passenger trains normally consisted of three coaches plus a guard's van. Because of the age and condition of the carriages used, the service became known locally as the Marsden Rattler. Marsden Cottage Halt was reputed to be the smallest station in the country with only room for one carriage. Although officially being called Marsden Cottage all who knew it, knew it as Salmon's Halt. This passenger train service provided a life line for the families. Food was obtainable from the local farms and most of the miners grew vegetables and fished, but if a shop was needed the nearest was a walk over Down Hill and along Harton Back Lane to Harton Village.

Salmon's Hall (Marsden Cottage) was a small close knit community being so isolated. The coast road, following much the same line as the railway, was built in 1928 but life at Marsden Cottage was still hard, with no electricity or internal running water and a wind that could blow directly from Russia.

On the 11th of March 1930 *The Shields Gazette* carried a photograph on the front page entitled *A Sturdy Family of Pit Workers.* **The photograph was the one shown above of Mr and Mrs Cauwood of Salmon's Hall with their ten sons, all of whom worked at Whitburn Colliery.**
Reproduced by kind permission of Brian Cauwood.

Marsden Cottage was demolished in 1937 and in that year *The Shields Gazette* ran an article entitled *Memories of No-Man's Land* to coincide with the start of the demolition. The article featured an interview with Mr and Mrs Miller, the oldest couple and the last to leave the Hall. The couple had lived at Salmon's Hall for 37 years and reminisced about that period.

With the light from a smoke stained oil lamp sending shadows flicking over the walls, Mr and Mrs Miller sat in their age-old cottage at Salmon's Hall and told of the tragedies and happiness of the place they called *No Man's Land.* Mr and Mrs Miller explained that, from the house there was an underground passage leading to the shore. One occupant Ned Phillips liked to walk along the passage for a smoke. One day he went and never came back. The only trace that they ever found was his cap and handkerchief at the end of the tunnel.

They also explained how the mother of another family that lived there would always watch for her son coming down the drive from work. This day she looked out of the window and saw some men carrying his dead body, such was the shock that she dropped down dead. *The Shields Gazette* reported this incident on 1st October 1887.

A WHITBURN MINER KILLED.

A SAD SEQUEL.

P.C. Harbottle of the South Shields Borough Police reports that at two o'clock this morning, a miner named William Makepeace, aged 26 years, and employed at Whitburn Colliery, was in the act of jumping from a train in motion on the Whitburn Coal Company's line, near Marsden Cottages, when he stumbled and was crushed in the lower part of the body by the wheels of the carriage. He was conveyed to the Ingham Infirmary, where he died shortly after six o'clock. The body was afterwards conveyed by four men to deceased's home, Marsden Cottages. His mother, an old woman, 62 years of age, on learning of her son's death, fell down and instantly expired.

Tragedy struck again as *The Shields Gazette* reported on Friday, 29th November, 1889:

FATAL ACCIDENT AT WHITBURN COLLIERY. A serious accident happened to young man named James Makepeace, aged 21, at the above colliery on Wednesday. It appears that Makepeace was engaged as weigh-man, and at the time of the accident he was in the act of pushing railway truck off the weighing machine when some waggons which were behind him ran the waggon he was pushing, and striking him on the thick of the thigh so crushed him that the locomotive engine had to be employed to draw the waggon off before he could be liberated.   Dr Lumley, of Whitburn, was the spot at the time, and bound up the wound, and had him conveyed to the lngham Infirmary, Westoe, where he died last evening.

Makepeace, it is said, had a brother killed at the same place two years ago, and when the body was taken home his mother suddenly died through the shock. The young man whose death took place last night was well known in connection with temperance concerts and entertainments for charitable objects in South Shields, where he resided.

James' headstone is in St Peter's churchyard records that it was was erected by the Baring Street and Victoria Road Choirs and Friends.

Mr and Mrs Miller's most vivid memories were of the war days (WW1) when bombs dropped by a zeppelin fell into a field next to Salmon's Hall tearing away doors and shattering windows. *When the air raid was on I was so frightened I ran outside,* said Mrs Miller, *It was amazing that I was not killed.* She later saw the humorous side to it. Apparently the look-out man was coming down the hill when he saw Mrs Miller in her white nightgown, he actually thought it was a ghost and took to his heels.

Press Bureau, Official Message.

"A Zeppelin visited the North-East Coast on Tuesday night (15th June, 1915) and dropped bombs. Killed 16; Injured 40."

The Midnight ASSASSIN

The above contemporary illustration is of a zeppelin raid over Jarrow on the night of the 15th June, 1915.

The newspaper report of the incident explains that 15 people were killed and 15 injured.

This might not have been the night that Mrs Miller remembered as various raids took place at this time.

IR RAID ON NORTH-EAST COAST.

FIFTEEN DEATHS: FIFTEEN INJURED.

VISITOR A ZEPPELIN.

Press Bureau, Wednesday.

THE SECRETARY OF THE ADMIRALTY MAKES THE FOLLOWNG ANNOUNCE-MENT:—

A ZEPPELIN VISITED THE NORTH-EAST COAST LAST EVENING AND DROPPED BOMBS.

SOME FIRES WERE STARTED, BUT HAVE BEEN OVER-COME.

FIFTEEN DEATHS ARE REPORTED FROM THE DISTRICT AND FIFTEEN WOUNDED.

Not all the newspaper articles record tragedies. Some record truly heroic acts and Mr Thomas Varley who lived in Marsden Cottage as we have seen on the 1901 census, received a presentation for one of his acts of heroism. *The Shields Daily Gazette* of Saturday, 23rd September, 1893 recorded the joyous occasion:

THE RESCUE OF SHIELDS PILOTS. PRESENTATIONS TO VARLEY. There was a large gathering of South Shields pilots and townsmen at the County Hotel, Westoe, last evening, the occasion being series of presentations to Mr Thomas Varley, a Marsden miner, in recognition of his heroic performance in saving the lives of Thomas Purvis, pilot, and his assistant off Souter Point, on the 21st August last. —Councillor Peter Thornton presided, and was supported by Councillors T. D. Marshall and Mr Stainton, Mr Robert Henderson, proprietor of the hotel, Mr Thomas Gibson, hon. secretary of presentation fund, Mr J. Hart Burn. North Shields, Mr J. J. Runciman, Mr Thomas Purvis, Mr Charles E. Walton, Mr John Dodds. Dr McNab, Dr Turnbull and Mr Varley, the hero ef the occasion.

The Chairman said they were met there to do honour to a man who deserved it. Englishmen bad always recognised bravery, but no act in recent times had aroused such feelings of admiration on the North-East Coast as that performed by Thomas Varley, who put off in a stormy sea and rescued two pilots. (Cheers.) He had that afternoon seen the beat in which Mr Varley went to sea, and was more than ever impressed with the gallantry of the deed performed by the Durham pitman. (Cheers.)

Councillor T, D. Marshall made the first presentation on behalf of the South Shields pilots. He said that he thought there were no two classes of men, who had to face extreme danger, as civilians, more prominently than the man who sought his living upon the sea, and the man who had go down into the bowels of the earth to earn his livelihood. It was a remarkable and rather, happy coincidence that two men, who almost lived upon the sea and were thoroughly accomplished in the management of boats, should rescued from watery grave by one, who, from the nature of his calling, would hardly be expected to know anything about boats all. (Applause.) He would like to repeat to them a few lines which had just struck across his mind.

> In the bivouac of life,
> Be not like dumb driven cattle;
> Be a hero the strife.
> (Applause.)

Mr Varley had certainly been a hero in the strife, and if had gained no other recognition of his bravery than the meeting together of the brave men who ventured their own lives for the sake of others the at the mouth of the Tyne he would have been well recognised. (Cheers.) Our seagirt island had from time immemorial produced men like Mr Varley - men who were ever ready to lend a helping hand to fellow creature in distress —(applause)—and it was pleasing to think that such acts, more frequently than not, were acknowledged in tangible and deserving manner. Mr Varley had proved that was possessed of the right sort pluck, and therefore he bad much pleasure in handing him purse of gold and a gold medal. (Loud cheers.) The latter was inscribed as follows:—

Presented to T. Varley by Tyne pilots for saving the lives of Thomas and Wm. Purvis. August 21st. 1893.

Councillor Stainton made the second presentation, which consisted of an excellent gold watch, chain, and seal from his admiring townsmen, and handsomely mounted pipe from Mr Collier, of King Street, South Shields. He thought that Mr Varley's heroism was equal to any of that which they now read about having been performed by heroes in the brave days of old. (Applause.) would recite to them, if they would permit him, some lines which had composed specially for that occasion. (Yes, and cheers.) then recited as follows:

> He is pitman and works in the Marsden Mine,
> His name is Varley. and he deserves line.
> A capsized coble in south-west gale
> In the wild North sea - no sight of sail.
> Two are clinging the upturned boat,
> With keen cruel waters circling each throat.
> Helpless and hopeless, and with failing breath
> Waiting together, certain of death.
> Desolation, despair, thoughts of the past
> Crowding around them, not long last.
> A sorrowing look on the distant shore,
> Their feet again never to touch—never more.
> But what this that is seen the beach.

Almost more than their eager eyes can reach
Lad, what is it? Why it's only a speck,
But it's coming—and coming to the wreck—
A hero, escaped from dangers in the pit
Has launched his cockle shell, his brow firmly knit,
His life uncared for through the choppy wave.
One thought only - their forlorn lives to save.
And saved them, without delay or parley
He is a miner, and his name is Varley
(Loud applause.)

The recipient of the gifts returned thanks in a feeling manner, and expressed his readiness to perform another such deed if occasion required it, He would follow the motto Shields. Alway* ready." (Loud cheers.)
In the course of the evening an excellent programme of vocal and instrumental music was rendered.

YACHT ACCIDENT AT MARSDEN

MR. VARLEY TO THE RESCUE.

About seven o'clock last Wednesday night, a sailing yacht, containing five men, was making for Marsden Bay, but on getting into the broken water the yacht became unmanageable, and the sea broke aboard and filled it, after which the craft drifted on to the rocks. At this point, Mr Thos. Varley, who was a witness of the incident, waded into the water up to the waist, and got a rope from the man, and by this means got the whole of the men ashore. He then went aboard and tossed the ballast overboard, and with the aid of the rescued yachtsmen managed to drag the vessel off the rocks and place it above high water mark. The men were very thankful for the aid rendered them, as but for the ready help received some of them might have been drowned. Their clothing being soaked through a coastguardsman took them to his house and did all that was necessary for their comfort, and provided them with a substantial tea. It is stated that the men belong to Wallsend.

Amazingly three years later Mr Varley gets the chance to prove his promise. *The Shields Gazette and Shipping Telegraph* of Monday, 29th June, 1896, held this article about his second act of bravery when he rescued five Yachtsmen in trouble in Marsden Bay.

A photograph of Salmon's Hall (Marsden Cottage) taken by Janet Cauwood in the 1930s. Many thanks to Brian Cauwood, whose paternal and maternal grandparents both lived at Solomon's Hall, for much of the information contained in this chapter and his willingness to share information from his website: *The Marsden Banner Group*.

Brian Cauwood writes:
People using The Leas today will be walking over the spot where Marsden Cottage stood. They will be totally unaware of the opulence and grandness that once stood here, when some of the most powerful and influential people in 19th century South Shields society owned and graced the building or that 70 years ago this was a small hamlet providing homes for workmen and their families who helped power the might of British industry. The lives, hardships, joys and tragedies that had occurred, underfoot, long ago but now forgotten.

179

Aged Miners Homes

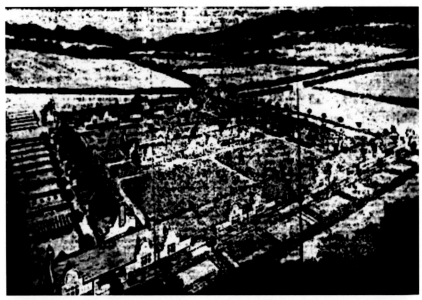

An illustration, reproduced in *The Shields Daily News* **Saturday, 11th July, 1914; showing the Dutch gable style roofs of the proposed single story cottages and all the fields that would be surrounding this community in 1914.**

The Aged Miners Homes at Harton, which in 2021 are still offering accommodation to elderly people, are clearly visible on the 1921 map. One hundred years ago they were situated among the fields on the eastern side of Harton village. Harton House Farmstead was their nearest neighbours and the views from their outward facing kitchens would have swept over to Horsley Hill Farm, Harton Down Hill Farm and Cleadon Hills.

The Durham Aged Mineworkers' Homes Association (DAMHA) was founded in 1898 and grew from the vision of Joseph Hopper, a miner and lay preacher. He believed that a man who had served in the coal mines all his life deserved better than to be evicted from his tied colliery home when he retired. A small weekly levy voluntarily donated from miners' wages, plus donations of land and materials from mine owners and others, allowed the homes to be constructed and let free of charge. The first Marsden Road homes were opened in 1914 and had indoor toilets when they were built, demonstrating the commitment to high quality care that the DAMHA had from the outset.

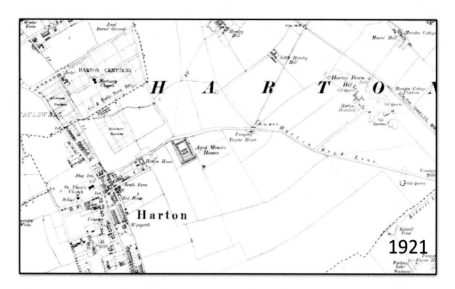

1921

On Saturday, 11th July, 1914 a field day of entertainment was held to mark the laying of the foundation stones of this 48 housing complex in the new garden style layout, designed by the eminent local architect, Mr J M Morton.

Thirty foundation stones were laid by prominent local residents and leaders of the miners at Harton, St Hilda and Whitburn Collieries. These can be seen under windows in various parts of the complex.

A photograph go one of the Marsden Road miners' cottages with one of the commemorative foundation stones beneath its sitting room window. Two of thees cottages are currently being reproduced at Beamish Museum as part of their 1950s village.

Foundation Stones of a Garden Village Laid Near So. Shields.

The miners of South Shields and district had a "field day" on Saturday, when the foundation stones were laid at Harton of 48 homes for aged mine workers and their wives.

The houses, which are being provided by the Durham Aged Mine Workers' Homes Association, will be grouped in the form of a garden village, and will be occupied by mine workers who have been employed at the Harton, St. Hilda, and Whitburn Collieries. This scheme is the second and most important part of a project for the provision of 64 homes in the area of the Harton Coal Company, the first 16 being now in course of erection at Boldon Colliery.

The miners of the district turned out in great force, and headed by bands and banners, marched from South Shields to the sites of the new homes, which are delightfully situated on the road from Harton Village to Marsden. The procession was headed by the Marsden Miners' Lodge, whose beautiful new banner, showing the homes as they will be in their finished state, attracted much attention.

Dr. John Wilson, M.P., president of the Homes Association, presided over the proceedings, which were opened with a prayer by the Rev. G. H. Ashworth, Vicar of Harton. Immediately afterwards 30 foundation stones were laid, the gentlemen performing the ceremonies including Dr. Wilson, M.P., and the Rev. J. R. Croft, of the Homes' Association, representatives of the Harton Coal Company, the Mayor of South Shields (Ald. R. H. Pettler), and other prominent residents, and the leaders of the miners at the three collieries.

A public tea was held afterwards, followed by a meeting and concert in the evening.

The newspaper cutting and accompanying photograph below are taken from the St Peter's Church Scrapbook vol II, 1907-1915.
Reproduced with kind permission of the vicar and churchwardens of Harton St Peter.

Mr. Richard Thornton, the music-hall prop rietor, laid one of the stones. On the right is Mr. Edwin Winter, the manager of South Shields Empire.

Richard Thornton was certainly a celebrity of his day; a self made Shields lad. He died in 1922, aged 83, at his residence in Gosforth and was laid to rest in St Peter's churchyard beside his first wife. The Gazette recorded the event explaining that:

The remains were conveyed by a motor hearse from the residence at Eden Villa, Gosforth, to North Shields, and thence, by ferry, to South Shields. At the ferry landing there was an immense gathering. Two open landaus and a motor car were filled with beautiful wreaths and other floral tokens from members of the family and a wide circle of friends. At the head of the cortege was the St Hilda's Colliery Band, which played Chopin's Funeral March.

Durham Aged Mineworkers' Homes
ASSOCIATION.

Programme of Proceedings

AT THE

Opening of 48 New Cottages at Harton,

ON

SATURDAY, OCT. 9th at 2·30 p.m.

CHAIRMAN, J. W. TAYLOR, Esq., J.P., M.P.

Prayer by Rev. G. H. ASHWORTH, Vicar of Harton.
Chairman's Remarks.

Presentation of Key to James Kirkley, Esq.,
OF CLEADON PARK, SUNDERLAND.

OPENING OF THE HOMES.

Address by ALD. S. GALBRAITH, J.P., M.P.
        JOHN EDMONDSON, Esq.
        T. H. CANN, Esq., J.P.
        JAMES LOWTHER, Esq.
        W. B. CHARLTON, Esq.
        JAMES WILKINSON, Esq.
        Rev. J. R. CROFT, M.A. (Hon. Treas.)
        RUSSELL REA, Esq., M.P.
        JOHN SUMMERBELL, Esq.
        W. J. HARTSHORNE, Esq.
        Coun. JOSEPH BATEY, J.P.

Each speaker not to speak more than seven minutes.

Vote of Thanks to Jas. Kirkley, Esq. for opening the
homes also to the Chairman and Speakers, moved
by JOHN ADAIR, Gen. Sec., seconded by Councillor
Jos. DAWES.

The St. Kilda, Marsden, and Harton Brass Bands
will give Selections on the grounds.

Reproduced with kind permission of the vicar and churchwardens of Harton St Peter.

The homes were officially opened on 9th October, 1915, by James Kirkley Esq. JP. as the stone plaque at the entrance proclaims. The other side of the entrance there is an identically shaped plaque and this bears the following inscription: **The greatest thing in life is to spread as much happiness as possible among those with whom we live.**

James Kirkley also furnished and completed a recreation and committee room for the people of the Harton Aged Mineworkers' Homes in February, 1916. It was furnished with: tables, armchairs, bookcases, books and various games consisting of dominoes, draughts, etc. There was also a large clock and other necessary furnishings. The recreation room can still be seen above the main entrance archway.

West Harton

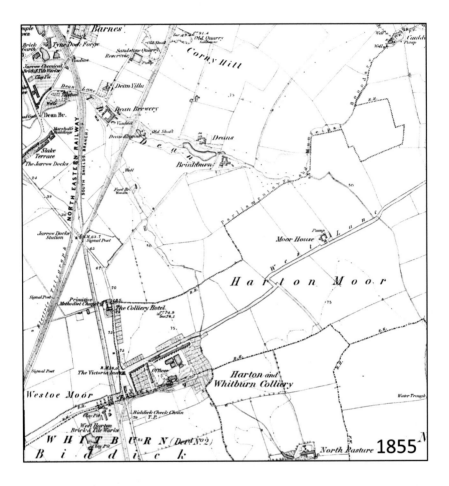

All of West Harton, except the Union Workhouse was taken into South Shields in 1901, hence this chapter only looks at the situation prior to that date. Looking at the 1855 map, West Harton seems to comprise of two pubs and some houses near the newly established colliery (the brick and tile works were outside the Harton Township boundary) with Slake Terrace in Jarrow being the nearest other housing.

Twenty years later, in 1875, we have a colourful individual impression of the houses that comprised Harton Colliery written in the *Newcastle Weekly Chronicle* under the heading, *Our Colliery Villages:*

Saturday March 7 1874 Newcastle Weekly Chronicle
Our Colliery Villages: Harton

This noble Colliery stands far enough away from the village from which it derives its name. As the crow flies, the distance would be a mile or more, but the lane connecting the two winds considerably and makes the journey by so much longer.   It stands right in the country as a colliery should do.

It has, however, clustered around it not only the customary pit town but a hamlet of fair pretentious to the rank of an independent village. Indeed a village with such a big sail cloth factory in its midst and such a fine row of middle class houses is in a promising way of becoming a town. And it would be still more worthy to be ranked as a town if all the four or five hundred people employed at the pit resided on the spot. Unfortunately for some of them they are doomed to live at Templetown, of which we gave some account last week. It is not very far - indeed those whose lot is cast there must often in their hearts wish it further.

Very different and yet outwardly very similar, is the little lot of houses which once constituted the entire homestead of Harton Pit. Probably there are something short of a hundred of these forty year old houses occupying two sides of the great pit yard. The double houses are next the road and their situation throws into unpleasant prominence for every wayfarer the ovens, coal-places and ash-holes provided for the accommodation of their inmates. As to conveniences of another sort, it ought by this time to be sufficient for the readers of these articles to call attention to the fact that the pit has been working since between 1830 and 1840, and in those remote ages builders, owners and miners paid small regard to decency. The march of science has done wonders for the development of the mine, but little or nothing for the comfort of the miners.

Still they are better off here than in some pits in the county. They have garden lots over the way; and they are so lavishly supplied with pig crays and other wooden buildings, roughly constructed that railings appear to constitute the favourite crop. The inner or yard side of the double houses presents an unusually neat and clean appearance for a row so old and low.   There is quite an air of respectability and many indescribable proofs of attention to neatness and general effect.

There may be something in the fact that most of these homes are occupied by master's men, and the master of the master's men living in a home that commands the entire range many have something to do with the orderly appearance of things as far as the eye can reach. Besides, the row is so near the workshops that broken panes and dismantled doors can hardly fail to be attended to with tradesman like promptitude and zeal.

The photograph above was taken in 1904 and is of Quality Row.
The photograph below was taken by James Henry Cleet on 11th March, 1935 and shows the rear of Double Row prior to its demolition.

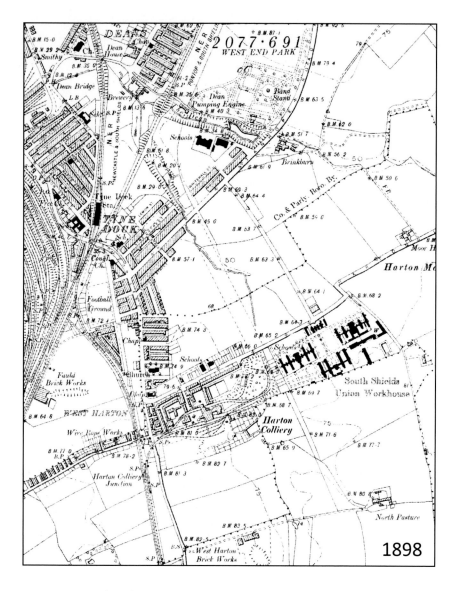

1898

Twenty years after the newspaper article this 1898 map records the growth in housing that has taken place both inside and outside the Township. A fact clearly shown in the census returns which become page after page of families living in the area. The population of Harton Colliery had grown rapidly from 1839 when this area was fields, a part of the farming community, to having a population of 4,062 in 1891 living in 389 dwellings which is an average of 10.5 people in each dwelling. Most dwellings having fewer than five rooms, the majority having two rooms.

ENGLAND AND WALES, 1891.

Enumeration District, No. _52_

Name of Enumerator, Mr. _Charles R. Marshall_

ON OF ENUMERATION DISTRICT.

lumn 9 from the Copy supplied to him by the Registrar. Any explanatory notes or observations calculated to make is especially necessary that the names of the various Local Sub-Divisions should be inserted in Columns 1 to 8.]

9

Description of Boundaries and Contents of Enumeration District.

[handwritten entries:] Straker Terrace, Young's Ville, D'Arcy Street, Eleanor Terrace, Wilkinson Terrace, Harton Terrace, Jacks Terrace, Tyne Terrace, Metcalfe Terrace, Pearson's Buildings, Strakers Buildings, Scotts Buildings, Isaac Buildings, Daglish's Buildings, Golden Lion Inn, Jordisons buildings, Heckels buildings, Raeys buildings, Halders buildings, Green Lane cottages, Hope St, Green Lane Villa Green Lane Villa, Railway New Cottage, Greenfield St, Simonside Hall & lodges Simonside, Bilton Villa

Boundary I.-

Bounded on the North by the Borough Boundary, on the East by the said Boundary to West Row, on the South by the Boldon Township Boundary, and on the West by Westoe Township Boundary. Also a formerly detached part of the parish of Southwick comprising Brockley Whins Station & cottages, West Simonside Farm House & cottage.

Also a formerly detached part the Parish Monkwearmouth comprising High Simonside Farm House.

Also a formerly detached part of the Parish of Whitburn comprising Biddick Hall Farm. Parliamentary Division of Jarrow (part of)

Eng.

The 1891 enumerator's list for this area of Harton Township records the newer streets, terraces and buildings: Straker Terrace; Young's Villa; D'Arcy Street; Eleanor Terrace; Wilkinson Terrace; Harton Terrace; Jack's Terrace; Tyne Terrace; Metcalfe Terrace; Pearson's Buildings; Bailey's Buildings; Straker's Buildings; Scott's Buildings; Issac's Buildings; Daglish's Buildings; Golden Lion Inn; Jordison's Buildings; Heckel's Buildings; Raey's Buildings; Halder's Buildings; Green Lane Cottages; Hope Street; ?Villa; Green Lane Villa; Railway New Cottages; Greenfield Street; Simonside Hall and lodges Simonside; Bilton Villa. The older properties nearer the colliery such as (West Row, Quality Row and Double Row) appear on another census sheet.

Few of these streets now exist and the named buildings are difficult to locate, if indeed they still exist. A few street signs remain to bear witness to their existence. Above is the sign for Tyne Terrace and Wilkinson Terrace and the to right the sign for Jack's Terrace.

James Henry Cleet (1876-1959) was a local photographer who in the 1930s was employed by South Shields Council to photograph areas before they were demolished as part of their slum clearance programme. These two black and white photographs are part of his official record, as was the one on the previous page and the one on the following page. The photograph on the left is dated 6th January, 1938 and provides a rear view of numbers 6 and 8 Straker Terrace. The photograph on the right taken on the same day shows the backyard shared by numbers 13 and 15 D'Arcy Street; washing is in progress as can be seen through the open wash house door.

The Cleet photograph above shows Straker Terrace and on the corner a shop. This section of 1898 map shows West Harton at the time of the photograph, long after it had been taken into South Shields, but it helps, I believe, to put a lot of the information about streets and building names into some sense. Straker Terrace can be seen slightly above centre.

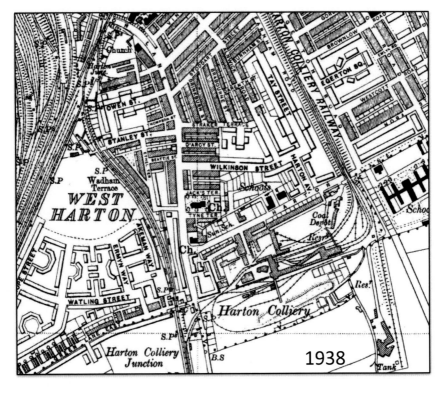

Straker Terrace ended at Boldon Lane, which is still a shopping street (see photograph showing the Jack's Terrace sign on page 186).

The last name on the 1894 Trade Directory, shown on the following pages, is that of Mrs Sarah Jane Younger, a grocer in Straker Street. The 1891 census places in Young's Villa, a Sarah J Younger head of the family, a widow and a grocer, she is 58 years old. Is Young's Villa then situated in Boldon Lane between Straker Street and D'arcy Street? This naming of sections of roads as individual terrace blocks is still be visible on certain properties though out the town and would explain the number of small terraces and buildings on the trade directory and the census returns which are not visible on maps.

At home on the night of the census are Sarah's three daughters and a granddaughter; Jane 21, Edith 18 a Board School Teacher, Isabella 15, and Sarah J 12 (granddaughter) a scholar. There are five properties listed in Young's Villa: The next family recorded on the list may well be one of Sarah's sons and his family, for the census records Joseph Younger 28 a fireman on the railway, with Alema his wife 28, Thomas 7 scholar, Joseph 6 scholar, Janet 4, Frederick 2, and John 11 months; the next name on the census list is Janet Luck a widow 72, who is a retired confectioner; the next names are Richard Frizle 78, a retired coal miner, with Isabella Cook 71, a widow and a general domestic servant; then in the last property are the Oley family, John Oley 34 a coal miner, his wife Sarah 30, their children Mary Ann 8 scholar, Robert 6 scholar, Ethel May 4, and Sarah 1 year old. The next name on the census lives in D'Arcy Terrace, so Young's Villa would appear to have stretched between Straker Terrace and the next street running east west off Boldon Lane, D'Arcy Terrace.

Sarah's property must have been quite grand and included the shop as it had over five rooms, her son and his family lived in two rooms, Janet Luck one room, Richard Frizle one room and the Oley family three rooms. Further investigation of the 1894 Trade Directory links John Sadler, a boot-maker to Young's Villa and Thomas M Young a surgeon. Maybe these were the commercial premises at street level within the building, next to Sarah's grocer shop, and the living accommodation was above? Neither John Sadler nor Thomas Young were in the property overnight and so are not mentioned in the census.

It may well be that Thomas Young, the surgeon, owned the property and hence its name, Young's Villa, renting it out to the families already mentioned? His residence is given in the trade directory as 2 Chapter Row, South Shields.

WEST HARTON.

About ⅔ of a mile south-west of South Shields.

All Saints' Church, Harton ter
Harton Colliery
Harton National School; H. Hook, master;
  Miss M. Craigie, mistress ; infant
  school, Miss A. Moss, mistress
Harton Parish Council Office & Fire Station.
  --W. Bainbridge, clerk
Post & Money Order Office ; Edward
  Richardson, postmaster
Primitive Methodist Chapel, Eleanor ter
Primitive Methodist Mission, Green Lane villas
Public Vaccination Station, Wesleyan Sunday
  School, West lane ; attendance for free
  vaccination every Tuesday in January,
  April, July & October, at 3 p.m.--Frdk.
  W. Gibbon, public vaccinator
Registrar's Office for Births & Deaths, Wes-
  leyan Sunday School, West lane ; at-
  tendance every Monday & Thursday,
  3 to 4·30 p.m.--James Sedcole, registrar
Union Workhouse (So. Shields) E. Read, master
Wesleyan Methodist Chapel, Metcalfe ter

Adamson John, engine driver, 6 Wenlock rd
—— Shereton Anderson, fireman, 7 Weddle ter
Aitken John, platelayer, 17 Tennant st
Alexander John, foreman, 3 Madras st
Allan Bertram, joiner, Talbot rd
Armstrong Adam Latimer, Prince of Wales
  hotel, Green lane
—— Matthew, platelayer, 6 Wilkinson ter
Atkinson James, fireman, 17 Eleanor ter
—— Robert, wagonwright, 13 Tennant st
Auld James, miner, 7 Harton ter
Baglin Thomas, miner, Talbot rd
Bainbridge Wm. asst. overseer, 10 Harton ter
Bartlett Geo. engine driver, 8 Wenlock rd
Bartram Edwin, fireman, 21 Madras st
Bayfield Henry, grocer, South View ter
Bell Frank, engine driver, 1 Wenlock rd
—— George, engine driver, 17 Wenlock rd
—— Samuel, labourer, 14 Madras st
—— Stephen, engine driver, 21 Wenlock rd
Bix Robert, platelayer, 10 Tennant st
Blair Joseph, engine driver, 6 Metcalfe ter
Boden Joseph, musician, Talbot rd
Bowman Thomas, miner, 4 Wilkinson ter
Bradnum Lucy (Miss) shopkeeper, Greenlane.w
Brown Jane (Mrs) 9 Harton ter
—— John, platelayer, 22 Tennant st
Buckham Edward, guard, 7 Tennant st
Burns Jane Ann (Mrs) grocer, 6 Green lane
Cameron James, miner, 2 Tyne ter
Campbell Thos. engine driver, 10 Wenlock rd
Camsell George, miner, Scott's buildings
Carr George, tinsmith, Green lane
Chapman Ralph, labourer, 30 Madras st
—— Thomas, wagonwright, 30 Wenlock rd
Charlton Patrick, bootmaker, Bailey's bldgs
Charlton Ralph, engine driver, 29 Wenlock rd
Clark Robert Alexander, saddler, 8 Jack's ter
Colley Henry, farmer, Harton Moor farm
Collingwood Robert, guard, 16 Tennant st
Colman Frederick, labourer, 16 Madras st
Colville David, guard, 9 Wilkinson ter
Colwell J. & M. farmers, High Simonside farm
Conway John, shopkeeper, 7 Green Lane cres
Cook George, miner, 1 Wilkinson ter
—— Robert, miner, 13 Jack's ter
Cooper David, engine driver, 23 Wenlock rd
Coppock Geo. wagonwright, 36 Wenlock rd
Corner Wm. miner, 5 Jack's ter
Crabb John, policeman, 5 Metcalfe ter
Crooks John, trimmer, 11 Eleanor ter
Cummings Hry. engine driver, 4 Wenlock rd

Curry James, labourer, 12 Eleanor ter
Dack Henry, beer retailer, Green lane
—— Robert, chimney sweeper, Green lane
Davidson Matthew, platelayer, 27 Madras st
—— (W.) & Sons, mineral water mfrs. Green ln
Daws Edmund, miner, Scott's buildings
Deaton Elizabeth Wilson (Miss) shopkeeper,
  11 Harton ter
—— Wm. 1 Jack's ter
Ditchburn Thomas, guard, 23 Madras st
Dixon John, miner, Scott's buildings
—— Robt. Jas. manager, Green Lane villas
Douglas Robert, miner, 3 Metcalfe's ter
Dron Charles, engine driver, 26 Madras st
Dunn George, engine driver, 10 Madras st
Fairs Matthew, colliery surveyor ; r Stan-
  hope rd. Tyne Dock
Farrow George, joiner, 6 Weddle ter
Fishburn Joseph, engine driver, 7 Madras st
Foreman Wm. shopkeeper, Young's villas
Forster John, miner, 7 Wilkinson ter
Foster Wm. engineman, Talbot rd
Gallon John, engine driver, 34 Wenlock rd
Garlick Wm. engine driver, 24 Wenlock rd
Gibson George, timekeeper, 8 Madras st
—— John, platelayer, 23 Tennant st
Goodwin Daniel, labourer, 11 Tennant st
Gordon John, joiner, 18 Eleanor ter
Graham John, guard, 6 South View ter
Gray Joseph, fruiterer, South View ter
Green John, wagonwright, 28 Wenlock rd
Haddington Joseph, miner, Talbot road
Hall George, miner, 2 South View ter
—— James, miner, Docker's buildings
—— Joseph, grocer, South View ter
—— Robert, shopkeeper, Docker's buildings
—— Wm. engine driver, 35 Wenlock rd
—— Wm. miner, 15 Jack's ter
Hanney Peter, platelayer, 6 Madras st
Harrison Joseph, shaftsman, Kingston

Harton (The) Coal Company, Limited,
  Harton, Saint Hilda, Boldon and
  Whitburn collieries. General offices,
  South Shields ; Fitting offices, 17 Sand-
  hill, Quayside, Newcastle-on-Tyne
Hellam Thomas, machinist, 18 Madras st
Henderson Chas. Allan, guard, South View ter
—— George, clerk, 25 Madras st
—— George, farmer, North pastures
—— John, gateman, 5 Weddle ter
Heslop Hunter, miner, Kingston
—— James, overman, Quality row
Hook Henry, schoolmaster
Hopwood John, signalman, 18 Tennant st
Horn George, enginewright, 1 Eleanor ter
—— John, miner, Talbot rd
—— Wm. miner, Kingston
Howe Joseph, miner, Colliery row
Hunter George, engine driver, 20 Madras st
—— Wm. engine driver, 9 Tennant st
Huntington Joseph, miner, 19 Madras st
Hutchinson Ralph, wagonwright, 2 Madras st
Jackson David, merchant, 1 Harton ter
Johnson Wm. engine driver, 27 Wenlock rd
Jordison Henry, mason, 16 Wilkinson ter
—— Robert, trimmer, Jordison st
—— Sarah (Mrs) 15 Eleanor ter
Kelly John, miner, Scott's buildings
King Robert, engine driver, 22 Wenlock rd
Kirkup James, wagonwright, 6 Tennant st
Knox James, guard, 14 Tennant st
Leach Charles, miner, Scott's buildings
Leggett Henry, fireman, 4 South View ter
Leybourne Thos. Wm. cashier, Harton col-
  liery ; r 14 Logan ter. South Shields
Little George, labourer, 2 Tennant st

Lodge Harry, miner, Scott's buildings
—— Thomas, trimmer, 6 Jack's ter
Macdonald Hugh, miner, Scott's buildings
Maconochie Jas. Wm. joiner, 5 Wilkinson ter
Magee Michael, engine driver, 12 Wenlock rd
March John, farmer, Biddick Hall farm
Martin Barnard, engine driver, 18 Wenlock rd
—— Matthew, engine driver, 19 Wenlock rd
Massingham Wm. mariner, 19 Eleanor ter
May Geo. viewer; rSimonside hall, So. Shields
McQueen George, joiner, 10 Wilkinson ter
Mensforth Richard, platelayer, 4 Tennant st
Menzies James, newsagent, 6 Harton ter
Metcalfe Peter, dairyman, Kingston
Mitchell Peter, fitter, 20 Jack's ter
Mitcholson Wm. engine driver, 2 Wenlock rd
Modral John, engine driver, 33 Wenlock rd
Mordue Wm. foreman, Green Lane villas
Mort Thomas, engine driver, 17 Madras st
Nelson John, miner, 7 Eleanor ter
Nicholson Wm. 10 Jack's ter
—— Hodgson, miner, Scott's bldgs
Noble Daniel, miner, Scott's bldgs
Oliver John, grocer, South View ter
Palmer Imbrose Jas. carpntr. 8 Wilkinson ter
—— John, platelayer, 5 Tennant st
Park Wm. engineman, 13 Wenlock rd
Patterson Alexander, labourer, 1 Madras st
Pearce Henry James, 6 Kingston
—— Wm. engine driver, 13 Wilkinson ter
Pearson John Wm. 22 Jack's ter
—— Mark, miner, 9 Jack's ter
Potts Henry, engine driver, 3 South View ter
Proud Launcelot, fitter, 7 Wenlock rd
Purvis Wm. 3 Weddle ter
Read Edmund, master of workhouse
Reay Wm. engine driver, 11 Wilkinson ter
Richardson Edward, grocer, Victoria bldgs
—— George, grocer, Bailey's bldgs
—— John, wagonwright, 5 Wenlock rd
Riddle Charles, boilerman, 4 Weddle ter
Robinson Andrew, gland packer, 25 Wenlock rd
—— Geo. colliery manager, Harton colliery
Robley George, blacksmith, 3 Wenlock rd
Robson John, engine driver, 11 Wenlock rd
Rose Samuel, fireman, 19 Wilkinson ter
Rowland Robert, engine driver, 15 Wenlock rd
Sadler John, bootmaker, Young's villas
Sayers John, fireman, 12 Wilkinson ter
Scott Ralph, blacksmith, 13 Eleanor ter
—— Wm. signalman, 19 Tennant st
Scutton Sarah (Mrs) 4 Jack's ter
Shotton Charles, butcher, Green Lane villas
Sinclair James, engineer, Kingston
Sinton Mrgt. Emily (Mrs) grocer, Hope st
Smith Anthony, blacksmith, 22 Madras st
—— Edward, engine driver, 9 Wenlock rd
—— Edward, guard, 15 Tennant st
—— Isabella (Mrs) 11 Madras st
—— James, guard, 8 Weddle ter

—— John Geo. engine driver, 38 Wenlock rd
—— Wm. 16 Eleanor ter
Spears Robert, guard, 29 Madras st
Sponton John, engine driver, 31 Wenlock rd
Steel Michael, platelayer, 21 Tennant st
Stephenson Henry, mariner, 3 Wilkinson ter
—— Joseph, grocer, Green lane
Stoker Thomas, miner, 7 Jack's ter
Stokoe Matthew, engine driver, 5 Madras st
Storey George, engine driver, 16 Wenlock rd
Sword John P. agent, 19 Eleanor ter
Symons John, ticket colletr. Harton colliery
Tate Thomas, blacksmith, Harton colliery
Taylor Irving, platelayer, 1 Tennant st
—— Thomas, platelayer, 8 Tennant st
—— Wm. inspecting engineer, Biddick hall
Telford Wm. engine driver, 15 Madras st
Temple John, Golden Lion hotel, Green lane
Ternent John, engine driver, 20 Wenlock rd
Thorret John, guard, 12 Tennant st
Thurlwell Isabella (Mrs) 14 Wenlock rd
Todd George, draper, West Harton house
—— John, engine driver, 9 Madras st
—— Wm. engine driver, 26 Wenlock rd
Trenholm Robt. Whitfield, butcher, Green lane
Turnbull Wm. joiner, 3 Tyne ter
Tweddle Wm. platelayer, 20 Tennant st
Urwin Mthw. colliery engnr. 20 Eleanor ter
Vardy Joseph, painter, 1 Tyne ter
Varty Margery (Mrs) Talbot rd
Waites Wm. engine driver, 32 Wenlock rd
Waterson Peter, platelayer, 3 Tennant st
Watson Edward, weighman, Green lane
—— Hume, joiner, 14 Jack's ter
—— James, miner, 4 Harton ter
—— John, fireman, 3 Jack's ter
Watters George, fireman, 24 Madras st
Waugh Michael, miner, 14 Wilkinson ter
—— Wm. grocer, Green Lane villas
Wayte Nicholas, foreman, 40 Wenlock rd
Weddle John, engineman, 2 Harton ter
Whitelock Wm. engine driver, 13 Madras st
Wilson Anthony, miner, 15 Wilkinson ter
—— John, miner, Scott's buildings
—— Matthew, check weighman, Green lane
—— Wm. wagonwright, 37 Wenlock rd
—— Wm. weighman, 17 Wilkinson ter
Winchley Edw. engine driver, 28 Madras st
Winskell Andrew, 23 Jack's ter
—— John Andrew, Victoria inn, Harton coly
Winter Nicholas, fireman, 12 Madras st
Wood Thomas, bootmaker, Green lane
Woodbine Henry, miner, 21 Jack's ter
Wright Wm. storekeeper, 18 Wilkinson ter
Young Ralph, machinist, 4 Madras st
—— Thomas M. surgeon, Young's villas; r
    2 Chapter row, South Shields
—— Wm. engine driver, 30 Wenlock rd
—— Wm. miner, Double row, Harton colliery
Younger Sarah Jane (Mrs) grocer, Straker ter

Two pages taken from an 1894 Ward's Trade Directory.

Many of the businesses mentioned in the Trade Directory on the previous pages were situated on Green Lane, a road under the control of Harton Township which acted as an artery linking Simonside with West Harton until 1901, when both areas were taken into South Shields.

Green Lane Crossing. Looking Westward.

Green Lane Crossing Looking Eastwards.

Two photographs by James Cleet offering a view of the dame area go Green Lane but from opposite directions.

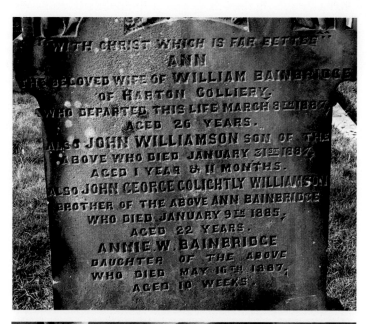

As much as the census returns and the trade directories, the photographs and the newspaper articles, the headstones of those who lived at the colliery and now lie in St Peter's churchyard speak of the lives they lived.

Simonside

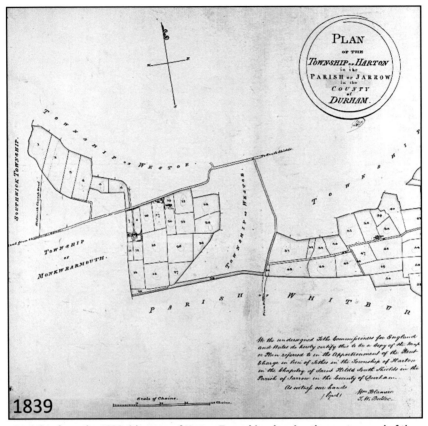

1839

A section from the 1839 tithe map of Harton Township, showing the western end of the township and the other townships that surrounded the section of Simonside allocated to Harton at some time in the seventeenth century.

Robert Surtees in his book *The History and Antiquities of the County Palatine of Durham*, published in volumes between 1816 - 1840 explains that: **There is a tradition that the village of Simonside was entirely depopulated about two centuries ago by the plague, and the nearest townships divided the deserted lands....parts of Simonside now lie in Harton, Westoe, Monkwearmouth, Southwick and Fulwell.**

Hence possibly from the early seventeenth century Harton Township was responsible for a part of the area we still call Simonside: the area around Simonside Hall; Simonside Lodge; Bilton Hall; including two farms (p122).

These appear as two bubble like attachments to the west end of Harton held there by the thin thread of Green lane. This is obvious in the section of the 1839 tithe map opposite and until 1901 can be picked out in other maps denoting the boundaries of the townships. In 1901 along with most of West Harton this area was taken into South Shields.

Three substantial houses dominated this area: Simonside Hall, Simonside Lodge and Bilton Villa. Both Simonside Hall and Simonside Lodge can be seen on the 1839 tithe map, and by 1855 all three exist. All have glorious, panoramic views over to the river and the salt marshes, full of birds and wildlife, while at the same time being close to the Wrekendike Roman Road (Leam Lane) which was a significant road leading from Chester le Street to South Shields.

The narrow strip of land known as Green Lane would become filled with shops, small industrial units and houses and a small collection of miners' houses would be built within the Simonside area. The miners' houses, like two of the large houses: Simonside Lodge and Bilton Villa, still exist.

In the 1851 census we find at Bilton Villa John Mease 21, an alkali manufacturer, living with his sister Elizabeth 22, and brother George 15, plus a house servant Margaret Hills 26.   In the two lodges belonging to the house: Bilton Villa Lodge, John Huntley 24, a carter, his wife and their young son, plus his sister-in-law a child of 11; Bilton Villa West Lodge we find the Hellewell family, William who is 33 and a mason, his father-in-law who is a cordwainer and 67 years old and his wife and five children.

Bilton Villa, 2021. The property is now divided into a number of separate residences.

John Mease would die at the house in 1857 and the 1861 census would find George Meade now 25 living at the villa supported by two servants. John and George were the sons of the wealthy Solomon Mease of Tynemouth, a prominent industrialist and shipowner. George became proprietor, with his father, of the Lake Chemical Works, Jarrow. Solomon lived at Cleveland House North Shields but Bilton Villa was most probably one of his properties.

Bilton Villa was sold in 1878 and again in 1895 when it was described in this advert in *The Shields Gazette*, Friday, 4th October as:

> FOR SALE or TO LET, the MANSION with south aspect, known as Bylton Villa with about 3 acres of ornamental grounds and gardens, conservatory, vineries, 2 stalled stable, entrance lodge, &c., situate about midway between Jarrow and Tyne Dock. The House may be viewed by permission of the present tenant, and particulars may be obtained at the office of the Hedworth Barium Co., Ltd., East Jarrow, or No. 1 St. Nicholas Buildings, Newcastle-on-Tyne.

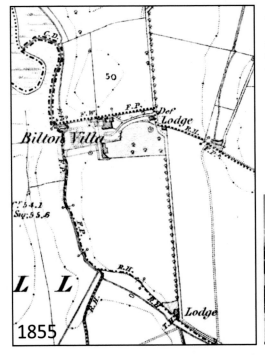

A small blown-up section of the 1855 map, shows Bilton VIlla and its two lodges positioned at the very western tip of the land within Harton Township.

Below is a photograph from 2021 showing the remaining lodge.

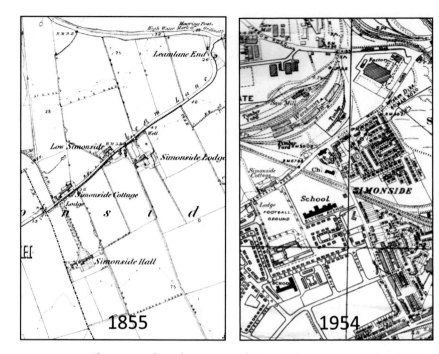

These maps show the same area but are 100 years apart: 1855 and 1954.
Simonside Lodge and Simonside Hall are visible on both.
Simonside Hall would be demolished in 1968.

In Simonside Lodge in 1891 lived John Thompson 58, a ship owner, his wife Elizabeth 39, and their son John 26, a ship broker, Sarah Widdle 20, a domestic servant and Ellen Snetels 19, a housemaid. In Simonside Lodge Gate lived Christopher Baker 66, a coachman, his wife Sarah 54, and his daughter Fanny 29.   In 1901 Christopher and Sarah are still living in Simonside Lodge Gate. At the main house, Simonside Lodge, Elizabeth Thompson is now a widow living with her niece and two domestic servants.

Simonside Lodge Gate and Simonside Lodge in 2021.

Few photographs exist in the public domain of Simonside Hall. Here it can be seen in the background of this image, a large five windowed central building with side wings and a dutch gable style, stable roof just visible. From the 1920s onward the hall went into decline, was divided into apartments, and by 1938 it was a social club. The estate was bought by South Shields Football Club in 1947 and was their ground until it was sold for housing in 1968. Indeed on the section of 1954 map on the previous page the area in front of the house is marked as a football ground. Below is an aerial shot of the new housing estate being built in the early 1970s on the site of Simonside Hall.

Simonside Hall may have been built by Robert Wallis the pioneer Shields shipbuilder but is more likely to have been built by his son John at the the end of the eighteenth century.

After John Wallis the next occupier of the Hall was Henry Major. The Hall was by all accounts a pleasant country house surrounded by orchards with fine views of the wetlands of Jarrow Slake albeit in a relatively lawless area. There are newspaper reports of him being robbed by a highwayman in Boldon Lane in 1821. Saturday, 19th May, 1821 one report reads:

> On Wednesday night se'nnight, about half-past ten o'clock, as Henry Major, of Simonside, Esq. was returning home from South Shields, he was attacked in Boldon-lane by two men, who, with a violent blow on the head, felled him from his horse, and robbed him of his watch, £5 in notes, and some silver. Mr. M. was very much cut about the face and head, and there is no doubt that the ruffians left their victim believing him dead. Mr. Major, with much difficulty, reached the house of Mr. Blenkinsop, near the spot, covered with blood.

The next occupant George Cairns was a speculative shipowner who bought large American wooden ships cheaply and put them mostly into the wood trade from Canada. His most notable ship was probably the *Zambesi*, a 1,089 tons nitrate clipper built in St John's Canada in 1857, which he bought in 1866 and had a reputation as a flyer, but he had others including the 1,111 tons *Exodus*, the *Frank Shaw* which was wrecked on the Goodwin Sands in 1869 with the loss of 8 lives and the *Charles Ward* lost in 1872.

The golden age of Simonside Hall was from the mid-1870s when George May and his family lived there. He was a mining engineer who was the general manager of the Harton Coal Company, a local politician, and at one time President of the Mining Institute at Newcastle. The house became the centre of an active social circle. In 1891 he was 62, Fanny his wife 47, Helen Maud their daughter 25, and Ethel Bertha their second child 20, plus a cook, a waiting maid and a house maid, Elizabeth Pattinson 28, Elizabeth Johnson 24, and Elizabeth Longley 58.

George May was the honorary clerk of works for St Simon's Church and either he or his wife or daughter laid the foundation stone of many buildings in Harton Colliery and Boldon including the two methodist chapels at West Harton, the Miner's Hall at Boldon, Boldon Colliery Board School, and Boldon Colliery Co-op.

His wife Fanny ran a celebrated amateur dramatic company from the Hall which gave performances in Shields, Durham and Sunderland principally in support of the RSPCA but also in support of the Ingham Infirmary and the Sunderland Eye Hospital. Their eldest daughter Helen Maud known generally as Maud was the star of the company and something of a local celebrity. Maud advertised in the *Era* for plays to be written for her *with a strong female lead* and appeared at charity balls which were fully reported in the papers in exotic costumes (Venus was one of her favourites).

George May moved from the Hall to Clevaux Castle near Darlington in the early twentieth century (he was by then a very wealthy man who left more than £186,000 in his will when he died in 1915) but Maud stayed at Simonside until her marriage in 1908. She had a second career as a dog breeder. Below is a picture of her is from the *Tatler* where she featured regularly in its pages.

The far image is of George May in his working clothes as the Mining Engineer for Harton Collieries 1872-1902. He was also President of the Mining and Mechanical Engineers Institute , 1896-1898.

The nearest image is of his daughter Maud May printed in the *Tatler* 20th January, 1915 with two of her greyhounds.

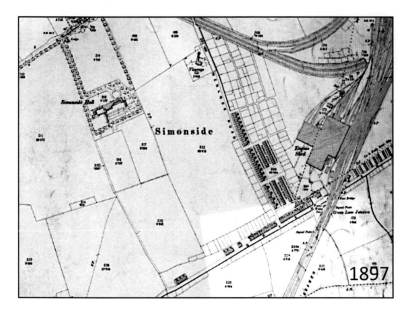

Above on this section of the 1897 map of Simonside is Simonside Hall and just a little to the south east of the Hall are a collection of terraces probably built by the Harton Coal Company for their workers at the colliery or the engine depot right beside these streets. Also see on this map along that thin line of Green Lane are the footprint of buildings, shops and small industrial units. Of the Green Lane buildings little remains, but the terraces are still standing

Wenlock Road and Madras Street in Simonside, 2021.

Harton
Coastline

Chapter 4

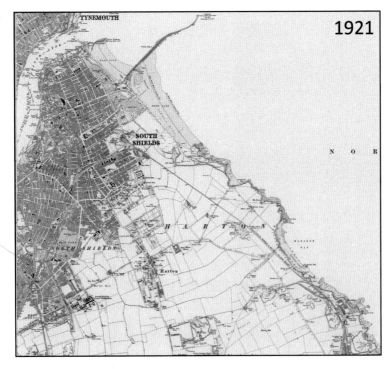

Introduction

Although the western boundaries of Harton Township changed in 1901 there were no changes made to the eastern, coastal boundaries as a comparison of the 1862 and 1921 maps opposite show. From Trow Rocks to the beginning of Marsden Bay, the coastline lay not in South Shields but in Harton Township. This chapter will deal with the coastline of Harton Township, the buildings and people who lived along it.

This is a rugged stretch of coastline made up of magnesium rocks, cliffs, caves and coves. It became part of South Shields in 1932 and is now managed by the National Trust for all to enjoy.

The nineteenth century saw many reports in newspapers that spoke of the fearfulness of the sea along this coastline, the wrecked ships and lives lost. There are, however, very few accounts of smuggling, but many believe it must have taken place, there is even mention (p218) of a tunnel leading from Marsden Cottage to a sheltered cove called Man Haven. Maybe the coastguards were very efficient or those involved were too good to get caught.

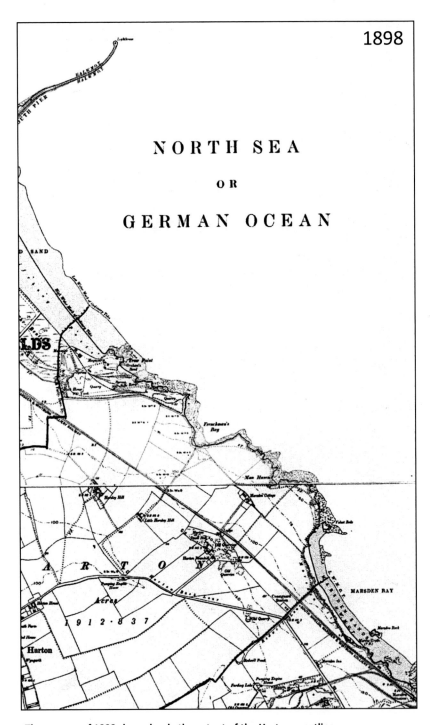

These maps of 1898 show clearly the extent of the Harton coastline.

Bays and Caves

The Velvet Beds

The coastline which lay within Harton Township can be clearly seen on the 1898 map opposite. It stretched from just before Trow Point in the north and south down to Marsden Bay. The boundary line following what is still known as Redwell Bank. It did not include Marsden Rock but rather a small tidal island called the Velvet Beds, which was then a huge tourist attraction.

Pleasure boat trips ran long before the piers were built bringing people from Shields for a relaxing time at this celebrated beauty spot. An early description from 1834 can be found in Mackenzie and Ross' *An Historical, Topographical and Descriptive View of the County Palatine of Durham Volume 1:*

.. the Velvet Bed, a small island covered with smooth grass and which is often the scene of festivity and amusement during the bathing season, when 'Gypsy parties' from Tynemouth and other neighbouring towns visit this spot. A cottage has just been erected on the beach where visitors may be accommodated with refreshments; and steps have been cut in the rock which render the ascent and descent safe and easy.

We do not have any illustrations from the Georgian or Victorian period, but some superb early twentieth century photographs are in South Tyneside Library of boat trips leaving the harbour possibly on their way to

The Velvet Beds was very popular. This could be accounted for by the fact that in the nineteenth century many of the visitors to Marsden came by rowing or sailing boats, later it was 'steamboat' trippers. The South Pier was not completed until the 1890s; and the distance from the mouth of the river would be considerably shorter and the water more shallow than it now is.
Doris Johnson South Shields in Old Picture Postcards Vol 2.

the Velvet Beds and of the 1930s corporation built cafe and tent hire at the bottom of Redwell Bank (which always intrigued me as to why it was called the Velvet Beds, not Marsden Bay).

Sadly time has taken its toll on the little tidal island on the north end of Marsden Bay (see photograph on previous page) and it is no longer the lush and verdant place it once was and is now locally known as Camel's Island. There are various rings still visible in the rocks at the base of Camel's Island which were most probably where these pleasure boats tidied up.

A photograph from the 1920s of pleasure boats leaving the Harbour in South Shields possibly bound for the Velvet Beds in Marsden Bay.

The upper photograph is captioned 1950s the lower one 1930s, both show the original
buildings at the base of Redwell Bank on the beach at Marsden Bay.
Notice they are known as the *Velvet Beds Carter for Tents.*
The sign offers: *Tea Trays for the Beach, Confectionery, Cigarettes, Ices, etc.*
Tents and Beach Chairs for hire.
Last year all remains of the concrete bases or steps of these buildings were removed
by the National Trust, having become very dangerous as the constant erosion of the
sea won its battle.

Man Haven

A little further north of the Velvet Beds is a much frequented cove, still displaying remains of twentieth century winches and boathouses.   This landing Bay is called Man Haven. Mackenzie and Ross in their 1834 topographical description of the Harton coastline mention Man Haven;

>.......a place called Man Haven, above which is a crane by which the cobles of South Shields Pilots, with their crews, are lowered into the sea, during such stormy weather as prevents them from crossing the bar at Tynemouth. The cobles are carried in carts to this place.

This quite amazing statement is confirmed by other accounts and fully described in a newspaper article by Thomas Marshall which appeared on 11th April, 1924 in his local history column. At this point he is writing about John Salmon (1824-1912) who lived at Salmon's Hall on the cliff tops in Harton (p164).

>John Salmon only spent a portion of his years at the Hall near Man Haven. He possessed a coble which lay in the haven and which he used frequently. At one time the mouth of the Tyne had a heavy sandbank known as the Bar, now almost non-existent owning to extensive dredging and the lengthening of the harbour seawards. Only at high water could the bar be crossed by vessels of any great draught, and at low water, the sea often broke heavily, making it impossible for a pilot's coble to pass out to meet a ship without running great risk. Many lives had lost on the Bar and the pilots were forced to cast about for some alternative means of embarkation, and they at last hit upon the idea of carrying their cobles overland and launching them in Man Haven, where Salmon had erected ways for the lunching of his own boat. No sooner was this rash expedient suggested than it was carried out, and the strange spectacle of boats travelling along the coast on wheels was seen. A winch was used for hauling up the cobles, the pilots could easily judge the depth of water on the bar from the Whaleback Rock a reef at the end of the haven, which was submerged at high water......It was Salmon who did much to secure them their Commission which has now become the Tyne Pilotage Authority. The Tyne pilots at a later date requested Trinity House to provide them with some manner of steamer, and so obviate the unnecessary risk they ran putting out from the coast in open cobles, and the result was that they were assisted to purchase their first steamer. They had then no longer to rest upon the hospitality of the owner of Salmon's Hall.

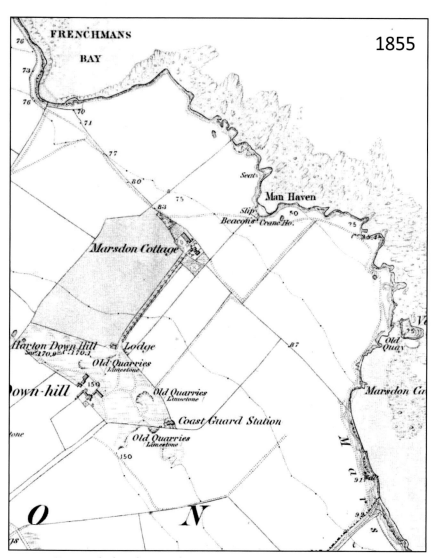

Note marked on the map above Man Haven: the slip, beacons and crane house.
The map also marks an old quay between the Velvet Beds and the cliff, which is where
the metal rings, such as the one shown on page 214 can be found among the rocks.
The original Harton Coastguard Station is also marked on Harton Down Hill.

Cobles as shallow light working boats had a long history on the north east coast but in the middle of the nineteenth century they became of interest to the leisure middle classes too. Unlike the owner of a conventional yacht, a coble owner required no deepwater mooring for his craft in a river or a dock, a coastal beaching station sufficed for much of the summer and at winter layup it was simply hauled ashore up the bank. Cobles also offered exciting prospects for competitive racing and coastal cruising. Indeed in June 1876 John Salmon helped form the Whitburn Coble Yacht Club, using Whitburn and Marsden Bays, with social events at the hostelry in Whitburn named *The Jolly Sailor*.

A photograph from the 1920s showing two cobles in the harbour at South Shields. The boat on the right is the pilot's coble 72, named *Jubilee*.

As well as being used for coble landings and by the Tyne pilots, there are lots of stories about Man Haven being used for smuggling purposes and even the repeated story of a tunnel leading from the bay to Marsden Cottage.

Brian Cauwood remembers his grandmother, Ada Cauwood née Burn, born in 1894, explaining that when the Burn family moved to Marsden Cottage they moved into the kitchen area, which was part of the main house that had been converted into an individual dwelling. In the pantry area was a door that lead to the passageway. Ada said as children she and her siblings used to often go this way to the beach.

Hodgson on pages 489-9 explains how that:

Between Frenchman's Bay and the next inlet known as Man Haven - from which the pilots used to launch their cobles when the weather was too rough to enable them to put off from the Tyne - there was formerly a deep cave now silted up with sand, which still bears the appellation of the 'Smuggler's Cave' and is said to have been used as a depot for contraband goods brought in from overseas. Indeed, so late as 1851, the smuggling schooner *Rob Roy* was captured off this point with 8000lbs of tobacco and cigars, valued at £4,000, stowed away on board of her; while about 600lbs were found in a cave on shore, possibly the cave now referred to.

It has not been possible to find records of this incident, but in *The Newcastle Chronicle* Saturday, 6th April, 1850 this similar smuggling event was reported:

THE CAPTURE OF A SMUGGLING VESSEL.—The smuggling vessel captured off Tynemouth Castle on Thursday week, the particulars of which were given in our last number, proved to be the *Rob Roy*, of London, John Pritchard, commander, and was from Nieuw Diep, in the Texel. She was about 32 tons burthen, and was an old revenue cutter. She had 137 bales of tobacco, 60 lbs. in each bale, and 61 cases of cigars, on board, and the customs officers were not above two hours from the New Quay, until they returned with their prize. The men said the master was landed at Yarmouth ill, but it is understood that he had gone ashore at Marsden Rock to arrange for the landing of the cargo. It was the first trip for the vessel. The crew consisted of five noble looking fellows. Their names are John Botcher, ―te, Thomas Dawkins, Wm. Jewson, Thos. Frogler, and ―.. ―as Petit. They said they had no idea that the steamboat was going to play them a trick, else neither they nor even a boat on the north-east coast would have touched them, as their little cutter sailed like the wind. The men were brought up before the South Shields Magistrates on Wednesday. They pleaded guilty to the charge, and were committed to Durham House of Correction for nine months each, with hard labour. The quantity of tobacco and cigars was upwards of 8,000 lbs. both of superior quality. If it had been got into the country, it would have deprived the revenue of nearly £2,000; and of course the fair trader would have been injured to a corresponding extent. The vessel is forfeited and will be sold by the crown.

Other newspaper reports remind us of the danger of the sea:

On the night of Monday 18th October 1869, the Prussian Brig Muritz Reichenheim of Zingst bound for Shields from Shoreham in ballast was being towed by the tug Reynard when at 10.30pm the tow rope broke off Trow Rocks. A violent NE by E gale give the Brig no chance of clearing the land once she was adrift, so she put up a staysail in a desperate attempt to run ashore at a safe place but struck a little to the north of Man Haven and went to pieces in very heavy seas. One man survived by lashing himself to a spar which was later washed ashore, but nine men including the captain drowned. The tug stood by for a time attempting to take off the crew and reattach the tow rope while shining her light to try to guide the brig to a safe place. The light was seen by brigadesmen on watch at the life brigade watch house at South Shields who searched the coast from Trow Rocks to Souter Point in appalling conditions but failed to find the wreck. Search parties went out again at daybreak and they found the pitiful remains of the ship at Man Haven. The sole survivor, Alfred Shunrokk, managed after spending more than five hours in the sea to crawl to Marsden Cottage where he was kindly treated by Mr Shaw, and recovered enough to be able to visit the Prussian Consul in the afternoon.

Frenchman's Bay

The handwritten note at the side of this postcard is written: *This is Frenchman's Bay beside South Shields.*
Collection of Ernest Lewthwaite

Hodgson explains on page 489 of his *History of the Borough of South Shields* that this beautiful bay derived its name, *as Richardson's Terrier of Survey tells us, from the circumstances of a French Ship being wrecked there many years ago.* Again it is difficult to prove this, as is the story then expanded from this one, that some of the sailors found refuge in Harton Village. They were carrying the plague and the ancient village was razed to the ground to destroy the virus.

An advert in *The Shields Gazette* on Tuesday, 17th September, 1935 for a play which it is stated will offer an explanation for the title of Frenchman's Bay.

At 8.45 a play of special interest to Shields will be presented; this is "Frenchman's Bay." The action takes place at Frenchman's Bay, South Shields, in 1793 and 1815, where, tradition has it, a great deal of smuggling took place. In this play Edwin Lewis offers an explanation for the title of the bay.

Hodgson continues his description of Frenchman's Bay:

In the early part of this century (1800) the bay was the chosen abode of an eccentric character known as Willie the Rover. He built himself a rude hut under the overhanging rock at the head of the bay, on the level platform to which a flight of steps now leads down from the top of the cliffs. The hut, the foundations of which were visible until past the 1850s, was of the rudest type. It had a small unglazed aperture which served as window and chimney combined, and Willie was accustomed to sleep in a sack on the floor in front of the fire. He earned a precarious living by mending boots and shoes, and was suspected of not being too scrupulous in the methods by which he provisioned his larder at the expense of the flocks and crops of neighbouring farmers. At length he disappeared announcing that he had had a fortune left him and was going to walk to London to obtain it.

Frenchman's Bay with Salmon's Cottage sitting up above the cliffs. It is incorrectly labelled South Shields, being in Harton Township when this postcard was produced. *Collection of Ernest Lewthwaite.*

Postcard showing the steps leading down form the cliffs into Frenchman's Bay *Collection of Ernest Lewthwaite.*

Lady's Bay

A 1960s postcard showing Lady's Bay after quarrying. The rock in the centre, now gone due to coastal erosion, was known as Graham's Rock.
Collection of Ernest Lewthwaite.

Hodgson then goes on to mention Lady's Bay, which is the next Bay to Frenchman's Bay, where in 1854 Trow Quarry had been established (p226):

Many interesting legends are attached to the caves and bays of the beautiful coast-line immediately southward of the Borough. Charming cave in the Lady's Bay at Trow Rocks (destroyed in April 1884 by the operations of the Tyne Commissioners) contained the famous, 'Fairies Kettle', a beautiful circular basin, scooped in the rock by natural action and kept full with sweet fresh water by an ever flowing stream. There is a similar spring in a large cave on the south side of Frenchman's Bay, which, although covered at high water by the tide, furnishes a plentiful supply of fresh water at low tide.

An oil painting of *The Fairies Kettle* **by by local artist James Shotton (1824-1896).**
North Tyneside Council the Quadrant, Art Uk Website.

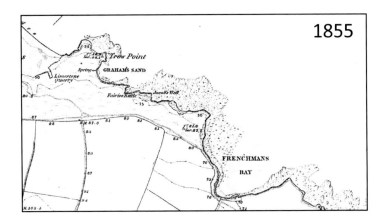

Doris Johnson in Volume 1 Postcards of South Shields, explains that:
What is now Lady's Bay was shown as Graham's Sand on the 1855 OS. Jacob's Well and the Fairies Kettle are also shown between this and Frenchman's Bay. Mr Wallis of Westoe wrote down the story of the Fairies Kettle which was actually a circular hollow in a large cave which was only accessible at low tide. Legend has it that it once contained a golden cup and after a hazardous adventure a young man gained possession of it and brought it to the chapel of St Lawrence at Westoe . After consideration, the priest took it to Durham and gave it to the shrine of St Cuthbert. The Tyne Commissioners had undertaken to preserve the famous cave but a heavy fall of rock, partly due to heavy quarrying nearby destroyed it completely.

A 1920s photograph of ladies at Trow Rocks returning from Lady's Bay which is off to the right.

The heavy-handedness of the Tyne Commissioners often resulted in letters of complaint to the local newspaper.

July 10,1879.

To the Editor of the Shields Daily Gazette. Sir, ——I am glad that the attention of the public has at last been called to the deliberate infringement of their rights in the neighbourhood of the Trow Rocks, the closing of footpaths which have been used uninterruptedly for so many years, especially the one leading to Ladies' Haven. Doubtless it is owing to the over zeal the servants of the Commissioners, as I really can't believe that public body like the Commissioners, who should assist the people in preserving their rights instead of attempting to rob them of them, has been guilty of this act. I, at any rate, am quite determined not to be prevented from walking over any portion of the locus in quo, and now that a move has been made that means will once taken reverse (if necessary force) the obstructions complained of, I for one will be ready any time to lend a helping hand.

Yours truly,
Robert Blair.
5 King Street,
South Shields,

These two photographs from the early twentieth century show that Trow Point returned to its prominence as a pleasure spot once the quarry had ceased major production.

A photograph taken almost in the identical spot to the one on the opposite page of the boundary of South Shields and Harton Township at Trow Point. This one was taken at the end of June, Race Week, in 1908.

223

Trow Quarry

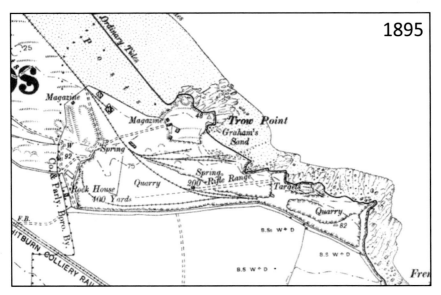

As the 1895 map above shows the coastline boundary of Harton Township extended to a little beyond Trow Point. That is where we see the long sandy beach of South Shields end and the magnesium cliffs rise up out of the sea which form the coast line south to the mouth of the River Wear.

The contemporary photograph on the opposite page shows the entire coastline that was once within Harton Township and the two magnificent piers at the mouth of the River Tyne, feats of engineering achieved at the end of the nineteenth century to offer safe protection to many of the merchant ships coming into the river.

By the mid-nineteenth century the rapid growth in trade and industry led to a growing need for improvements to the poorly-maintained River Tyne. On 15th July, 1850, the Tyne Improvement Act received Royal Assent and stewardship of the river passed to the newly-created Tyne Improvement Commission. In 1854 the commissioners began a programme of development and improvement to the navigation of the river that continued into the twentieth century; this included dredging and deepening the channel and constructing new infrastructure including docks, coal and shipping staithes and a pair of piers (North and South Piers) to protect the mouth of the river at Tynemouth and South Shields. The Tyne subsequently became one of the principal ports of the United Kingdom and enabled the development of the great ship building and ship repairing industries for which the river became world-famous. On 31st July, 1968, the Tyne Improvement Commission was dissolved, and replaced with the Port of Tyne Authority.

Good quality stone was needed to build the piers and a perfect site, a mere mile away was found. In April 1854 the Commissioners purchased for £6,793 the freehold and leasehold interests in thirty-six acres of land at Trow Rocks, in Harton Township, from which to quarry the material for the piers from the Ecclesiastical Commissioners. A single track railway was constructed along the level coastal edge and thence to the stone yard at the site of the South Pier, in South Shields. (This is not the Marsden Rattler, which can be seen in the corner of the map opposite labelled as the Whitburn Colliery Railway.) More than three million tonnes of stone was used in the construction of the piers, and the stone used on the lower courses, facings and both lighthouses was magnesium limestone quarried at the Tyne Commissioners Trow Quarry.

The map opposite shows the footprint of the quarry and the railway tracks, rifle range, magazines and buildings which formed part of it. There are some superb accompanying photographs in South Tyneside Libraries which present its buildings, railway trucks, steam engines and cranes. Quarrying finally ceased in the 1950s and the area was used as land fill site through to the 1970s. It is now managed by the National Trust as a recreational area.

A selection of photographs of Trow Quarry during its working life.
The Quarry cut into the cliffs away from the sea and left Trow point which was
in use as a civil defence area as can be seen by the guns visible in the above
photograph .

The small pillar shaped rock was known as Graham's Rock.

Another large area of rock was left as protection between the sea and the
quarry as at Trow Point and as this had been the area of the rifle range it
became known as Target Rock.

The photographs opposite show the cranes and some of the buildings
associated with the quarry, none of which now exist. Most of the photographs
on these pages date from the early 1900s

The photograph below from 1937 captures the steam train heading off from
Trow Quarry to the stone yard at the pier head. In the distance along the
promenade can been seen the columns of the shelter known locally as
Ghandi's Monument and now converted into Colman's Seafood Temple.

Postcard in the collection of Ernest Lewthwaite

On the edge of the quarry the 1895 map names Rock House. This may locally have been known as The Nest, which, as can been seen from the above, was so well known locally at that time, that postcards were produced of it. Doris Johnson writing in volume 1 of her book, *South Shields in Old Picture Postcards*, page 72 states that:

The Nest, the old thatched cottage near Trow Quarry, was the home of the first on site foreman for the building of the south pier. There was quite a number of these cottages put up by workers, as when they came in the 1850s there were few building regulations and no Medical Officer of Health. The Nest was quite close to the old borough boundary stone which was to the south of the road which now runs from the Broadway down to Trow Rock Car Park. Hence placing it exactly in the same position as Rock House.

Another house clearly shown in the images opposite sitting on top of Trow Rock was linked to the military defence site on the rock and will be discussed later in this chapter. Then there were, according to the census returns of 1871, 1881, 1891 and 1901, two other dwellings on the site.

In the 1891 census the following families are living at Trow Quarry:

1 John Marshall 54, a general labourer, born in Nottinghamshire, a widower with three of his children, Sarah Medley 28 married, acting as his

housekeeper, Isabella 14, and John 12, all three born in South Shields. Also Frances Beecroft 3 years old born at Trow Rocks, and Henry Dining 82, John's father-in-law, a retired pitman from Hebburn,

2 Henry Dack 36, a general labourer from Norfolk. Alice Dack 36, his wife from Leicestershire and Frank Dack 21, his brother, a general labourer from Norfolk.

3 Thos Skimmings 40, a Corporal in the Royal Artillery and Harriet Skimmings 31, his wife, both born in Essex. With William Geo Skimmings their one year old son born at Trow Rocks.

4 John McDonald 55, quarry foreman, his wife Margaret McDonald 58 and John McDonald 28, their son, a general labourer, all from Scotland.

The 1901 census places the following families at Trow Quarry, two are still the same families as in 1891:

1 Trow Rock Cottage John McDonald 65, Margaret 68, John 38, all from Scotland and Isabella 25 (from South Shields, married to John), Margaret 5 and John 4, both born in Harton.

2 Trow Rock Gun station Charles Moore 46, Gunman Royal Artillery, from Suffolk and his wife Margaret 40, from Morpeth Northumberland,

3 Joseph Spooner 47, joiner and his wife Elizabeth 47, both from Norfolk, plus their six children, 5 girls and a boy all except the youngest born in South Shields while Beatrice, 4 years old, was born in Harton.

4 John Marshall, a widower of 62, a worker at the limestone quarry from Nottinghamshire and Frances Beecroft, his granddaughter, 13 years old, born in Harton.

Along with the four dwellings and the engine house and warehouse stores there are two magazines mentioned on the 1895 map. One was for the defence emplacement on the top of Trow Point the other for the quarry. The quarry one down in the sand frequently needed to be dug out, as can be imagined from the photograph opposite.

The quarry magazine in the sand at the foot of Trow Point, shown on the 1895 map on page 226.

A view from Trow Point looking over Graham's Sands in 2021, nothing but the void created by the quarry exists. This is the bay which was known locally as Lady's Bay and it was here that for a time as well as quarry machinery there was a rifle range, the rock in the distance is still frequently referred to as Target Rock.

The top photograph is of the first drill of the 3rd Durham Artillery taken in 1860. Many named in the shot became prominent local men in their later lives. Such as Robert Blair who was later to live in Harton Lodge and to lead the 1875 excavation of the Roman Fort in South Shields (*The People's Roman Remains book and Harton Village 1900 book*) and John Salmon the son of the then current Town Clerk of South Shields who was to become the owner of Marsden Cottage.

A photograph on page 228 shows the guns positioned on Trow Point.

The lower photograph from 2021 shows the mount for the later guns used by the 3rd Durham Artillery as part of the coastal defence system.

The 205 (3rd Durham Volunteer Artillery) Battery Royal Artillery, are still present in Harton/South Shields, their drill hall is just off the coast at Northfield Road; nicknamed Frenchman's Fort.

Coastal Defences

The cliffs in Harton Township offered a good coastal defence position.

In 1864 Major Stevenson of the South Shields Volunteer Corps was successful in obtaining from the Tyne Commissioners a suitable site to position a practice battery for the newly formed Third Durham Artillery Volunteers at Trow Point. *The corps now (1901) have a battery of two 32 pounders and one 64 pounder in position there.* (Hodgson p462.) Later there would be two 64 pound guns. (the

The photograph opposite shows the first drill of the Third Durham Artillery Volunteers with one of their 32 muzzle loaded smooth bore guns mounted on a garrison carriage.

The colour photograph shows the holdfasts for the mountings of the two 64 pounder rifle muzzle loading guns on traversing slides, which are still visible at Trow Point.

Industrialisation and technology moved forward in the Victorian period. But war and the threat of invasion was never far off, the unification of Germany in 1870 and the rise of its navy caused many in the government to consider the weakness of industrial ports and ship building centres like the Tyne. New weapon systems were explored and one experimentation took place in Harton Township beside the Trow Quarry on Trow Point in 1887:

Hiram Maxim and his company (more infamous for their invention of the machine gun) designed and constructed a disappearing, or floating, gun emplacement. The concept of this was that a gun could be mounted in a low, robust, concrete emplacement set into the cliff top, that would be hard to spot and harder to hit. The gun would be housed and loaded down inside the emplacement and then, using hydraulics and pneumatics, raised up briefly to fire before dropping down again.

The Trow Rock Floating Platform was also known as the Clarke-Maxim Disappearing Platform for barbette mountings. The Clarke-Maxim mounting first appeared in 1885. The trial for this new maxim mounting took place one and half miles south of the mouth of the Tyne at Trow Rock (NZ385667), hence its name.

233

A replica six inch gun was mounted on the emplacement in 1987.

The Durham Artillery Volunteers had three obsolete 32pr guns mounted there for practice. Also a small magazine for which they paid a nominal annual sum to the Tyne Improvement Commissioners who owned the site. In 1885 they were asked to lease/lend the site to the War Office. It was leased for a year and in May 1886 the pit was excavated to a depth of fourteen feet for the mounting. In October 1886 Maxims agreed to construct the emplacement at their own expense and to have it ready for trial within four months. It was not ready until December 1886 and the trials took place in December 1887 with the 6inch B.L. Mk IV gun.

The Elswick mounting at Shoeburyness proved to be more successful and was adopted for service. The Clarke-Maxim mounting was declared 'unlikely to be of any value and no more should be constructed'. The lease of the land was terminated in 1894; the machinery was removed and the emplacement filled. The site reverted to its use for volunteer practice.

The extensive growth of the adjoining limestone quarries had left the site on an island of higher ground. A late 19th century map shows a rifle range, presumable for the use of volunteers, established in the floor of the quarry.

Hodgson explains on p463, about the splendid range at Harton:
In July 1900 the proposal, made as an outcome of the South African War then raging, that Civilian Rifle Clubs should be formed throughout the country, was enthusiastically taken up in South Shields. A Club was formed, with the Earl of Durham as President, and obtained nearly 300 members in a very brief period. The members practise at the Harton Range (por at Trow Rocks in the summer months, while a Morris Tube is provided for practice during the winter.

The small magazine used by the 3rd Durham Volunteers was augmented in the 1880s by a shell filling room and accommodation for a resident gunner and his family, who served as caretaker for the sight. Quite a dangerous place with dynamite stores for the quarry too.

As well as the site on Trow Point a further defence site on the cliffs just to the south of Trow Quarry was planned in 1882, and finished in March 1905. I The fort at Frenchman's Point was designed as a counterpart to the battery at Tynemouth Castle. It had two 6 inch guns, and one 9.2 inch. The shells were raised on a hydraulic lift. There was a caretaker's house, stores and a camping ground.

AZETTE AND SHIPPING TELEGRAPH, WEDNESDAY, JUNE 24, 1903.

THE NEW FORT
AT FRENCHMAN'S POINT.

THIRD DURHAM VOLUNTEER ARTILLERY CAMP.

VISIT OF LORD ROBERTS.

No. 1. No. 2

No. 3 No. 4

1.—The Volunteer Camp. 3.—The Cliffs at Frenchman's Bay.
2.—Two of the Big Guns. 4.—The New Fort.

Just months after opening, it was downgraded to practice only, to have some of its guns reinstated again by 1911. In 1913, realising the importance of the arms production and shipbuilding trade on the Tyne (which at this time accounted for 30% of naval production in Britain) the Admiralty rearmed Frenchman's Point Battery accordingly. Huts were built for the permanent soldiers. A large galvanised steel fence with prongs around the top to deflect bullets was constructed. Frenchman's Point Battery served throughout WW1. Four years after hostilities ended, in July 1922, the site was dismantled and cleared, being redeveloped as a holiday camp, however it was resurrected at the start of WW2 as an anti-aircraft artillery battery.

The newspaper report of Wednesday, 24th June, 1903, recording the visit of Lord Roberts, Commander in Chief, to the camp offers this description of Frenchman's Fort:

THE NEW FORT AT FRENCHMAN'S POINT. THIRD DURHAM VOLUNTEER ARTILLERY CAMP. VISIT OF LORD ROBERTS.

The new fort at Frenchman's Point, although its construction is of recent days, has quite a long history as a part of the general scheme of

coast fortifications. Fully quarter of a century ago the situation was mapped out by the War Office authorities as eminently suited for coast defence purposes. But the War Office are proverbially slow to move, has been reserved for the great movement in the direction of shore defence works to witness the consummation of the scheme. The construction of this new stronghold has, so far the masonry and excavations are concerned, taken over two years. It is built bed rock foundation and fortified with powerful ordinance and equipment of the most modern type. The armament includes two 6-inch Q.F. breach loading guns, and a heavy 9.2, the latter being of new type B. I. The whole of the guns have been made the Elswick Ordnance Works.

Only the two quick-firing guns have, so far, been placed in position for permanent service. They were used for the first time by the volunteers in camp last week, and then only on the occasion of the visit of the inspecting officer when the charge was reduced to one half. They weigh seven tons each, have muzzle velocity of 2,154 feet per second, and fire a projectile 100lbs in weight, the rate fire being approximately four rounds per minute. Their range is effective, being seven to eight miles.

The 9.2-inch gun will not be ready for official trial before the end of August. Although in the British Army the 9.2-inch gun is not known as a quick firing gun, its rate of fire—once in three-quarters of a minute—compares favourably with similar guns in foreign armies, which are called "quick firing". It weighs about 23 tons, fires projectile weighing 380 lbs, which leaves the muzzle of the gun at the high velocity of 2,600 feet per second. Its penetrating power Harveyed steel is 20.5 inches, and it has an effective range of 14,000 yards. It could easily, therefore, drop a shell into Blyth.

The fort completely equipped with means for securing precision and efficiency in marksmanship. With recent developments in the science of gunnery a remarkable system has been perfected for the regulation and practice of the fire of a fortress such as this. The invention and adoption of instruments known as "position finders" and "depression range finders" enables the fire to be directed with great precision upon given spots likely to be passed by ships, and the equipment of the fort in this respect is complete in every detail. Besides being a formidable fortress it therefore promises to be a valuable training school as well for our volunteers, upon whom presumably would devolve the responsibility of running the fort—with small stiffening of Royal Garrison Artillery—in the event of an unexpected invasion.

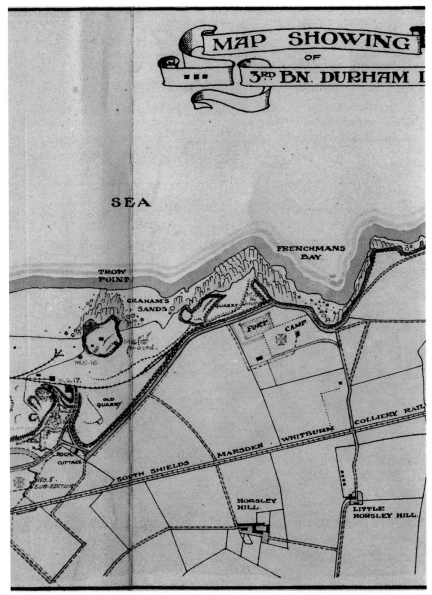

DLI Costal Defences Map from WW1, showing the area within to Harton Township.
Reproduced by permission of the Trustees of the former DLI and Durham County Record Office.
Durham County Record Office D/DLI 2/3/10

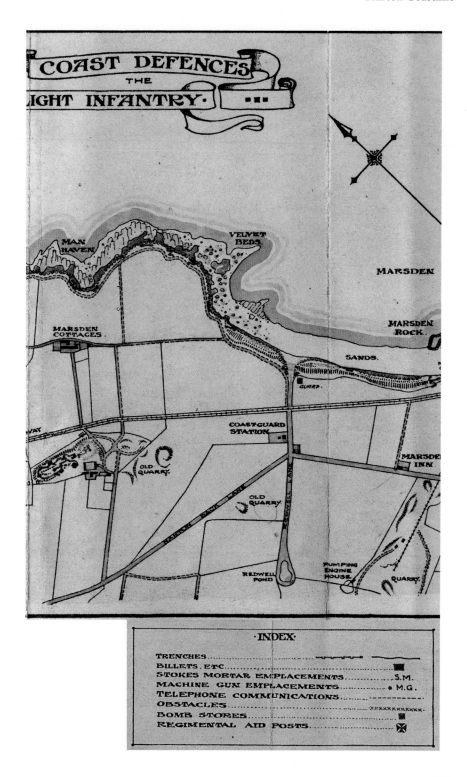

COAST DEFENCES
THE
LIGHT INFANTRY. ...

MAN HAVEN

VELVET BEDS.

MARSDEN

MARSDEN COTTAGES.

MARSDEN ROCK

SANDS.

GUARD.

COASTGUARD STATION

OLD QUARRY.

OLD QUARRY

MARSDEN INN

REDWELL POND

PUMPING ENGINE HOUSE

QUARRY.

·INDEX·

TRENCHES	
BILLETS, ETC.	
STOKES MORTAR EMPLACEMENTS	S.M.
MACHINE GUN EMPLACEMENTS	• M.G.
TELEPHONE COMMUNICATIONS	
OBSTACLES	xxxxxxxxxxxx
BOMB STORES	
REGIMENTAL AID POSTS	

1914: DEFENDING THE TYNE

JONATHAN JONES recalls the life of Leslie Robert Tilley, a battery gunner at South Shields during World War One:

LESLIE Robert Tilley was born in Enfield, Essex, on 11th April 1889, into a family of light engineers, predominantly well sinkers. The family business, Thomas Tilley and Sons Limited, had been started by Leslie's grandfather, who'd started life as a coppersmith, approximately 100 years before the birth of his grandson.

Leslie was the second child of Ernest John Tilley and Ellen (Nellie) Kain. He was educated at the Royal Grammar School, in Enfield, and studied for a brief period at London University, from which he was removed for, in his own words, 'lack of progress', in 1908. Apparently his love of the rowdy music halls of the time, did not sit well with the academic standards of the university.

After leaving London University he was articled to a firm of water engineers in Walton-on-the-Naze, in Essex. Following the failure of the family business, 25-year-old Leslie found himself apprenticed to another firm of engineers, and spent the summer of 1914, just prior to the outbreak of WWI, supervising the laying of water pipes in the Sunderland area, taking every opportunity, in his spare time, to go sailing along the North East coast.

It was only natural that when war broke out, Leslie signed up, as soon as his contract in Sunderland permitted. He was among the first volunteers, all who had bought the promise that the war would be over by Christmas. Thankfully, his previous career and training had left him with the technical skills to join one of the 'specialist corp', and he joined a reserve company of the Royal Garrison Artillery, based in North Shields, in December 1914.

Here he takes up the story of his WWI career:
As I liked sailing, knew how to use a shotgun, and the technicalities of sending water through several miles of pipe, it seemed only natural to the powers that be that I would be best suited to the principles of long range gunnery. I was commissioned as a second lieutenant in the Royal Garrison Artillery (Special Reserve), a 'one pipper', or 'terrier' and a temporary gentleman. I was posted to the Frenchman's Point Battery, at Trow Point in South Shields. This had two six-inch guns covering Tynemouth and a 9.2-inch gun at the southern end of the position. Our battery was in the No.3 Military Fieldwork zone, in the local defence scheme.

It was described to the public as **the area lying between the sea and an imaginary line drawn from Trow Point westward to Horsley Hill Farm, and thence through Little Horsley hill, Harton Down Hill Farm, and Marsden Cottage, to the sea.** *Our gun batteries weren't terribly secret. Plenty of foreign seamen were familiar with the layout of the port facilities. Merchant ships from Germany had been regular visitors to the Tyne before the war. The gun-battery at Frenchman's Point was an open secret, tucked away below a stretch of railway. So it made no difference to the war effort when the gun position was spelled out in the newspapers. However, the newspapers also warned that anyone approaching the position without warning, in darkness or in fog, would be shot.*

The 'Gambardiers', as servicemen in the RGA were known, were prized for their understanding of so-called 'technical' or 'slide-rule' gunnery. We understood the mysteries of range tables, basically how to hit the target at very long ranges. We also knew the plan for a navigational 'box', set up a mile and a half offshore. This had been worked out before the war. All vessels wishing to enter the Tyne were to anchor there to be boarded by the crew of an examination steamer. All this took place under the gaze of the 6 inch guns at Spaniard's Point under Tynemouth Castle. In the event of a ship behaving suspiciously, a single warning shot was allowed. If this was ignored, all guns in range would let fly.

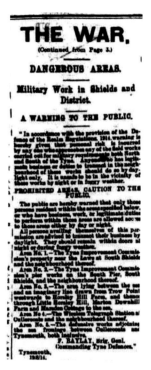

THE WAR.

(Continued from Page 3.)

DANGEROUS AREAS.

Military Work in Shields and District.

A WARNING TO THE PUBLIC.

Second Lieutenant Leslie Robert Tilley and opposite the newspaper article he recalls in his description of his time at Frenchman's Fort during WW1.

In those early days we were subjected to almost daily battery drills, including the use of searchlights and floodlights, test firings and security exercises, until we could have carried them out as we slept. The ink had barely dried on my commission when we were put on high alert. On December 16th, 1914, the German Navy launched an audacious attack on the British mainland, including sending six battleships to bombard coastal towns of North Eastern England. Scarborough was one of the towns hardest hit. Its inhabitants didn't stand a chance, as one tonne shell after one tonne shell rained down on the town. It's estimated that as many as 1,150 shells fell on Scarborough on that mid-December night, killing several hundred people, and injuring dozens more. However, closer to my battery, in Hartlepool, the German battleships didn't have it all their own way, and were forced to withdraw, after suffering damage from the defender's guns. A small victory for our side, considering what had happened further down the coast.

But it wasn't all defending British shores against the German navy. The garrison at Frenchman's Point also had to be alert to help shipping that got into trouble in the sometimes treacherous seas around the North East coast. One such incident involved a Dutch merchant ship, the Sliedrecht, which went ashore on rocks close to Frenchman's Point. Again, Leslie takes up the story:

On the 18th of March, 1915, the Sliedrecht went ashore at the cliffs at Frenchman's Point. The officers and men from our battery, and some troops garrisoned on the coast, went to help.

Under law all ships had to carry rockets to launch ropes ashore, if they got into trouble, although on this occasion they didn't do much good. Someone at the battery called for more rockets to be brought to the cliff-top. An officer of Tynemouth RGA, 2nd Lieutenant Nisbet, was a member of Tynemouth Volunteer Life Brigade and knew how to fire a rope to a ship. While that was in hand four gunners from Tynemouth RGA scrambled down the cliff. When the ship ran out of rockets after only getting a single rope ashore, Lieutenant Nisbet came up with an expedient, lowering a length of metal on a rope. The ship was only five yards from the cliff-face by this time. With two ropes attaching her to the land all 26 crew were saved by the gunners from the battery.

The Dutch captain, and a few of the crew, went back on board once it became clear that the ship wasn't severely holed. The ship was later salvaged and brought into the Tyne.

Danger didn't only come from the sea, as Leslie explains:
On the 15th July, 1915, Zeppelins launched a major raid on the Tyne causing 18 dead and many wounded, the heaviest casualties in any air raid on Britain so far.

On the 23rd July 1915 I was promoted Lieutenant. Through the Autumn, Winter and the Spring that followed, I waited for an enemy fleet that never arrived. I could see most of the Tyne defences from my battery position, but we gradually realised that we weren't really needed. The Admiralty had no further need to call on the coastal defence gunners. Depending on your point of view, we were either a body of skilled artillerymen dying on the vine, or a pool of useful labour awaiting redeployment.

I saw my last enemy Zeppelins over the Tyne in April, 1916. Newcastle's defence lay increasingly with aircraft and the Admiralty also ordered dozens of 'spotter' dirigible balloons for routine naval patrols.

Shortly afterward any involvement between myself and the Frenchman's Point battery ended. The following month I was off to Shoeburyness in the Thames Estuary for instruction in anti-aircraft fire. From there on, I would be on the Western Front with the First Army.

I later heard that the Frenchman's Point Battery was emptied in 1922. After the war I believe a Mr Wilson bought the land around the gun battery and the battery itself. He later abandoned attempts to dynamite the gun-placements and magazine, and operated the remainder of the site as a holiday camp, until it was abandoned in the late 1930s.

Although Leslie's involvement ends there, the history of the battery does not. In WWII the position was re-occupied by the Royal Artillery and searchlight crews, who created a small military village behind the cliff-top. Unfortunately, the gunners had no previous fort book to refer to when they tried to write a history of the site, when it was decommissioned in 1945. The only information that was available was that the battery had contained two 6" guns and a 9.2" gun during the period 1914-18.

By Jonathan Jones, assisted by Mark Tilley

A WW2 aerial photograph of the fort and camp plus the new Little Horsley Hill Council Housing Estate behind the Coast Road. The Coast Road was built in 1928 and Little Horsley Hill Estate in the 1930s.

Opposite are advertising materials for the camp between the wars when it was being used as a holiday camp. In the lower post the photograph shows a caravan and tents but also the original brick and wooden buildings of the fort.

Frenchman's Bay Holiday Camp

(Near the famous Marsden Rock & Grotto)

- Every accommodation including Field for Sports, Bathing, Boating, Fishing, Football, Cricket and Dancing. Also Large Recreation Hall.

Provision Stores in the Camp.

- Bungalows and Bell Tents with every convenience for Hire.
- Sunday Schools, Boy Scouts, Girl Guides, Boys Brigade, Cycling Clubs, and all Picnic Parties Catered for at moderate prices.
- Garage and Good Parking Ground.

BOOK EARLY AND AVOID DISAPPOINTMENT.

G. B. WILSON
FORT HOUSE, FRENCHMAN'S BAY, South Shields

Telephone : South Shields 1204

FRENCHMANS BAY SO.SHIELDS
HOLIDAY CAMP.
BUNGALOWS & BELL TENTS FOR HIRE
APPLY G.B.WILSON. PHONE 1204.

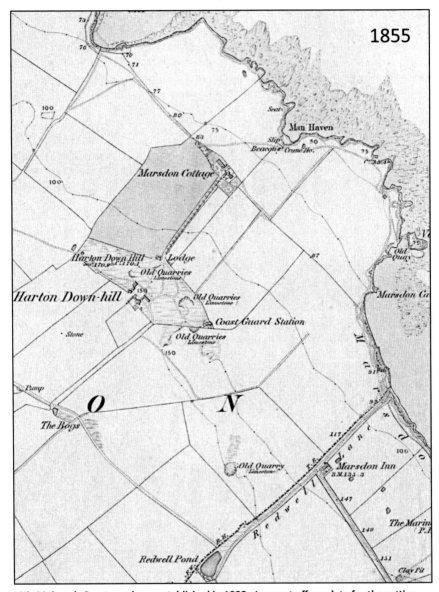

1855

His Majesty's Coastguard was established in 1822. I cannot offer a date for the setting up of a Coastguard Station in Harton Township, but there on this 1855 map, on the superb natural lookout position of Harton Down Hill is recorded a *Coast Guard Station*.

The Coastguards

As Historic England explains in their introduction to Coastguard Stations:

Britain is a maritime nation, and since Roman times has had structures adorning the coastline dedicated to maintaining a watch over shore and coastal waters. In recent centuries these have been constructed for various reasons including the prevention of smuggling, locating and co-ordinating assistance to ships in distress or as part of defensive facilities against attack or invasion. Since 1822 many of these sites have been occupied by, and constructed for, Her Majesty's Coastguard. When first established, the Coastguard inherited facilities from previous government initiatives to counter the clandestine transportation of goods. These provided the basis of what became a national network of coastguard stations.

The initial purpose of the Coastguard was revenue protection, but this altered during the 19th century to that of a naval reserve. The service also had some life-saving responsibilities and in the 1920s this became its primary role, along with coastal observation. These shifts in function were often accompanied by administrative change, as control of the service was passed between different government bodies. The duties were carried out from land-based stations but also sometimes from ships. The Coastguard has also maintained a close association with other coastal rescue services, most particularly the lifeboat service and life-saving companies and brigades.

Until the late 20th century the basic elements of a Coastguard station usually consisted of accommodation for Coastguards, a watch room or house, boathouse and equipment store. These facilities were sometimes supplemented by subsidiary lookouts or watch towers. In the early years of the service the premises were often leased, but from the mid 19th century they were increasingly purpose-built. Over the last two centuries the numbers of stations has fluctuated, probably reaching a peak of over 500 in the early 20th century. Their locations have varied from isolated coastal or estuarine situations to seafront positions in towns and ports. Architecturally there has been a considerable variety in the style and building materials of the station buildings although a degree of standardisation seems to have taken place from the turn of the 20th century.

The section of the 1855 map on the previous page shows a coastguard station at Harton Downhill. It was not until 1881 that Marsden, the part lying in Harton Township, received purpose-built coastguard houses; two cottages and a rocket-cart house. *The Shields Daily Gazette* of Wednesday 20th June, 1881 ran the following advert on the front page calling for tenders.

Coastguard Contracts
To Builders and Contractors

Tenders for the erection of TWO Cottages and a ROCKET-CART HOUSE for the Coastguard at Marsden, in the County of Durham will be received at this Office, at noon on Tuesday 5th July 1881.

The drawings and specifications may be seen at the Watch Room, Coastguard Station, South Shields.

Bills of quantities may be received on application to this Office.

Director of Works Department, Admiralty,

71 Spring Gardens, London, S.W.

June 1881

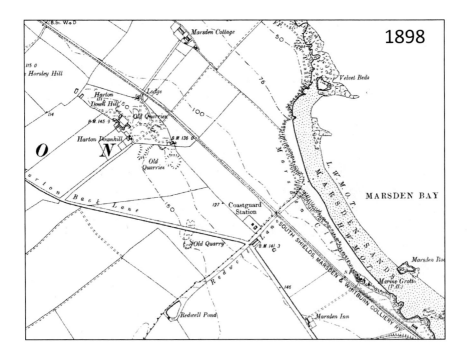

The 1898 map opposite shows the location of the purpose-built coastguard houses on Redwell Bank. Photographs exist as they were not demolished until the later part of the twentieth century and replaced by some bungalows, but the impressive front garden wall still remains.

A photograph from the 1960s showing the coastguards' houses on the lefthand side of Redwell Bank

The census returns show how these coastguard families were not local people, initially one assumes because of their need to be apart from whatever illicit smuggling maybe happening with in the community. The advert is for two cottages and the early census of 1871, shows that it was two coastguard families that lived at the Harton Down Hill Station.

In the 1871 census the coastguard families recorded at Harton Down Hill were:

1 John Harvey 33 and his wife Mary Ann Harvey 30, both from Devon and their eighteen month old son, born in Harton, John James Godfrey Harvey and Mary Ann Godfrey 66, John's mother-in-law, from Somerset

2 William Baser 36 and his wife Jane Baser 34 and their children; Robert James Baser 7 Eliza Maria Jane Baser 2, and Henry Charles Ryde Baser 9 months old. The baby was born in Harton, the others are from Devon, so the Baser's obviously only arrived in Harton in the previous year or two.

In the 1891 census the two families are
1 Joseph Podesta 34, his wife Shirley 38, their daughter Annie 6, all from Hampshire.

2 J T Tagget 37, his wife Evangeline 36, both from Cornwall

In the 1901 census the two families are:
1 John T Burgess 44, from Lambeth London and his wife Mary 41, from Whitehaven, Cumberland, their children; John 15, a coal miner, underground, Frederick 14, coal miner, underground, William 12, Albert 8, Florence 5 and Beatrice 4. All except Beatrice were born in Northumberland while she was born in South Shields

2 Charles E Richie 29, from Limehouse, London, his wife Linda 34, from Blackheath, London, their four month old son Charles, born in Harton and Mary Wakeman, Charles' aunt, a widow of 75 living on own means, originally from Devon

ROAD WORKS ... Redwell Bank before the last war, with the Coastguard House on the right.

The coastguards although originally empowered to catch smugglers, must by these dates have become an integral part of this ever watchful community living so near to the cliffs in Harton. That the local Harton community, small though it was along the coastline, were always aware of the sea and its threat and often supported and assisted the coastguards is recorded in various newspaper articles. A few are mentioned in other chapters, such Mr Snowdon the farmer of Harton Down Hill (p110) rushing to assist the coastguards which were at that time stationed right next to his house and Mr John Varley of Marsden Cottage (p178) raising the alarm for the coastguards. The following are a selection from the numerous reports in the local newspapers concerning shipping disasters and loss of life in the area; often the coastguards had a major role to play.

Sunderland Daily Echo, Friday, 2nd April, 1886:

A DEAD BODY FOUND AT MARSDEN.

Yesterday afternoon, about four o'clock, four men found the body of a woman, apparently about 45 years of age, amongst the rocks at the Velvet Beds, near Marsden Rock. It was laid below high water mark, and did not appear to have been long immersed in the water. The men removed the body to the Coastguard station at Marsden. It has not yet been identified.

The Newcastle Daily Chronicle, Wednesday, 9th April, 1890:

VESSELS IN DIFFICULTIES OFF MARSDEN.

A telegram from South Shields, last night, states that the coastguard at Marsden reports seeing a schooner, name unknown, in difficulties. She was in tow of a tug, when the tow lines broke. Rockets were fired, and another tug came to her assistance, but a second tow rope which was got on board also broke, and the vessel drove seawards. A Danish schooner has also been driven seawards.

SUPPOSED DISASTER OFF MARSDEN.

On Saturday about noon the coastguard stationed at Marsden were informed by a man who had been fishing beside Manhaven that he had seen a vessel founder about half a mile from the shore. A coast-guardsman hurried down to the beach opposite to where the occurrence was said to have taken place, taking lifebelts for use in case of need, but there was nothing then to be seen, except that he thought there was some small object on the surface of the water, which might be a bladder used in a fishing boat, or it might be the head of a man who was swimming, but it disappeared almost immediately. All day a strict watch was kept along the shore, but nothing cast up, and a search along the beach yesterday was also fruitless of result. The person who gave the information said the vessel had the appearance of a Scotch herring boat. There was a very heavy sea running at the time, the gale being at its height The boat was coming from the south as if bound for the Tyne, and whilst he was watching her the sail split and she immediately gave a lurch and went down. The most careful inquiries are being made as to any boat answering the description that may be missing, and it was stated that one of the fishing fleet that should have returned to the Tyne on Saturday has not turned up, but she was expected to be lying with her nets till the gale abated.

Above is a newspaper report of Monday, 24th August, 1891, with a follow up report the following night, Tuesday, 25th August, 1891 stating that:

A tiller, such as would be used on a Scotch herring boat, had been picked up on the beach at Marsden, and it has been taken possession of by the Coastguard.

So intrinsically linked to the sea, reports of shipping were of constant interest to everyone reading the local newspapers of the day. Ships coming in and out the Tyne were reported on daily and the local newspaper, for a time, was called *The Shields Daily Gazette and Shipping Telegraph*.

The Shields Daily Gazette and Shipping Telegraph, Thursday, 14th August, 1890:

WRECKAGE NEAR MARSDEN.

The coastguard authorities at South Shields yesterday received information that some wreckage had been cast ashore at Lady Bay, near Marsden. Coastguardsman Lapsley, directed by Chief Officer Lorden, proceeded to the place, and found the wreckage, which appeared to be portions of a fishing boat. There were also near the place a mast and a brown sail, as well as a number of bladders, such as are used by fishermen. The wreckage is supposed to be that of the salmon coble Willing Lass, of North Shields, which foundered while making for the Tyne, during a strong westerly gale, on the morning of the 22nd ult., when two men were drowned.

The Shields Daily Gazette, 14th April, 1902:

BODY OF A MAN FOUND AT THE TROW ROCKS, SOUTH SHIELDS.

Last night the body of man was found on the sands near the Trow Rocks, South Shields, and P.C. Owen and a coastguardsman removed it to the mortuary at the Laws. There were five wounds on the left side of the face, having apparently being caused by deceased being washed about amongst the rocks. The body that of a man fairly well dressed, between 45 and 50 years of age, 5 feet 8 or 9 inches in height, stout build, fresh complexion, dark brown hair, bald on the top of the head, and ginger moustache. The clothing consisted of a grey woollen under shirt, lace boots, white collar and front, black tie fastened with two brass studs, and brown checked suit. A purse was found on the body containing two keys with a label attached belonging to the Key and Property Registry, Hope Street, Glasgow, and numbered 17,947. From appearances, the body seams to have been in the water only few hours.

The Shields Daily News, Saturday, 20th January, 1917:

THE BODY FOUND ON MARSDEN BEACH. Inquiry at Harton.

An inquest was before the Deputy Coroner (Mr A. Shepherd) the Harton Institution, on the body of an unknown man found on the sands at Marsden Tuesday the 16th inst.

Arthur Reginald Jones, 14 years a sea scout, stationed Marsden, and living in Eleanor Street, South Shields, said at 5 o'clock the 16th inst. he was walking along the sands at the north end of Marsden Bay, in company another sea scout, named Robert Wilkinson, when they came across the body of man partly covered with sea weed. The top part of the head was gone, and the face was unrecognisable. The body was nude. Witness informed the coastguard, and also P.C. Reed, who had the remains removed. There was nothing beside the body.

P.O. Geo. Reed, of the Durham County Police, stationed Marsden Colliery, said on receipt of the information from the Sea Scout Jones, he proceeded the north end of Marsden Beach, and found the body there as described. The top part of the head was missing, and the left leg broken. The body had apparently been left by the tide. It appeared to have been in water for some time. With the assistance of the coastguards he removed it the mortuary at Harton.

P.C. Simpson of County Police, stationed at Harton, said he had made every inquiry, but had failed to got the body identified. There had been a large number people at the mortuary, but none of them had been able to identify it. He (the sergeant) did not think himself, it was possible for the body to be identified, having regard to the state it was in, the fact that there were no clothes and no tattoo marks. A woman came down from Newcastle yesterday, to see if it was the body of her husband, a soldier, who had been missing since a week past Monday, but she failed to recognise it. He (the sergeant) didn't think it could be that this particular man as he had only been missing a week, whereas this body appeared to have been in the water three weeks or a month. ....

The Deputy Coroner said the curious thing to his mind was the fact that the body was entirely nude. It might be the body a member of the crew of a ship that had been torpedoed. That seemed to him the most likely explanation of this peculiar circumstance might be that the man had only his trousers on and came up on deck just as the ship was struck. He would then probably toss his few clothes off with the idea of trying to swim ashore. He thought, however, they should return a verdict of "Found dead on the beach," because there was no evidence that he had heed drowned.

The jury returned a verdict as suggested by the deputy coroner.

WIRELESS TELEGRAPHY AT MARSDEN.

The site of the proposed Marconi signalling station at Marsden has been selected, and the motive power, generating plant, and other apparatus will be in buildings which will be erected between the Marsden Coastguard Station and the colliery, a short distance inland. The installation will be provided at a point on the cliff tops to the north of Marsden Bay, and it is expected that telephonic communication will be established with the fort at Frenchman's Bay.

On Friday, 5th August, 1904 this newspaper report explains that a leap forward in communication was being brought to Marsden. A Marconi signalling station was to be erected. Coastguard lookout positions continued to be of great importance for many further decades. This one positioned so precariously on the cliff edge between Trow and Frenchman's Bay, was photographed in the 1960s though no longer operational by that time.

DIG THIS ... Trow Quarry and the old coastguard lookout in the early 1960s.

Two photographs of the twentieth century coastguard look on Harton Down Hill. The upper one showing the rear view, with the lookout positioned to have commanding views of the coastline.

The advert for the construction of the 1881 coastguard houses at Redwell Bank (p250) does not mention a look out and it may have been that the coastguards maintained their original look out on Harton Down Hill, which was just a short walk from their new station. A concrete building supposed by many to be a WW2 gun emplacement may have been a twentieth century coastguard lookout on the site, as it is exactly the same construction as that on the promontory at Trow, with a thin concrete roof and open front and sides offering uninterrupted views of the coastline, rather than a small gun portal as seen in WW2 bunkers. Similar indeed, to many coastguard stations up and down the coast still in use today.

Hengtisbury Head Coastguard Station.

This article from Tuesday, 2nd June, 1903, shows the breadth of incidents the coastguards were involved in and also has so much resonance with incidents we still report today.

MARSDEN ADVENTURE.

CAUGHT BY THE TIDE.

Two visitors to the seaside, yesterday, had a narrow escape with their lives through being overtaken by the tide on a base of rocks just a little south of Marsden Bay. It appears that John Liddle, of Newcastle, and a Miss Hall, of Manchester, had been spending the day at the seaside, and had found their way on to some low lying rocks at a point a little distant from Marsden, underneath the cliffs, which at this part are over 100 feet high. They had apparently not see the danger of their position until they discovered that their retreat was cut off by the rising tide which was fast creeping upon them. They raised an alarm and attracted the attention of several people on shore. Their position was extremely perilous, for they had reached the rocks evidently when the tide had been back, and the rising tide had made them prisoners, with no means of escape. Their predicament gave rise to grave fears by those who had seen them from the sea banks, and it was at first suggested that a boat should be launched and taken round from Marsden to their rescue; but this idea had to be abandoned on account of the difficulties which would have to be overcome in order to get the boat near enough to enable them to be taken off. A message was quickly despatched to the coastguard station at Marsden, and the chief officer (Mr Williams) was communicated with at the South Shields station. In the meantime the coastguard at Marsden took prompt action with a view to effecting, if possible, the rescue of the lady and gentleman who were fast becoming surrounded by the rising sea. Coastguardsmen Matters and Ritchie promptly got out the cliff ladders, and commenced their work of rescue. In their efforts they were assisted by the Marsden Life Saving Company. Matters descended at considerable risk to himself, whilst Ritchie superintended operations from the cliff top. An enormous crowd had by this time been attracted to the scene, and considerable anxiety was manifested for the unfortunate people down below. Eventually Mr Liddle and Miss Hall were rescued from their predicament, and brought safely up the ladders to the top of the cliff. The couple were naturally very much exhausted and unnerved by their most trying experience. They state that their rescuers came to their aid just in the nick of time, for their position was becoming more dangerous every minute, and they were completely surrounded by the rising tide. Mr Liddle, it appears, resides in Clumber Street, Newcastle.

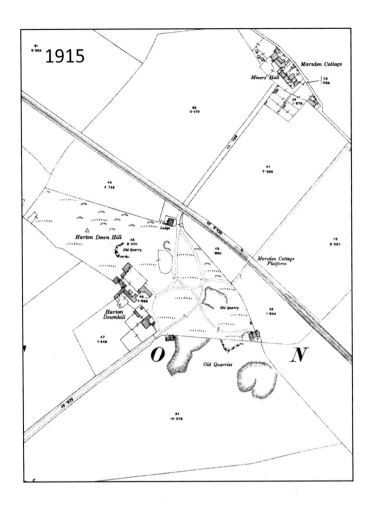

Marsden Cottage Platform

The Marsden Rattler is the local nickname for a railway which ran along the coast from Whitburn Colliery a mile or so south of Harton Township to a station in South Shields renamed in 1900 as Westoe Lane. It had one stop or rather halt midway and that was Marsden Cottage Platform, on the coast at the eastern side of Harton Down Hill, visible on the map opposite. The railway had been built as a private enterprise without an Act of Parliament in the late 1870s by the Whitburn Coal Company. It was two and three quarter miles long and a single track line.

Before the colliery at Whitburn was built, Marsden was a very small village consisting of farms, a few cottages and a lighthouse at Souter Point, the only industry in the area was limestone quarrying which was on a small scale. The Whitburn Coal Co. bought five quarries, two of which were developed as the Lighthouse (Marsden) Quarries. The Lighthouse Quarries were found to have huge reserves. The need for a greater workforce led the Whitburn Coal Company to build a new village to the north of Souter Lighthouse and in front of the quarry; 135 houses were built and about 700 people lived there. Further miners and quarrymen were needed many living in nearby South Shields. In 1888 the Board of Trade sanctioned the running of passenger services along the line. The workmen from South Shields were then able to use the railway as a means of getting to work as the direct road along the coast linking South Shields and Marsden, did not exist until November 1928.

So as well as being a mineral line the South Shields, Marsden, Whitburn Colliery railway line began to run trains to get the workforce to and from work. This is why Marsden Cottage Platform was created. By 1891, the Whitburn Coal Company was in financial difficulty, and was amalgamated with the Harton Coal Company, which continued to work the line. The Harton Coal Company bought Marsden Cottage, (locally called Salmon's Hall p164) once a huge summer home for the wealthy, turning the outbuildings into cottages and dividing the main house into separate dwellings for men working at the nearby Whitburn Colliery. Marsden Cottage Platform, a request stop, hence a halt, was provided to take the miners living at Marsden Cottage to work and their families into South Shields, where there were a choice of shops. In 1911 67 men, women and children lived in this isolated hamlet. Marsden Cottage was demolished in 1937 but the halt remained open to serve the Little Horsley Hill housing estate which had been built in the 1930s. The service eventually stopped running in the early 1950s.

The Shields Gazette Wednesday, 25th March, 1891:

MARSDEN ROCK.

MARSDEN AND SHIELDS RAILWAY.

GOOD FRIDAY AND EASTER HOLIDAYS.

On GOOD FRIDAY, Trains will run as follows :—
Leave Shields—7·10, 10·40, 11·20, 12·0 a.m., 1·20, 2·0, 3·0,
4·0, 5·0, 6·0, 7·0, 7·40, 8·20, and 9·30 p.m.
Leave Marsden—8·20, 9·0, 11·0, 11·40 a.m., 1·0, 1·40, 2·30,
3·30, 4·30, 5·30, 6·30, 7·20, 8·0, and 9·0
p.m.

On EASTER MONDAY and TUESDAY, Trains will run as
follows :—
Leave Shields—9·0 a.m., 1·30, 2·20, 3·20, 4·50, 5·35, 6·15,
7·20, 8·20, and 9·30 p.m.
Leave Marsden—9·20, 11·0 a.m., 2·0, 3·0, 4·35, 5·15, 6·55,
7·0, 8·0, and 9·0 p.m.
The Whitburn Coal Co., (Ltd.), South Shields.

The first timetable only shows a weekday service but Marsden was convenient for Marsden Rock and the beautiful bay there, so quite quickly the line began to attracted tourist traffic with a Sunday service which was slightly more frequent than the weekday service being introduced. This 1891 advert in *The Shields Gazette* 25th March, suggests extra trains ran during holiday periods. Normally the passenger trains consisted of three coaches, plus a guard's van. The railway always used secondhand coaching stock usually worn out and in quite poor condition. The riding quality of the carriages gained some notoriety and the service was given the nickname, *The Marsden Rattler* which remained with it until the service ended.

Until 1913 there were separate trains for the public and workers but after that date the same train was used with separate carriages for the miners. The coaches used by the miners were stripped of all interior partitions and fittings and fitted with wooden seats. Non-workforce passengers were directed to the correct carriage by the guard.

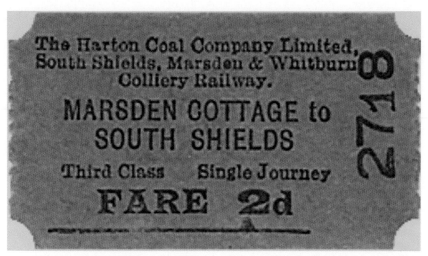

This ticket is from 1913, at that time an adult single fare for the entire journey from South Shields to Whitburn was 4d and a return ticket for the journey 6d.

The halt had a short unlit platform on the east side of the line with a brick waiting shelter. After nationalisation in 1947 the National Coal Board also provided two corrugated iron shelters, one either side of the brick shelter. The three shelters stretched the full length of the platform.

Paper tickets were issued by the conductor. Trains stopped by request only. If passengers wished to alight at the platform they would tell the guard at Westoe Lane or Marsden and he would inform the driver that the train needed to stop *half way*.

A photograph taken by Alan Snowden of Marsden Cottage Platform post-nationalisation.

The above photograph is of a passenger train leaving WhitburnColliery in about 1930.

Of a similar date is this photograph of the old bridge carrying the Marsden Rattler line at the bottom of Redwell Bank leading to Marsden Bay.

The Shields Daily Gazette and Shipping Telegraph, Monday, 30th March, 1896:

FATAL RAILWAY ACCIDENT AT MARSDEN.

A dreadful accident, attended with fatal result, occurred on the Harton Coal Company's Railway from South Shields to Marsden on Saturday night; whereby a man named Richard Newton, 51 years of age,— and who has been at the Whitburn Colliery ever since the sinking operations were in progress—lost his life. Newton, along with other three men named Robert Stafford, Alexander Wallace, and Robert Forster, all belonging to Whitburn Colliery, was going from Marsden Inn to Marsden Village, at about a quarter past ten o'clock, when nearing the railway instead of using the sub-way, they proceeded with the intention of going over the line, just before going on to the rails his companions saw the head-lights of an approaching engine and attempted to prevent deceased from crossing. He, however, freed himself from their grasp, and made the attempt, but was struck by the engine, which was running from Shields to Marsden. His lifeless body was picked up in the six foot way, having been knocked or dragged some fifteen yards. The head was fearfully mutilated and death must have been instantaneous. The rest of the body was without a scratch, although the trousers were torn.

One of the most recognised graves in St Peter's Churchyard relates to a death on the South Shields, Marsden and Whitburn Colliery Railway. It was reported in *The Shields Gazette* on Wednesday, 8th July, 1891:

AN ENGINE DRIVER KILLED NEAR MARSDEN

Robert Smith, aged 28, engine driver, engaged on the South Shields and Marsden Railway, was instantly killed last evening, through his head coming into violent contact with the wooden footbridge which spans the line near Trow Rocks. The deceased was, it appears, on the top of the engine repairing the whistle when the accident occurred, the train being in motion at the time. The deceased was conveyed to the mortuary at the Ingham Infirmary. He resided at Harton Village.

A photograph of the remains of Marsden Cottage platform in the 1960s. Norfolk Road in the new Marsden Estate is seen in the distance on the right. Hence this image shows the exact position of the platform, at the bottom of Harton Down Hill and the coast road running alongside.

The lower photograph looking from the opposite direction is taken as the train approaches Marsden Bay with the rear of Grotto Road houses on the left side.

Harton Moor

Chapter 5

Introduction

Harton Moor, lying on the west side of the hill where Harton Village stands was never entirely in Harton Township, indeed only a small portion of it was, but a very significant portion. In 1901 the industrial, heavily populated section of Harton Moor, was taken from the control of Harton Township and passed into that of South Shields County Borough.

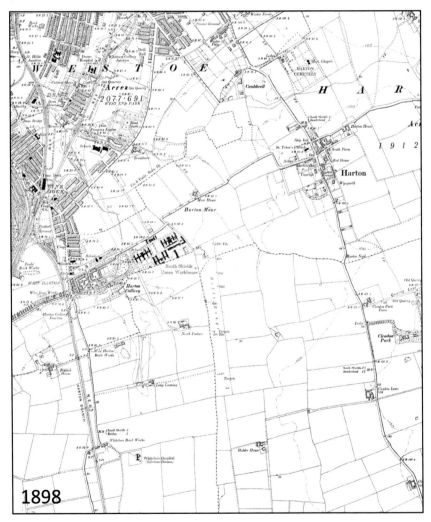

A large area of flat and sometime poorly drained land the dotted line on the 1898 map opposite shows the the extent of the ownership of this area by Harton Township.   Three years later, in 1901, Harton Colliery, the new Harton Laundry plus Moor House Farm would be taken into South Shields. What did remain after 1901 was the Union Workhouse; the clue might lie in the title. Although this would in turn become Harton General Hospital, it was never officially given the name Harton Workhouse, that was a local derivation denoting its geographical position.   It was home to over a thousand inmates in 1901 but not all were from Harton nor were they solely the responsibility of Harton Township.

Interestingly when removed from the governance of Harton Township neither the colliery nor the laundry changed their names. The Harton Coal Company and Harton Laundry and Dye Works would make this little area well known during the first part of the twentieth century.

The following chapter aims to give an introduction to Harton Colliery, Harton Laundry and the Union Workhouse at Harton but it will also mention two other areas not in the Township as they offer a uniquely different insight into life on Harton Moor.   Moor House Farm is dealt with in the chapter on Harton Farms (p116).

Harton Colliery

The main workings commenced when the proprietors of the Harton Coal Company, Messrs. Anderson, Blackett, Philipson and Wood took over the interests of the St. Hilda Colliery and began to expand. The Harton Coal Company was registered 6th August 1885

Mrs Brandling cut the first sod of green grass at Harton when the shaft sinking began on 10th May, 1841. The sinking ended after four years on 10th July, 1845, when the Bensham Seam was won at a depth of 1,260 feet (384m) at a cost of £60,000, being the greatest depth reached in the Tyne district at that time.

The Harton Coal Company's operations had a lot to do with the layout of South Shields. They developed a railway system which linked the four collieries owned by the Harton Coal Company; St. Hilda, (1822); Harton, (1841); Boldon (1866); Whitburn (1874); as well as the Marsden Quarry (stone dust); the Coal Cleaning Plant at Bent's Farm, later Westoe Colliery (1909); Harton Staithes on the river near Mill Dam; and the various coal depots in the town like Victoria Road, Claypath, West Holborn, etc.

Harton Colliery has a very particular claim to fame. In 1854 the Seventh Astronomer Royal, Sir George Biddell Airy (1801-1892) used the shaft at Harton Colliery to conduct an experiment to measure the mean density of the earth. Harton was chosen because, as at that time it was one of the deepest excavations into the earth's crust. Airy set up two observation stations connected by electric signals, one on the surface the other at the bottom of the shaft. In each, on a solid foundation, was fixed an astronomical clock with a compensated pendulum exactly regulated. In front of each of these was a free Kater's pendulum suspended on a knife edge of very hard steel.

The principle on which the experiment was based is that the number of vibrations of a free pendulum is an exact measure of the power of gravitation. The difference in the number of vibrations in a given time of the free pendulum on the surface and that at the foot of the shaft enabled

The above engraving shows the pendulum room at the bottom of Harton coal pit.

George Airy to calculate the weight of the earth. He gave a lecture in the Central Hall, South Shields in 1854, explaining his findings and thanking the Harton Coal Company for their most kind services. His estimate was quite close to what we now accept as the earth's density, 5.5153g/cm3.

Harton Colliery expanded over many decades and was a successful pit, conditions were as those in other collieries at the time. Happily no major disasters are recorded. In 1909 a second shaft was sunk at Harton.

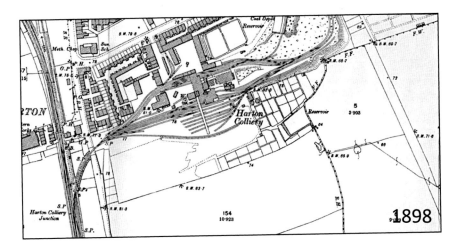

A photograph from about 1890 in Harton pit yard. Teams of horses were at that time used to transport coal wagons to Green Lane.

Showing the pit head and winding wheel at Harton colliery in about 1900. The photograph is taken from the south, looking northwards.

In 1913, the Harton Coal Company's peak year, there were 4,000 men working in the four pits owned by the company, with 2.4 million tons of coal being won and brought to the surface from the South Shields District. The years between the wars were healthy enough years for the company, but production never again reached the heights of 1913. The colliery closed on the 25th July, 1969, with the loss of about a thousand jobs.

A photograph taken in the 1920s of Harton screens where coal was sorted and graded.

A view of Harton Colliery from the south taken in the 1930s. The large timber yard in the foreground was the store for the pit props.

Harton Laundry

Situated amongst fields and some distance from Harton Village was this long, low building that became known as Harton Dye Works. In the late 1800s, when many homes did not have running water, wash-houses and laundries were essential businesses.

Harton Laundry is not recorded on the 1898 (p270) which would have been surveyed at an earlier date. However it was opened in March 1897 as the newspaper report of Thursday, 18th March declared. It was only in Harton Township for five years, but geographically remained so and like the Harton Coal Company became a well recognised name throughout the area.

Harton Moor Laundry
Opening Ceremony

Introduction of machinery to do away with any labour is now getting quite common and soon it will be difficult to find work for many who now obtain their living by manual work or labour. Steam Laundries have for some time been quite common in London and the big cities in the provinces, but now they are being introduced in every town worthy of the name. Quite a huge laundry has been promoted at Harton Moor, and this was opened yesterday under very interesting auspices. The site which is a very eligible one, covers an acre of ground, and is situated near Moor House Farm on the West Lane leading from Harton Colliery to Harton Village.

The buildings consist of a laundry, 147 feet by 40 feet, and boiler and engine houses, 40 feet by 40 feet, with stabling in the rear. The building is approached from the West Lane by large entrance doors for the vans to enter into the receiving and delivery vestibule, and abutting to which in a central position, are the clerks and private offices, surrounded by clear glass partitions and commanding a view of all departments. On the left is the sorting or receiving room, 50 feet long, fitted with bins, table, etc for the reception and sorting of the soiled clothes, each customer's work being treated quite separately. Behind this is the general wash house, a 100 feet room, fitted with all the latest improvements for steam and mechanical washing, consisting of washing

A photograph from 1900 Of Harton Moor Laundry looking east toward Harton Village; Phillipsville, Willis' Cottages and West View House are in the distance.

machines, hydro extractors, etc. So that the most delicate fabrics can pass through without injury, two drying rooms 30 feet long are provided for drying the clothes, superseding the old fashioned sliding horses. The clothes are dried by a current of purified air, worked by Blackman's fans the external air warmed and purified passing through the drying rooms. The ironing room is of a similar size to the washhouse and contains an immense ironing machine with steel cylinders weighing several tons, also tiny tyler irons heated by gas and air, weighing only a few ounces. The airing chamber is heated and ventilated so as to contain a perfectly dry atmosphere at a temperature of about 100 degrees Fahrenheit, in which all goods are thoroughly aired before passing on to the final stage in the packing room. The packing room, 44 feet by 22 feet is fitted up with divisions so that each customers' goods may be sorted, and then transferred into baskets for delivery.

The buildings are lined with white glazed tiles and efficiently lighted by continuous roof lights filled with patent glazing. The whole of the rain water from the roof is collected into tanks in the grounds and thoroughly filtered and used in washing. In addition to these there is a large reservoir capable of holding 60,000 gallons. A mess room is provided for the work people, and furnished with tables, seats, and cooking stove.

A large number of dignitaries were present for the opening ceremony which was conducted by Mr J M Moore amid great celebration as he declared the Harton Moor Laundry open.

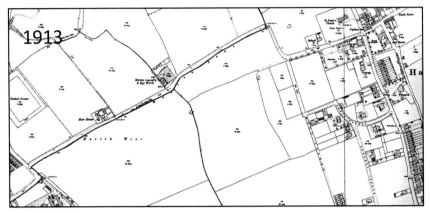

With the change of the boundary line in 1901, Harton Laundry would become part of South Shields.

The American machinery was installed in the Harton premises by William Bird, a young engineer from Wales who had recently moved to Tyneside. Mr Bird became managing director of the business and by the 1930s was a majority shareholder. Other laundries were later brought into the business including the Snowdrift Laundry from Scarborough and The Tynemouth and District Laundry. New aspects such as carpet cleaning and dry cleaning became a part of the service which continued to change with the times. The dry cleaning and dye works business continued on the Harton site when the laundry aspect of the business transferred to Newcastle in 1926.

By the 1940s the firm had a recognised logo of a leaping deer; Harton meaning Hill of Harts/deers. The firm eventually closed in 1970.

Advertising was always an important element of the laundry and newspaper after newspaper carries daily adverts such as this one from Thursday, 2nd July, 1903.

THE
HARTON MOOR
CLEANING & DYEWORKS,
SOUTH SHIELDS,

HAVE THE LATEST AND ONLY

CARPET BEATING & CLEANING
MACHINERY

IN THE DISTRICT.

Send us a Post Card and you will be attended to at once.

CARPETS RETURNED WITHIN 24 HOURS WHEN REQUIRED.

FIFTY YEARS
OF HARTON

When horseless carriages rattled through the cobbled streets and can-can-girls can-canned, Harton were beginning to make a name for themselves with their dyeing and dry cleaning service. The years that have passed have made "The Harton Service" no empty phrase, but something on which you can rely for quality workmanship at a reasonable outlay . . . . made possible by science, machinery . . . . and the enthusiasm of our workers.

Be smart and gay
the Harton way

HARTON DYEWORKS LIMITED
Branches in all districts

An advert from *The Berwick Advertiser*, Thursday 7th April, 1949.

The Workhouse

The Poor Law Amendment Act of 1834 resulted in the 15,000 or so parishes in England being formed into Poor Law Unions, each with its own Union Workhouse. The South Shields Poor Law Union was formed on 10th December, 1836. Its operation was overseen by an elected Board of Guardians, 25 in number, representing its 6 constituent parishes as listed below (figures in brackets indicate numbers of Guardians) Boldon (1), Harton (1), Monkton (1). Jarrow (1), South Shields (9), Westoe (9), Whitburn (1). Hebburn became part of the union in 1894 and Boldon Colliery 1895.

The population falling within the Union at the 1831 census had been 24,427 with parishes ranging in size from Harton (population 217) to Westoe (9,682) and South Shields itself (9,074). The average annual poor-rate expenditure for the period 1834-6 had been £9,029 or 7s.5d. per head. The first South Shields Union Workhouse was erected in 1837 on the north side of German Street (Ocean Road). By the 1870s, the German Street building was proving too small and in 1875 it was decided to build a new workhouse at a site on the edge of Harton Moor.

The foundation stone for the new building was laid in September 1877 by the Chairman of the Board of Guardians, W M Anderson JP. The architect for the scheme was J H Morton who was also involved in the design of the nearby workhouse at Gateshead. Construction of the building cost £43,361 but the total cost, including the purchase of 17 acres of land from the Ecclesiastical Commissioners, was in the region of £55,000.

The new workhouse started admitting paupers in 1878 although the building work was not finally completed until early in 1880. It initially accommodated 700 inmates and comprised an entrance block, main building, infirmary, and schools. The main buildings were based on the then common pavilion layout, see map opposite.

Under the new Act, the threat of the Union Workhouse was intended to act as a deterrent to the able-bodied pauper. Life inside the workhouse was was intended to be as off-putting as possible. Men, women, children, the infirm and the able-bodied were housed separately and given very

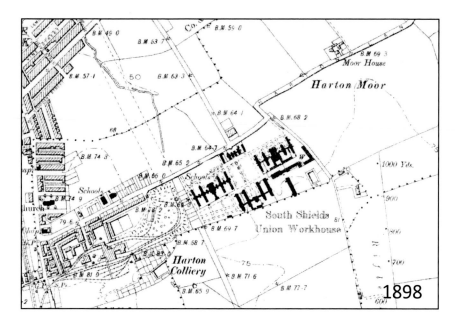

basic and monotonous food such as watery porridge called gruel, or bread and cheese. All inmates had to wear the rough workhouse uniform and sleep in communal dormitories. Supervised baths were given once a week. The able-bodied were given hard work such as stone-breaking or picking apart old ropes called oakum. The elderly and infirm sat around in the day-rooms or sick-wards with little opportunity for visitors. Parents were only allowed limited contact with their children — perhaps for an hour or so once a week on Sunday afternoon.

By the 1850s, the majority of those forced into the workhouse were not the work-shy, but the old, the infirm, the orphaned, unmarried mothers, and the physically or mentally ill. For the next century, the Union Workhouse was in many localities one of the largest and most significant buildings in the area, the largest ones accommodating more than a thousand inmates. Entering its harsh regime and spartan conditions was considered the ultimate degradation.

The workhouse was not, however, a prison. People could, in principle, leave whenever they wished, for example when work became available locally. Some people, known as the *ins and outs*, entered and left quite frequently, treating the workhouse almost like a guest-house, albeit one with the most basic of facilities. For some, however, their stay in the workhouse would be for the rest of their lives.

The Shields Gazette in an article of Wednesday, 2nd January, 1884 presents this account of the workhouse: A VISIT TO THE SOUTH SHIELDS WORKHOUSE. The following written by "A. Visitor," is sent to us for publication :—
On Friday last I, with a few friends, availed myself of the permission to visit the Workhouse, granted to the public by the Guardians of the South Shields Union, and I do not regret having done so, for I enjoyed quite a holiday treat on that afternoon,

A banner floating over the outside gate at one o'clock announced that the gates were opened to the general public, and on entering soon after, amidst a throng of eager visitors, we were received the master John Craik, with whom were twelve young lads, aged from 10 to 13, dressed very smartly with white rosettes on their breasts and in their hats, and looking the picture of health and comfort. These were the chaperones appointed by the master to conduct the several groups of visitors over the Workhouse and its grounds, and to initiate them into the various handicrafts and industries pursued by the inmates. A right busy time these young attendants had of it. They most courteously discharged their duties. Leaving the lodge for the main building, we passed along an avenue lined on either side with trees and pleasure ground tastefully laid out, till we turned to the house itself, when we got the first information of the great responsibility resting upon the officers of the Institution, and were somewhat startled seeing on a board, judiciously placed so all who ran might read, that the number inmates that morning reached no less a total than 615. Here we could not help inquiring of the master how he managed to govern so great number. He told us that being assisted by able staff of officers, he found things pretty easy—that "use became second nature," and that those he had to deal with were not so unruly and disorderly as an outsider might be led to think.

We were then brought by our attendant through the entrance hall, fragrant still with Christmas, and adorned with holly, mottoes, and flags, round by the women's day and into the sleeping rooms, where one could not fail being struck with the neatness and cleanliness on every side. Returning down the corridor, we passed through the spacious dining hall, where, on ChristmasDay, 626 inmates were regaled by the Guardians with plentiful supply of roast beef and plum pudding, accompanied by moderate allowance of beer, kindly given by friends. Spacious in its proportions, it was most beautifully and tastefully decorated with mottoes, banners, and our ever welcome Christmas holly; and festooned with flags and ensigns, kindly lent for the occasion by friends and well-wishers. Passing through this dining hall, we were led along the day-rooms and the sleeping apartments of the male inmates, and into those allotted to the married couples, noticing still the same signs of comfort, warmth, and cleanliness in every place. other groups of eager visitors were pressing on our heels, our young and civil guide next conducted through the various workshops, where box-making, shoe-maklng, and joinery working is done. From hence we passed to the engine house, where all the blocks of wood are cut by machinery, and passed into the stick-room to be made into firewood, and counted and packed in bundles, ready for the consumer's use. Here, also, we saw the brick machine, by which several thousands of bricks have been made, and we were rather surprised learning that these very workshops were largely, if not entirely, built of bricks manufactured on the spot. Passing on from this busy scene of industry, were then conducted over the hospital, first through the various wards alloted to the male patients, and afterwards through those allotted to the females; and here, where we might have expected to see or hear something that might hurt or pain the ear or eyes, we saw nothing but what was pleasant. The different wards through which we passed, were most tastefully decorated, and this had been done, as were afterwards informed, by the inmates themselves, who had cheerfully taxed their own slender pockets to make their wards look bright and gay at the festive happy season. On all sides we were struck by the order and cleanliness that prevailed, reflecting the greatest credit on all concerned in the management of the place. We thought our work was done, but our little chattering guide reminded us we had the gardens and schools yet to see, so on we went from the female side of the hospital into the gardens. A workhouse without its garden is something like friend Jack without its Jill. Passing through the gardens at length we reach the schools, the haunt of childhood and the home of merry laughter, and here we were struck with the bright eyes and cheerful faces of the children. The care and sorrows of a Workhouse seemed to sit lightly, yea not to sit on them at all. One place in the schools where all was order and happiness arrested our attention. This was the children's hospital, where the little ones, with their toys and picture books, were all pleasantly grouped around a cheerful fire, looking radiant with joy. The neatness and the spotless-cleanliness of the place seemed to speak of peace and home. With this final bright and happy memory fresh in our minds, we closed our pleasant visit to the South Shields Workhouse, thankful most heartily that to us the privilege still remained to struggle on in life amidst the busy crowd outside the Workhouse walls; but thankful also that for the helpless years of childhood, and declining life, and for those wounded in the battle of life, stricken down by sickness, or the pressure of immediate want, a safe and calm retreat is found, and where, if luxuries seldom come, its inmates at least are sheltered from the bitter cold, the glaring vice, the misery and punching want which, alas, prevails so largely, even in this our Christian land.

Photograph taken in 1912 of the male ward.

Towards the end of the nineteenth century, conditions gradually improved in the workhouse, particularly for the elderly and infirm, and for children. Food became a little more varied and small luxuries such as books, newspapers, and even occasional outings were allowed. Children were increasingly housed away from the workhouses in special schools or in cottage homes which were often placed out in the countryside and old *well conducted* couples were provided with cottages detached from the remainder of the house.

Successive additions were made to the Harton site and by 1910 it was estimated that the cost to date had been £94,750 with the workhouse now able to accommodate 1,200 inmates, excluding those in the separate lunatics' block at the south-east of the site. This was even before the countrywide depression of the 1920s.

South Shields workhouse has now become associated with the name of the novelist Catherine Cookson (1906-1998). Born into a poor family at Tyne Dock in South Shields, Catherine left school because of ill health before she was thirteen and followed her mother into domestic service. However, she began to try and educate herself through reading and night classes. At the age of 18, she obtained a job in the South Shields workhouse laundry as a checker. She remained in this job for about five years.

Two 1912 photographs, the upper one showing the workhouse laundry where some of the occupants were expected to work, the lower photograph showing the female infirm ward.

The upper photograph taken in 1912 shows one of the hospital wards at the workhouse.

The lower photograph of 1908 shows Able Seaman Charles Amey, a Burma, Baltic and Crimean veteran, being released from the workhouse and taken to comfortable lodgings. He was born in 1830 and died in 1911.

After 1930, the workhouse became Harton Institution and General Hospital, then South Shields General Hospital in the late 1940s, and later South Tyneside District Hospital. Only a few of the original workhouse buildings now survive.

A photograph of one of the entrance buildings of the workhouse taken in 1912. The wards for the occupants of the workhouse were much plainer in design and one can be glimpsed on the right hand side of the photograph.

The Union Workhouse remained in Harton Township when the rest of West Harton was taken into South Shields in 1901. The boundary line after 1901 came down Harton Lane and looped around the perimeter of the workhouse before heading back eastward.

Harton Rifle Range

Harton Rifle Range was never in Harton Township but on its very outskirts and it is such a tantalising piece of information I thought to share it. On the 1898 map below we see it marked just to the south of the Union Workhouse. It was established in 1887 and is often referred to alongside the Rifle range at Trow Rocks, this one was longer and offered more for both the soldier and the civilian enthusiast. The rifle range existed in this position for twenty seven years and was much used judging from reports in the local newspapers.

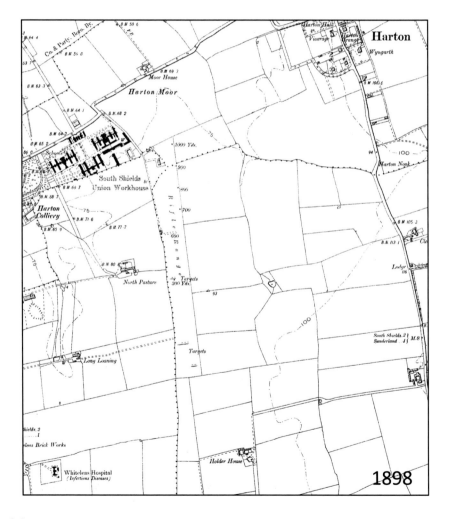

Thursday, 10th March, 1887:

TYNE DOCK RIFLE RANGE.

This week, operations have been commenced to clear the ground intended to be used as a rifle range at Tyne Dock. The field is at the back of the Union Workhouse at West Harton, and about ten minutes' walk from Tyne Dock Railway Station. A large staff of unemployed members of the corps are engaged in erecting the necessary fencing, building the butts, and demolishing a hedge which runs through the field, and it is expected that in about five or six weeks everything will be in readiness for the formal opening. The total length of the range—which, by the way, is almost as level from end to end as a billiard board —at which firing can take place will be 1,000 yards. According to present arrangements about one dozen targets will be erected, at which twenty men will be able to fire at one time. The firing points are so arranged that competitions can be carried on at 600, 500, and 200 yards from the same spot. Great interest is already taken in the affair, a large number of officers and others interested having visited the place, and all speak most highly of the site, which will, undoubtedly, be one of the best ranges in the country.

The Shields Gazette frequently lists in details events taking place at the range, such as the annual prize meeting of the Durham Rifle Association, listing all the prize winners or discusses the:

BUSY DAY AT HARTON BUTTS. SHOOTING FOR THE HUNT SHIELD. Harton Moor rifle range seldom presented more animated spectacle than it did last Saturday afternoon. There were representatives of almost every branch of the auxiliary forces shooting, or waiting to shoot.

287

Or explaining about: **THE annual prize shoot of the Northumberland Hussars Imperial Yeomanry took place on the Harton Moor Rifle Range.** Civilian Clubs like the Tyneside Rifle Club all used the range and had the results of their competitions announced in *The Shields Gazette*. In October 1900 improvements were made at the range.

HARTON MOOR RIFLE RANGE.

PROPOSED EXTENSIVE
IMPROVEMENTS.

Extensive alterations to the well-known Harton Moor rifle range are in contemplation which, when completed, will afford greatly enlarged facilities for rifle practice. The necessary plans have been finally passed, and these show that some 15 targets will be mounted. There will be six at 200 yards, five at 500 yards, and four at 600 yards. The canvas targets are to be adopted these being of greater utility and much more favoured than the iron ones. Great addition is to be made at the 200 yards butt, which will be considerably lengthened. The butts at 500 and 600 yards, especially that at 500 yards, are already of considerable proportions, and can soon be made of the requisite dimensions. The targets being placed en echelon, will allow firing at all three ranges to be carried on simultaneously, and allow competitors to conclude their practice in the least possible time.

On Saturday, 20th January, 1900, before these improvements a woman of 52, Ann Smith, was accidentally shot dead at the rifle range. A section of the newspaper article reporting on the Coroners' inquest into her death is reproduced on the opposite page. The Coroner recorded an accidental death, but expressed the opinion that the War Office authorities should be communicated with, with the view of increasing precautions at the range.

DISTRESSING SHOOTING ACCIDENT AT HARTON MOOR.

DEATH OF A WOMAN.

On Wednesday afternoon Mr A. T. Shepherd, deputy-coroner, held an inquest at the South Shields Union Workhouse, Harton, respecting the death of Ann Smith (52), of 16, Brunswick Street, South Shields, who was shot dead while working in a field behind the rifle range at Harton Moor during the shooting practice of the Yeomanry on Tuesday afternoon. Mr T. D. Marshall, solicitor, represented the relatives of the deceased; and Colonel Proctor, Captain Graham, and Lieut. Bowman were present representing the 5th V.B.D.L.I.

Jane Smith, daughter of the deceased, said her mother was 52 years of age. Her father, William Smith, a sea-faring man, was in the workhouse hospital. About a quarter-past two on Tuesday afternoon deceased was loading a cart in a turnip field on Mr Henderson's farm. Witness was also working in the field. Another woman ran down the field and told her something had happened to her (witness's) mother. Witness went and found her mother lying on her back at the top of the field, bleeding from the back of her head. Witness could not say whether her mother was alive, but she never spoke. Her mother lay till the servant man went and stopped the shooting, and then she was removed to the workhouse. The shooting had been going on all the morning about two fields off. There was a red flag on the top of the butt. Witness had not been warned to keep out of the way. She had been working there before when shooting was going on. She understood the flag was a danger signal. By Mr Marshall: She was not aware of any protection behind the butt. There were no soldiers or volunteers behind it to warn them.

Mary Kelly, single woman, Waterloo Vale, South Shields, said she was also working in the field. She was close to deceased when she heard a shot and deceased fell down. They were loading a cart with turnips at the time. Deceased was hit in the head. She got hold of the deceased's hand to pull her up, but on seeing the blood flowing she ran down the field and told last witness and the hind. Witness heard a lot of shots that day, both before and after the woman fell. Witness and deceased were in the second field from the butts. She saw the danger flag, but did not see any soldiers about. She and Mrs Smith had no fear. They thought they were out of danger.—By Mr Marshall: They were directly behind the butt in the direction of Cleadon. She did not know whether they were firing at the last butt.

Dr Appleton deposed to having seen the woman after the accident. He found life extinct. A bullet had gone completely through the head, causing fracture of the bone and laceration of the brain. In his opinion death was due to hemorrhage of the brain. The bullet had apparently come direct from the butt, as it would have collapsed if it had hit anything else.

Harton Moor Golf Course

The club was founded in 1922 as an 18-hole course. There was an initial membership of 370 peaking at 400 in the mid 1920s. Sunday play was allowed without caddies. The railway station at South Shields was 2 miles away there was also a tram service which had a stop at the clubhouse.

By the late 1920s the postal address of the club was given as Harton Moor Golf Club, Cleadon Park Estate and in 1940 Harton Moor Golf Club, King George Road.

Newcastle Daily Chronicle reported on Friday 23 February 1923.

Harton Moor Golf Club
Satisfactory Progress During First Year

The Harton Moor Golf Club, South Shields, has had a very successful first year, and the condition of the club's affairs shows every prospect of an equally prosperous current year. At the beginning of 1922 there were 103 gentlemen and 60 lady members. There was a rapid increase during the year, 120 gentlemen, and 74 ladies taking up membership. An equally strong financial position was shown by the balance sheet, the year's income totalling £1,455 including £907 members subscriptions. Samuel Rowe was appointed captain and W M Renton vice-captain. The following officers were re-elected; president, C J Devonport; vice-presidents C L Dobson and J T Bell; hon. treasurer, W Harle; hon. secretary, J Bell; committee – D Burns, G W Ellis, J J Ford, W B Mullin, A Ford, R Makepeace, S Rowe, E Richardson, J Spraggon, G Sigsworth, Rev. J Bradley, H Park. Mrs D Smith was appointed hon. secretary of the ladies' section, and Miss Henderson, captain. Ladies' committee; Mesdames D Burns, W R Bell, J Donovan, H Park and Miss Smith.

WW2 took its toll on Golf Clubs, members numbers decreased and courses were bombed, petrol for cutting the grass was rationed. In 1945 the Harton Moor Club members, then amounting to 53 males members and 59 lady members, decided to amalgamated with South Shields Golf Club and Harton Moor Golf Club ceased to exist.

Mortimer Senior School　　**Harton Laundry**　　　**St Peter's Church**

**Some amazing photographs have been posted on the Golf's Missing Links website which
show the level moor land and in the distance tantalising glimpses of
Harton Village, or Harton Colliery.**
With thanks to Paul Robertson.

SOUTH SHIELDS FOR SPORT

WHATEVER you want to do when on holiday you can do it at South Shields. Your favourite sport or pastime has not been overlooked here.

The splendid 18-hole course of the South Shields Golf Club, nearly 6,300 yards in length, commands grand views of the sea from its bracing situation on Cleadon Hill above Marsden. The commodious Club House of the Harton Moor Golf Club, the 18-hole course of which covers approximately 6,000 yards, adjoins the Cleadon Park Tram Terminus, while the beautiful 18-hole cliff-top course of the Whitburn Golf Club is situated roughly three miles from South Shields on the way to Whitburn and is easily reached by bus. This course has just been remodelled under the direction of a celebrated golf architect, and the result is gratifying to all who appreciate a grand course which is abreast of the most up-to-date developments in the great game.

Plenty of hard and grass tennis courts are available on the North Promenade and in all the parks and recreation grounds ; the South Shields Cricket and Westoe Rugby and Lawn Tennis Club holds an important Tennis Tournament in August Bank Holiday week. Excellent bowling greens will be found in the Marine, West, and Robert Readhead parks, also golf putting greens, and the charges are only nominal.

PAGE THIRTY

**This page from the 1935 Souvenir of South Shields pamphlet mentions a commodious
club house at Harton Moor.**

Conclusion

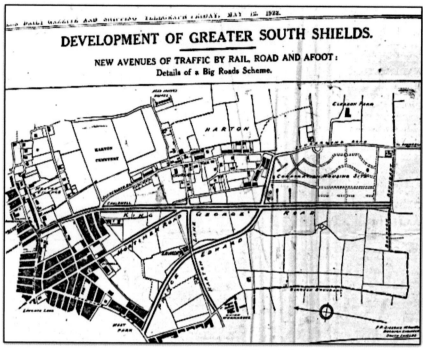

DEVELOPMENT OF GREATER SOUTH SHIELDS.

NEW AVENUES OF TRAFFIC BY RAIL, ROAD AND AFOOT:
Details of a Big Roads Scheme.

St Peter's Scrapbook vol III 1915-1936.
Reproduced by kind permission of the vicar and churchwardens of Harton St Peter.

This plan reproduced in *The Shields Daily Gazette and Shipping Telegraph* on Friday, 12th May, 1922, is glued into the last pages of the St Peter's Scrapbook Vol III. The accompanying article states:

The years that followed the war (WW1) will be an epoch marking period in the material growth and development of the County Borough of South Shields. The Town Council carried through an important extension scheme which brought 778 acres of added territory to the borough, including the whole of Harton Village, and housing site at Cleadon Park. The new boundary line extends westward and southward, and much of the new area acquired presents great possibilities as a future ideal residential quarter. The first essential in the development of big towns - is the provision of good roads - spacious avenues which carry not only the ordinary pedestrian traffic, but vehicles and light railways.

The article goes on to discuss the laying out of King George Road:

The centre portion 33 feet in width will carry the light railway. Abutting on each side is provision for a 24 feet carriage way, so that the current of road locomotion will be in one direction according to the going or coming; and footpaths on the outsides will be spacious and marked off by avenues of sheltering trees, out of which will evolve in years to come delightful boulevards.

The photograph above from 1923 shows the construction of the light railway which it was hoped would link Sunderland and South Shields, but never went any further than the Shields boundary.

The is now the central reservation of King George Road, which has matured to the splendid boulevard that was intended.

The article also discusses extending Mortimer Road so that it met this new King George Road, enjoyed the straightening and extension of Harton Lane and the completion of a section of Prince Edward Road.

Farms and fields vanished after 1921 and as the chapters in this book have shown what had been the rural Township of Harton did rapidly become, as South Shields Council had planned, a new residential quarter of South Shields. Hence in 2021 most of the houses in the Harton area of South Shields are less than 100 years old.

In this book I wanted to raise awareness that Harton Township existed; I hope I have done so. Progress is essential and homes are necessary; many thousands of people have enjoyed and do enjoy living in Harton. I hope they can also celebrate and take pride in the history of their area.

Thanks

I owe big thanks: to South Tyneside Libraries for their permission to use so many of the images in their archive, without which this book would be the less; to Rev Kate Boardman for her support; to David Kidd, Brian Cauwood, the National Trust and many others for the assistance they have given me in my research; to everyone who has shared their memories with me.

However grateful as I am for so much assistance it remains the fact that any mistakes and errors are totally my own for which I apologise.